Oligopoly

Oligopoly

An Empirical Approach

Roger Sherman
Department of Economics
University of Virginia

Lexington Books
D.C. Heath and Company
Lexington, Massachusetts
Toronto   London

Library of Congress Cataloging in Publication Data

Sherman, Roger, 1930-
    Oligopoly.
    1. Oligopolies. I. Title.
HD2731.S54   338.5'23   72-7019
ISBN 0-669-85050-0

Published simultaneously in Canada.

Printed in the United States of America.

International Standard Book Number: 0-669-85050-0

Library of Congress Catalog Card Number: 72-7019

To Char

Contents

List of Figures

List of Tables

Preface

By almost anyone's reckoning today, competition and monopoly are quite well understood. But for more than a century economists have struggled with far less success to understand markets that are neither competitive nor monopolistic, markets that are called oligopolies because they contain a few sellers rather than either the many sellers in competition or the one seller in monopoly. How can unique solutions be predicted among a few firms that can see their own interdependence? What one firm should do depends on what the others do and so, it is alleged, market price can lie anywhere between a competitive one and a tacitly collusive monopolistic one.

The work that follows rests on a presumption that in an oligopoly market the outcome will be influenced strongly by comparative rewards to each firm for its different alternative actions, in much the same way that other forms of economic behavior depend on rewards. Interdependence complicates the reward structure faced by each firm, but we can still focus attention on the reward structure and expect, on average, that it will influence behavior. This presumption is similar in spirit to that urged by Professor Edward Mason when the study of industrial organization was in its infancy. But here we explore its possibilities by the method of experimental economics first, before examining real industries. In turning to real-world industries, we emphasize slightly different variables but our purpose and methods are those used by students of industrial organization, and our results are intended to be of interest to the same audience. In tackling industrial organization issues we simply are attempting to make use of oligopoly theory and social psychology knowledge.

In preparing this work I have incurred more debts than properly can be acknowledged, let alone repaid. The most helpful benefactors are identified in acknowledgement footnotes at appropriate chapters. Chapter 1 and much of Part II constitute, with some revisions, parts of my Ph.D. dissertation at Carnegie-Mellon University. For their generous help I am indebted especially to Richard M. Cyert, Otto A. Davis, F. Trenery Dolbear, and Victor H. Vroom, who comprised my dissertation committee. In that work I benefited also from conversations with Lester Lave and Allan Meltzer. The two chapters in Part I report work carried out at Carnegie-Mellon by a group of seven faculty and fellow students. My joint authors, Gary Bowman, Trenery Dolbear, Lester Lave, Arnold Lieberman, Edward Prescott, and Fred Rueter, have very kindly permitted me to reprint the two papers that resulted. Two chapters in Part III are the joint work of Robert Tollison and me, and he also has been very kind in permitting me to include those two papers here. Most of the chapters in the book have appeared as papers in professional journals, and for allowing me to reprint them I thank the *Journal of Conflict Resolution*, the *Journal of Psychology, Kyklos*, the *Quarterly Journal of Economics*, the *Review of*

Economic Studies, the *Review of Economics and Statistics*, *Rivista Internazionale di Scienze Economiche e Commerciali*, and the *Southern Economic Journal.*

Roger Sherman

Charlottesville, Virginia
August, 1972

Oligopoly

1

Empirical Oligopoly

Few economists would argue that oligopoly theories are scarce; they seem plentiful, in part because they tend to be subjected only to tests of consistency or internal validity. Most oligopoly theories can be separated into two parts, one involving a choice structure which specifies payoffs for alternative actions, and another dealing with the behavior of those who face that choice and payoff structure. With respect to the behavioral part of oligopoly theories, an experimental test of validity is now at hand. Economic analysis will continue to play a crucial role in any elaboration of payoff structure, but we must confess (after one hundred thirty-odd years of development) that our precise, deterministic, and generally untested theories of oligopolistic *behavior* are inadequate.

Social psychologists, sociologists, and other social scientists have recently taken a great interest in individual behavior under the same types of payoff interdependence that arise in oligopoly. We thus have new knowledge of behavior under conflict that is relevant to the oligopoly setting, and new methods for adding to that knowledge as well. Economists should be and are employing these methods, because economists can pose many of the most fruitful research questions. Of course such experiments cannot fully validate theories of the real world; they can only validate individual (or group) behavior theories by themselves. Implications for the real world, based on a smaller number of validated theories of behavior, should then offer sufficiently greater promise of confirmation, however, to warrant greater investment in real world testing. Experiments give us an opportunity to try things out in a laboratory first, to weed out some less promising theories before proceeding further. Because economists have grown unaccustomed to such opportunities, a review of their relevance may be in order.

The Decline of Deterministic Behavior Theories

Early oligopoly models yielded unique solutions, but only by relying on very strong behavior assumptions. We can briefly trace the gradual decline in acceptance of these assumptions. Cournot's well known conjecture for each firm was simple; each assumed the other would produce the same quantity this period

Reprinted with slight adaptation by permission from "Experimental Oligopoly," *Kyklos*, 24 (No. 1, 1971), 30-49. I am indebted to Professors W.L. Breit, R.M. Cyert, F.T. Dolbear, and L.B. Lave for helpful discussions and comments.

as last period. [7][1] Without such a conjecture, each firm's profit maximizing problem would be indeterminate; with it, dynamic quantity adjustment paths converged to an equilibrium price and quantity.[2] Of course the most significant implication of the Cournot duopoly solution was its provision for *some* excess profit for each of the duopolists, an amount which decreased as the number of sellers increased.[3] Bertrand attacked that result when he claimed that sellers would set price instead of quantity, [3] so each would be motivated to cut price slightly below the other, until price equaled marginal cost and there was no profit.

Edgeworth elaborated on Bertrand's observation, adding limits on output, and determinacy was challenged; he found that if the firms had capacity limits or rising marginal costs, an oscillating price would result [13, pp. 116-21]. Edgeworth's firms began price cutting, as in the Bertrand case, but at some point one of the firms sold its entire output. Having committed its total output, the first firm would have given the second one a monopoly, but once the second firm exploited its monopoly position by raising price, the first firm would want to set a higher price too, just slightly below the price of the second firm. From there, the cycle would be repeated again and again.

Bowley's variant of the Cournot equilibrium relied less on obviously incorrect conjectures, but it also produced oscillations in price. [4] He let each firm consider reactions of the other to its own quantity changes. [4, p. 38] If only one firm, called the leader, knew the other's reaction function, there would be no price oscillation problem. Knowing how the other firm would react to any output of his own, the leader could solve a determinate problem for his own optimal output (which differed from his Cournot solution output). But Bowley

---

[1]For excellent description and early criticism of Cournot see [3] and [16], and for more recent evaluations [6], [14], [63] and [75]. For treatment of stability, which is not discussed here, see [51], [54] and [73].

[2]Cournot's conjecture is unrelated to expectancy in cognitive learning theory. In the learning theory, expectation is an hypothesis about causal relations. But for Cournot, the conjecture is merely an assumption, one which produces determinancy in an otherwise indeterminate situation. Moreover, the conjecture of Cournot is never tested, since feedback regarding a competitor's behavior can never shake the duopolist's reliance on his conjecture. If he were to test his conjecture before equilibrium was reached, he would discover it to be false. For an analysis of duopoly which relies explicitly on a theory of learning, see [15]. For an application of mathematical learning theory to duopoly, see [70].

[3]Cournot made very clear the effect of n in his model [7, pp. 79-89], and offered a set of possibilities linking monopoly ($n = 1$) at one extreme with competition (n very large) at the other. If a linear demand curve ($P = a - bQ$) is specified for his model, total market quantity becomes a function of n:

$$Q = \frac{n}{n+1} \cdot \frac{a}{b}$$

(If costs are assumed to be zero, the two extreme outputs are then $Q = (a/b)/2$ for monopoly and $Q = a/b$ for competition.) So independent maximizing behavior will produce a market quantity that is dependent on n, simply because of the structure of Cournot's model.

thought there would be oscillation; both firms would speculate–and be wrong–about what the other would do.[4]

Stackelberg accorded each firm complete knowledge of relations in the profit space *and* of reaction or behavior protocol, leader or follower, which would be most profitable for it. [66] The question of management psychology or learning was still side-stepped. Instead, by an analytical process, completely informed firms chose behavior protocols which were then mindlessly invoked. Such behavior protocols narrowed the set of feasible solutions, in a manner not unlike minimax or other decision criteria,[5] and that was their main purpose. They afforded no dynamic, interactive behavior, nor any feedback of results or reinforcement. Since they differed from minimax game strategies and lacked their equilibrium properties, it is not surprising that the protocol selections frequently produced oscillation.[6]

Stackelberg extended these behavior protocols to oligopoly markets, where any mutual agreement on a single leader became more remote and disequilibrium was even more likely. His exhaustive development of possible combinations of reaction functions reveals now in retrospect the weaknesses of this method for analysis of market behavior. From Cournot's unquestioning acceptance of competitor's actions, Bowley and Stackelberg had competitors' reactions antici-pated. Analytic determinancy was sacrificed if reactions proved inconsistent, and even when a determinate solution resulted, it was only because many possible actions were ruled out by the assumed reaction functions.

Chamberlin shifted from this extraordinary objectivity to a subjective view of each firm facing the rest of the market with a differentiated product and with price the parameter of action. [6] If the Chamberlin market contained few firms, they could 'recognize their mutual dependence' and consequently find a point of maximum total profits to all. The result was a 'cooperative' solution in which firms would share some of the advantages that would ordinarily accrue only to a monopolist. Such a solution can be traced to Adam Smith, but Chamberlin elaborated the means by which it could tacitly be agreed upon among few firms in a market without sub rosa communication or formal collusion,[7] and he clearly posed for the first time the possibility of either independent Cournot type behavior *or* cooperative behavior leading to tacit collusion.

[4]Many response patterns will not guarantee stability, even when two firms are identical.

[5]It is possible that by their prominence, such protocols afford coordination which facilitates agreement, even though they may not yield optimal results. See Schelling. [55] This approach was generalized by Henderson to include a choice among alternative decision criteria, each presuming a certain known form of market solution. [25]

[6]Stackelberg thought both (all) firms would usually battle to be leader, and called this 'Bowley's Case'. [66, pp. 19-20]

[7]Earlier writers (e.g., Cournot [7] and Fisher [16]) admitted the advantages of collective profit maximizing, but claimed that it would require outright collusion. For a summary criticism of Chamberlin's theory, see [67]. For references to a series of exchanges following Stigler's criticism, see [1].

The structure of payoffs could be emphasized now, rather than precise decision rules. And the dichotomy between cooperative and non-cooperative solutions could arise in all market situations, including Cournot's. It has been given its greatest generality in the game theory, [45] and takes convenient concrete form in the well known prisoner's dilemma setting. [39] Once this conflict structure is recognized, it is easy to see that behavior cannot be predicted in a deterministic way; social psychology and experimental economics have a useful role to play.

The Payoff Structure in Oligopoly

Many details of the structure of choices and payoffs in oligopoly have only recently been elaborated. For example, capacity limits can prevent unique solutions by destroying continuity. Continuous models follow a partial analysis technique, adopting a perspective as Chamberlin did of one oligopolist *vis-à-vis* the rest of the market. Shubik has demonstrated that this subjective view does not guarantee consistent models.[8] For a model to be internally consistent, it is necessary that each firm be able to contend with any demand situation that might arise as a result of any combination of competitors' actions. Shubik called such objective characterization of the demand faced by individual firms 'contingent demand,' and showed that when other firms have capacity limitations, the contingent demand for any one firm can have discontinuities. Thus, although finite cross-elasticity of demand among firms' products is a convenient property, its presence cannot be assumed in models that allow for capacity limits.[9]

What time period do the firms take into account in making their decisions? Oligopoly theorists usually assumed a short-run view, an exception being Bronfenbrenner who argued that a long-run time horizon normally determined a price which was then rigid over short-run periods. [5] The causal priority of price over capacity so well developed in competitive models need not apply in oligopoly, yet the same causal order has almost always been assumed. If long-run

---

[8]See [63, Chaps. 5, 7]. For an early exposition of both cost and demand indeterminancy where competition is imperfect, see Higgins [26].

[9]Other specific bases for continuity, through finite cross-elasticity of demand, give no assurance that it will be sustained even if capacity limits are ignored. In price variation models, sources of finite cross-elasticity among sellers include transportation cost, [30] product differentiation, [6] and imperfect information. [48, 67] Nichol showed that horizontal segments would arise in the sales curves of individual firms in markets with transport costs and in differentiated product markets. [46] Nutter, and later Fouraker, showed linear indifference curves were possible for differentiated products, and that they could produce horizontal segments on the firms' sales curves, or infinite cross-elasticities. [47, 18] Imperfect information cannot ensure finite cross elasticity in the situations examined by Nichol, Nutter and Fouraker.

marginal cost is constant over a wide range, as some empirical studies indicate, [2, 32] oligopolists have an opportunity to choose capacity. Expansion by some of them may eliminate dominant firms, as Worcester argued. [77] On the other hand, since capacity choices could determine the setting in which future price choices would be made by interdependent firms, they might reverse the causal order under which capacity depends on short-run price. They might restrain their capacities as a means to achieving cooperation on price. Without the force of an optimal size, capacity can thus become another dimension for negotiation and possible cooperation.

Until Bain and Sylos emphasized it, little explicit attention had been devoted to entry in oligopoly. Early oligopoly models simply assumed few firms (usually two!) and no entry. If collusion was achieved, it was at a price higher than the competitive one, and firms then adopted a size that was optimal for that price, usually the same size for each firm. Recently, for modest entry barriers, the Bain-Sylos 'limit-price' notion of oligopoly pricing has oligopolists depart from the competitive price to earn some excess profit, but not enough to attract new entrants. [2, 43, 62, 68, 71] Bain has also found that barriers to entry can be very high in many industries and warrant study of behavior when the threat of new entry is not immediate. [2]

Decision variables for oligopoly markets have gradually expanded in modern treatments. Fellner elaborated a number of considerations which would modify a firm's interest in joint profit maximizing solutions. [14] In the context of a ruin-game, Shubik made clear the importance of asset position as a determinant of price behavior, and problems caused by capacity limits. [63] Capacity choice has been emphasized by Sherman. [60] Cyert and March presented a many-variable, behavioral theory which enhances the prospect of fruitful study of real-world business firms. [8] These latter developments overcome a narrowness of scope that characterized earlier oligopoly models but they can make empirical testing even more complex.

Experiments, in contrast, simplify empirical confirmation. They create a different problem, however, inasmuch as verification occurs apart from the world, so interpretation of the experimental results, together with further verification, is still needed. Perhaps because of this, early oligopoly market experiments were confined to the settings of classical oligopoly theories. The main advantage of controlled experiments is that their results can be accumulated, however, so with time, elaborations of oligopoly behavior which are closer approximations of the real world may also be exposed to experimental investigation, part by part.[10]

---

[10]For a discussion of such methodological advantages of experimental economics, see [64]. Using human subjects in experiments is discussed in [56]. Having pairs of persons, and groups, as decision-makers is examined in [34] and [50].

Behavior in Experimental Markets

Hogatt carried out a simple quantity variation Cournot-type triopoly experiment in 1959. [27] The experiment involved only three markets and was not well controlled, but it supported a Cournot solution over a cooperative one. Fouraker and Siegel studied the Cournot duopoly and triopoly market under both quantity variation and price-variation (Bertrand) conditions. [3] Individuals acting as firms, made repeated simultaneous choices with no communication and either with or without complete information about the profits of other firms. Fouraker and Siegel found information an important variable in their triopoly and duopoly experiments; information about the profits of others increased the variance of outcomes. Without such information the Cournot solution was predominant. And they found triopoly more competitive than duopoly.

The Fouraker and Siegel results also tended to confirm Bertrand's claim that in a price-variation market with homogeneous products, behavior would be very competitive, for there was relatively little cooperation in the price-variation market even when participants were fully informed and few in number (two or three). Fouraker and Siegel ruled out a range of prices that could produce losses, however, and they also invoked an extra cost penalty for not having the lowest price. Thus, the model they used was one that would invite especially competitive behavior. Murphy later found that a threat of losses from lower prices could lead to more cooperation. [4][11] Cournot's model also lacked another ingredient of the oligopoly price-setting situation which could modify competition: limited capacity. So we cannot conclude that Fouraker and Siegel's results support competitive solutions in homogeneous product oligopoly as it usually is encountered.

Friedman examined behavior in duopoly, triopoly, and also four-firm markets, based on a Chamberlin differentiated product model under complete information. [20] He found more cooperation than Fouraker and Siegel had, possibly because his subjects played in more games and became more experienced. He has provided a careful criticism of his own results and also a review of Hogatt's and Fouraker's and Siegel's results. [22]. Because he has described the methods of these experiments, we shall not discuss them in detail here.

In experiments reprinted in Part I of this book, Dolbear, et al., also investigated market behavior in a differentiated product model, where they varied the number of firms and information conditions. [12] The number of firms was varied over two-, four-, and 16-firm markets. Under complete information, firms were given others' price and profit results; under incomplete information, only others' price was given. For both information conditions, fewer firms in a market led to significantly higher prices and profits.

There are two important structural differences between price-variation pay-

---

[11] In another replication of the Siegel and Fouraker experiments, graduate business students were shown to be less competitive than others, e.g., theology students. See [31].

offs in these Cournot (Fouraker and Siegel) and Chamberlin (Friedman, Dolbear et al.) models. First, the latter afforded *some* quantity to each firm even when other prices were lower, whereas in the Cournot market the low bidder would take all. Losses could be avoided at the low price in the Cournot experiments, too, but losses were still possible in the differentiated product experiments. As a result, the reward for price cutting was relatively greater in the Cournot (strictly speaking, Bertrand) market. A second difference involves the effect of n, the number of firms in each market. Following the Cournot model, Fouraker and Siegel compared the results of two and three firm markets in which the firms competed for the same total market quantity. If the firms cooperated, either three firms would split the joint profit or two firms would split it; the reward for cooperating was smaller as n increased. On the other hand, the reward for having the lowest price was the same regardless of n, since it was based on the same total market quantity. So as n increased, competing grew more attractive *relative* to cooperating. In either the Friedman or the Dolbear experiments, this was not so. As n increased, total market quantity was increased in proportion, to hold constant the balance between rewards for cooperating and for competing. Thus in the Fouraker and Siegel experimental Cournot markets, both structural and behavioral effects followed from changes in n, while in the Friedman and the Dolbear markets, structural effects of n were minimized if not altogether avoided. The finding of effects due to n in the latter experiments thus indicates that behavior is affected by changes in n even when structural effects are minimal. The Chamberlin argument that a small number of firms can reach a cooperative agreement tacitly is therefore supported in the experimental setting, without reliance on structural differences from the Cournot model which alone would tend to make cooperation more attractive as the number of firms grew smaller.

More recently, Hogatt conducted duopoly experiments in which one party or firm was a robot, performing in a programmed way. [28, 29] These experiments indicate that the behavior protocol of the robot will clearly influence the degree of cooperation, and that personality measures of the subjects will also. Although it forgoes genuine interdependence of participants, this method promises to allow subtle measurement of factors affecting individual behavior in oligopolistic conflict.

Behavior in Experimental Games

Observation of oligopolistic conflict behavior has by no means been confined to experimental markets.[12] One market-like but greatly simplified conflict structure used in many experiments is the prisoner's dilemma, which is illustrated in

---

[12]The vast majority of entries in Wrightsman's current 850 item bibliography of oligopoly-related work deals with games and other situations, not markets *per se*. [78]

Figure 1-1.[13] This simpler structure permits greater experimental control. It also narrows the scope of experiments, however, usually to two players and two strategies per player. The two alternative strategies represent cooperation or non-cooperation, extreme characterizations of what in a market could be a high price or a low price. In a paper reprinted in Part I below, Dolbear, et al., compared results in a market experiment involving 30 price strategies with those in a two-strategy prisoner's dilemma [11] and found less cooperation and lower average payoffs in the 30 strategy market experiment. Keeping this contrast in mind, factors that are found to affect the degree of cooperation in a two-strategy prisoner's dilemma are likely also to affect the degree of cooperation in market experiments.

The most interesting prisoner's dilemma experiments have involved repeated play of the game, an approximation to the continuing activity found in most markets and a practice followed in nearly all the experimental markets. Luce and Raiffa suggested [39, pp. 97-105] that iterated prisoner's dilemma games would yield more cooperative results than games played only once, because repetition offers an opportunity for each player to 'teach' the other. There is evidence that behavior does grow more cooperative when prisoner's dilemma games are played repeatedly. Experiments by Flood suggested this, [17] Friedman thought it was true, [21] and it has been confirmed over hundreds of trials by Rapoport and Chammah. [52]

Many independent variables which influence behavior in iterated games have been investigated, and although questions remain to be answered, cooperation has been controlled with considerable success. The most important variables have been: payoff structure, number of trials, communication[14] and information conditions, characteristics and strategy of one player, motivation,[15] and, as already noted, the number of strategies available. Most of these variables relate directly to recognizable market characteristics, so that their implications for the market context can be determined.

---

[13]This interesting problem is thoroughly described in [39] and experimental results based on the same dilemma structure are summarized in [3], [35], [36], [52] and [53]. For theory and experiments that emphasize learning, see [65] and [70].

[14]An opportunity to communicate has been shown to increase the cooperativeness of subjects under certain conditions. Such an increase was found by Deutsch for subjects given an individualistic motivation. [9] Loomis found that higher levels of communication increased trust and cooperation, [38] and Scodel, Minas, Ratoosh, and Lipetz found more cooperation after communication was allowed midway in a game. [57] But communication is difficult to relate to a market setting. Clearly, one firm *can* communicate with another. Through some institutions, however, particularly U.S. anti-trust laws, communication concerning price or pricing plans is expressly forbidden.

[15]Without using actual monetary payoffs, Deutsch instructed players to seek different objectives (e.g., individualistic, competitive, cooperative) in one play of a prisoners' dilemma game and found a direct relation between motivation induced and number of cooperative choices. [9] Absence of actual payoffs seriously limits the generality of these Deutsch results, of course, for without genuine rewards the experiment measures in part the obedience of subjects, not their own choices. The direction of any bias is not clear; it has been shown that absence of payoffs does not necessarily result in greater cooperation. [24]

Figure 1-1
Prisoner's Dilemma

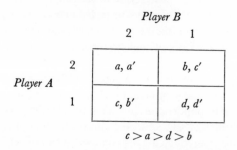

$$c > a > d > b$$

The structure of payoffs in a prisoner's dilemma can be related to market demand elasticity and cost conditions. Coincident choices (i.e., 1, 1 or 2, 2 in Figure 1-1) compare with the case when all firms in a market set the same price, making results depend on total market demand. Thus the difference between a and d in Figure 1-1 can be related to the elasticity of market demand. In a cooperative to non-cooperative range of prices, a larger value of $a-d$ corresponds to a less elastic market demand, and this is the economic property of a market that will favor price cooperation. But the proportion of costs that are fixed over the decision horizon, which is assumed shorter than the long run, can also influence the magnitude of $a-d$. The higher profit level, a, is achieved by restricting output, and as more costs vary with output, more expenses can be reduced by operating at a lower output level. Costs that are highly variable with output will thus encourage price cooperation.

Payoffs b and c in Figure 1-1 result from dissimilar actions by firms (i.e., 1, 2 or 2, 1 in Figure 1-1), and can be related to cross-elasticity and output capacity conditions. Player A's choice of the high price (smaller output) while player B chooses a low price will lead to payoff b for player A. Payoff b will offer less profit (greater loss) as a greater portion of costs are fixed. Payoff c will be greater and b smaller as cross-elasticities between firms' products are greater, as long as capacities do not limit quantities. So high cross-elasticity of demand and low cost variability will discourage price cooperation.

These relative payoffs have been shown to influence cooperation. A higher value of the ratio, $(a-d)/(d-b)$, will invite more cooperation, and a lower value of the ratio $(c-a)/(a-d)$ will tend to make cooperation persist. [53] Lave examined the influence of the number of trials, thereby introducing the time influence that is either implicit or explicit in all demand-supply relations in economics. [36] Using payoffs as shown in Figure 1-1, Lave argued that attempts at cooperation would become attractive and be made when n was large enough that $n(a-d) = k(d-b)$, where k was a constant, 3. This formulation combines a measure of the attractiveness of collusion, $(a-d)$, with the cost of being doublecrossed, $(d-b)$. Lave's theory implies definite attempts to cooperate as *n* grows very large. This is consistent with Luce and Raiffa's hypothesis and the results Rapoport and Chammah found in very large numbers of trials (300 to 700). [43] With the numbers of plays so large, cooperative behavior accounted for well over 50 per cent of the choices of males in experiments reported by Rapoport and Chammah. Pairs of females made only one-half as many cooperative responses as males.[16]

Personality measures have not been successful as predictors of cooperative behavior when subjects make interacting choices in a prisoner's dilemma. The sharpest effect is the Rapoport and Chammah finding the males cooperate more than females. Dolbear, et al., observed, however, that inclusion of student subjects' major fields can reduce the explanatory power of sex. [11] And results of earlier investigations of the effect of sex were equivocal. [23] Personality measures, including risk attitudes, have been disappointing predictors of cooperation in iterated experimental games. [10, 49] That risk attitudes do not predict cooperative or competitive behavior is especially disappointing because in a market context risktaking has traditionally played an important role.

Individual risk attitude has been related, however, to choice of prisoner's dilemma game in which to play. [58, 59, 61] Those who tend to avoid risky situations were found to prefer playing in prisoner dilemma games with greater opportunities for cooperation (higher value of the ratio, $(a-d)/(d-b)$). Further, pairs of subjects who both tended to avoid risk also cooperated significantly more in an iterated game that provided game matrix choices as well as strategy choices within the games. [60] When persons having different risk attitudes were paired, the person more fond of risk tended to earn more. In the same sense that a strategy choice within a game corresponds to a price choice, the game matrix choice can correspond to a capacity choice. So risk attitude may influence capacity decisions even though it has not been linked separately to a price decision. Thus, individual risk attitude does appear as an influential variable in laboratory choices corresponding to capacity or investment decisions.[17]

Measures of isolationism have served as predictors of behavior in a variant of the prisoner's dilemma which is called "chicken." This finding is interesting because another longer-run choice, the entry decision, can be represented by the "chicken game" matrix. [62] Figure 1-1 could be converted to a chicken game matrix if the *b* and *d* payoffs were reversed so the ordering of payoffs would become: $c>a>b>d$. The effect of this change is to make one simultaneous action (e.g., entry by two firms at once) less attractive to both players than if each selected a strategy different from the other. Persons with an isolationist attitude have been found to act more competitively (insist on entering) in the "chicken

---

[16]A rationalization for male cooperativeness that goes to their early need to cooperate in groups (while women remained in the caves) is presented in [74].

[17]Other factors have been shown to affect risk taking: (i) alcoholic beverages induce more risk taking, [72] (ii) young persons take more risk, [33] and (iii) groups take more risk than individuals. [34, 50] Risk taking has also been investigated as a value in itself. [37]

game." [40, 41] So where personality differences predict experimental game behavior, the choice seems to be of a long-run type.

Psychological variables already play an evident role in long-run oligopolistic choices, and they may also be detected as determinants of short-run choices by more sensitive measurement techniques (e.g., [29]). At the same time, payoff structure continues to play a crucial role in individual action even in the mixed-motive, analytically indeterminate conflict situation that characterizes oligopoly. Since the payoff structure faced by firms in any particular oligopoly market can be derived from information about economic variables, experimental game results can also be linked to economic variables, and can serve as a valuable source of hypotheses to be tested empirically in real markets.

Thus, since Cournot's explicit treatment of a few firms in a market, oligopoly theory has developed primarily as a short-run theory concerned with price or output decisions. Chamberlin characterized most clearly the cooperate or compete aspects of such an oligopoly choice. And we cannot now dispose of either the cooperative or the non-cooperative solution on analytical grounds alone. To investigate such contending solutions, researchers have turned from normative to descriptive techniques, including the controlled experiment. Cournot, Bertrand, and Chamberlin markets have been explored experimentally. Giving subjects more information tends usually to increase cooperation. And as n becomes smaller, subjects (acting as firms) cooperate more; that is, they set higher prices or smaller quantities and enjoy higher profits. This is so even when the structural effects of the Cournot model, which reduce the attractiveness of cooperation as n increases, are minimized. Subjects are able to achieve some cooperation without any communication save their price actions. But cooperation has been rare when more than two persons are in a market. Cost conditions can intervene, however, to affect the importance of n.

Other findings, from prisoner's dilemma games, are also relevant to oligopoly. The structure of payoffs influences the amount of cooperation achieved by subject-pairs, an important result because effects on the structure of payoffs can be traced to economic variables. Individual risk attitude affects game matrix choice, which is analogous to investment choice, and age as well as group discussion opportunity, and other variables, are known to affect risk attitude. Also, isolationist attitude affects play in a "chicken game," which can be related to an entry decision. Individual personality differences have not succeeded generally in distinguishing cooperators from competitors and a solely psychological basis for price collusion seems elusive, but psychological variables clearly can affect behavior in oligopolistic conflict situations. Experimental confirmation thus offers a promising way to test oligopoly behavior theories, at least as a preliminary check on their abundant supply. It affords a means of selecting most promising hypotheses to confront with real-world evidence. And it remains almost the only means of searching for psychological influences on oligopolistic behavior.

Behavior in Industry

Over the past twenty-odd years, without the advantages of laboratory control and on a scale very unlike experimental games and markets, the behavior of real-world industrial firms also has been investigated empirically. To overcome the lack of control inherent in real-world conditions, measurable elements of market structure that could be expected to influence firm behavior were defined, so their effect on firm behavior and industry performance might then be gauged in cross-section comparisons. Edward Mason first articulated some of the possible market structure elements, including product characteristics (e.g., whether a durable good, whether differentiated), the numbers and sizes of buyers and sellers, the relative ease of entry for new firms, cost characteristics of firms' operations such as the ratio of overhead to variable costs at given volumes of output or given variations in volume of output, and a number of others. [41] Prediction of the exact or even approximate effect of each element was not emphasized so much by Mason, for the classification according to market structure elements was intended mainly as a systematic means of gathering information about effects.

Joe Bain [2] and others have added predictions of the effects of elements of market structure on industry performance, usually stemming in one way or another from a paradigm that anticipates more cooperative behavior among a few oligopolistic firms if they are protected from new entry into the industry. And the difficulty of new entry and the extent to which a few firms control industry sales have each been found positively related to industry return on investment, or profitability. [2] Many other observations have been made as well, although substantial unexplained variance still remains. [76] Not all of Mason's suggestions have been pursued. Little attention has been given to the effect of cost characteristics on the firms' operations, for instance, and the exact effect of each element on the firm's rewards for alternative actions was never traced precisely.

Despite our inability to predict behavior exactly, we still can identify the reward structures that individual firms face in oligopoly markets. Each firm faces a whole structure of payoff values, one payoff for every possible combination of an action by that firm and an action by each of the others, and these payoffs are influenced by quite well understood cost and demand variables. One research strategy for attacking industrial oligopoly then is to fall back on these more complex but more reliably known payoff structures, on the expectation that firms will respond predictably, at least stochastically or probabilistically, to differences in payoff structures. All the experimental evidence we have suggests that payoff structure will influence behavior. We have only to trace the effect of economic variables on payoff structure, then, to be able to predict probabilistically from such economic variables the outcomes in oligopoly markets. That task is the subject of this book.

Our purpose here does not differ from that which has motivated other industrial organization studies. We rely more on the experimental method initially, though, for preliminary investigation of how reward structure and psychological variables can affect behavior. And when we turn to examine real industries we emphasize some different economic variables, too, because they can be linked more conveniently to reward structure. For instance, we examine cost function properties as Mason suggested. We also focus heavily on the firm's capacity choice, and concern for capacity as well as price choice probably is a distinguishing feature of the book. We presume that entry into many industries of interest will be difficult, and industry performance will depend then on whether the firms already in the industry can resist capacity expansion.

The book is divided into three parts. The first of these parts experimentally examines behavior in traditional short-run market games, where no new entry can occur. This work confirms the findings of others and adds some elaborations, making possible more exact interpretation in the oligopoly setting of other work by social psychologists. The second part introduces capacity as well as price choice into this oligopolist's payoff structure and experimentally examines new implications which result. Finally, in the third part, hypotheses for firm growth and advertising in oligopoly markets are tested, and the bearing these results have for the interpretation of previous market structure-performance studies is demonstrated. Implications for public policy toward industrial organization also are noted.

References

[1] Archibald, G.C., "Chamberlin *versus* Chicago," *Review of Economic Studies*, Vol. 29, 1961-62.

[2] Bain, J.S., *Barriers to New Competition*, Cambridge, Harvard University Press, 1956.

[3] Bertrand, J., Review of Cournot's "Researches . . . ." *Journal des Savants*, September 1883.

[4] Bowley, A.L., *The Mathematical Groundwork of Economics*, Oxford, Oxford University Press, 1924.

[5] Bronfenbrenner, M., "Imperfect Competition on a Long-Run Basis," *Journal of Business*, Vol. 23, 1950, 81-93.

[6] Chamberlin, E.H., *The Theory of Monopolistic Competition*, 8th ed., Cambridge, Harvard University Press, 1962.

[7] Cournot, A., *Researches Into the Mathematical Principles of the Theory of Wealth*, New York, Macmillan Company, 1927, translated by N.T. Bacon and Irving Fisher.

[8] Cyert, R.M., and March, J., *A Behavioral Theory of the Firm*, Englewood Cliffs, Prentice-Hall, 1964.

[9] Deutsch, M., "Trust and Suspicion," *Journal of Conflict Resolution*, Vol. 2, September 1958, 267-79.

[10] Dolbear, F.T., Jr., and Lave, L.B., "Risk Orientation as a Predictor in the Prisoner's Dilemma," *Journal of Conflict Resolution*, Vol. 10, December 1966, 506-15.

[11] Dolbear, F.T., et al., "Collusion in the Prisoner's Dilemma: The Effect of the Number of Strategies," *Journal of Conflict Resolution*, Vol. 13, June 1969, 252-61.

[12] Dolbear, F.T., et al., "Collusion in Oligopoly: An Experiment on the Effect of Numbers and Information," *Quarterly Journal of Economics*, Vol. 82, May 1968, 240-59.

[13] Edgeworth, F.Y., *Papers Relating to Political Economy*, Vol. I, London, Macmillan and Company, Ltd., 1925.

[14] Fellner, W.J., *Competition Among the Few*, New York: Augustus M. Kelley reprints of economic classics, 1960.

[15] Ferguson, C.E., and Pfouts, R.W., "Learning and Expectations in Dynamic Duopoly Behavior," *Behavioral Science*, Vol. 7, April 1962, 223-37.

[16] Fisher, I., "Cournot and Mathematical Economics," *Quarterly Journal of Economics*, Vol. 12, 1898, 119-38.

[17] Flood, M.M., "Some Experimental Games," *Management Science*, 1958, Vol. 5, 5-26.

[18] Fouraker, L.E., "Product Differentiation and Straight-Line Indifference Curves," *American Economic Review*, Vol. 48, pt. 2, 1958, 568-77.

[19] Fouraker, L.E., and Siegel, S., *Bargaining Behavior*, New York, McGraw-Hill, Inc., 1963.

[20] Friedman, J.W., "Individual Behavior in Oligopolistic Markets: An Experimental Study," *Yale Economic Essays*, Vol. 3, 1963, 359-417.

[21] Friedman, J.W., "An Experimental Study of Cooperative Duopoly," *Econometrica*, October 1967, 379-97.

[22] Friedman, J.W., "On Experimental Research in Oligopoly," *Review of Economic Studies*, Vol. 36, October 1969, 399-415.

[23] Gallo, P.S., and McClintock, C.G., "Comparative and Competitive Behavior in Mixed Motive Games," *Journal of Conflict Resolution*, Vol. 9, 1965, 68-78.

[24] Gumpert, P., Deutsch, M., and Epstein, Y., "Effect of Incentive Magnitude on Cooperation in the Prisoner's Dilemma," *Journal of Personality and Social Psychology*, Vol. II, January 1969, 66-9.

[25] Henderson, A., "The Theory of Duopoly," *The Quarterly Journal of Economics*, Vol. 68, 1954.

[26] Higgins, B.H., "Elements of Indeterminancy in the Theory of Nonperfect Competition," *American Economic Review*, Vol. 29, 1930, 468-79.

[27] Hoggatt, A.C., "An Experimental Business Game," *Behavioral Science*, Vol. 4, 1959, 192-203.

[28] Hoggatt, A.C., "Measuring the Cooperativeness of Behavior in Quantity Variation Duopoly Games," *Behavioral Science*, Vol. 12, March 1967, 109-21.

[29] Hoggatt, A.C., "Response of Paid Student Subjects to Differential Behavior of Robots in Bifurcated Duopoly Games," *Review of Economic Studies*, Vol. 36, October 1969, 417-32.

[30] Hotelling, H., "Stability in Competition," *Economic Journal*, Vol. 14, 1929.

[31] Johnson, H.L., and Cohen, A.M., "Experiments in Behavioral Economics: Siegel and Fouraker Revisited," *Behavioral Science*, Vol. 12, September 1967, 353-72.

[32] Johnston, J., *Statistical Cost Analysis*, New York: McGraw-Hill, 1960.

[33] Kogan, N., and Wallich, M.A., "Aspects of Judgment and Decision Making: Interrelationships and Changes With Age," *Behavioral Science*, Vol. 6, 1961, 23-36.

[34] Kogan, N., and Wallich, M.A., "Risk Taking as a Function of the Situation, the Person, and the Group," in: *New Directions in Psychology III*, New York: Holt Rinehart, Winston, 1967.

[35] Lave, L.B., "An Empirical Approach to the Prisoner's Dilemma Game," *Quarterly Journal of Economics*, Vol. 76, 1962, 242-36.

[36] Lave, L.B., "Factors Affecting Cooperation in the Prisoner's Dilemma," *Behavioral Science*, Vol. 10, 1965, 26-38.

[37] Levinger, G., and Schneider, D.J., "Test of the 'Risk is a Value' Hypothesis," *Journal of Personality and Social Psychology*, Vol. 11, 1969, 165-69.

[38] Loomis, J.L., "Communications, the Development of Trust, and Cooperative Behavior," *Human Relations*, Vol. 12, 1959, 305-15.

[39] Luce, R.D., and Raiffa, H., *Games and Decisions*, New York: John Wiley & Sons, Inc., 1957.

[40] Lutzker, D.R., "Internationalism as a Predictor of Cooperative Behavior," *Journal of Conflict Resolution*, Vol. 4, 1960.

[41] Mason, E.S., "Price and Production Policies of Large-Scale Enterprises," *American Economic Review*, Vol. 29, March 1939, 61-74, reprinted in R.B. Heflebower and G.W. Stocking, eds., *Readings in Industrial Organization and Public Policy*, Homewood, Ill.: Richard D. Irwin, Inc., 1958.

[42] McClintock, C.G., Harrison, A.A., Strand, S., and Gallo, P., "Internationalism-Isolationism, Strategy of the Other Player, and Two-Person Game Behavior," *Journal of Abnormal and Social Psychology*, Vol. 67, 1963, 631-6.

[43] Modigliani, F., "New Developments on the Oligopoly Front," *Journal of Political Economy*, Vol. 66, 1958, 215-32.

[44] Murphy, J.L., "Effects of the Threat of Losses on Duopoly Bargaining," *Quarterly Journal of Economics*, Vol. 80, 1966, 296-313.

[45] Neumann, J. von, and Morgenstern, O., *Theory of Games and Economic Behavior*, 3rd ed., New York: John Wiley & Sons, Inc., 1964.

[46] Nichol, A.J., "The Influence of Marginal Buyers on Monopolistic Competition," *Quarterly Journal of Economics*, Vol. 49, 1934-35, 121-35.

[47] Nutter, G.W., "The Plateau Demand Curve and Utility Theory," *Journal of Political Economy*, Vol. 63, 1955, 525-28.

[48] Ozga, S.A., "Imperfect Markets Through Lack of Knowledge," *Quarterly Journal of Economics*, Vol. 74, 1960, 29-52.

[49] Pilisuk, M., Potter, P., Rapoport, A., and Winter, J. Alan, "War Hawks and Peace Doves," *Journal of Conflict Resolution*, Vol. 9, 1965, 491-508.

[50] Pylyshyn, A., Aghew, N., and Illingworth, J., "Comparison of Individuals and Pairs as Participants in a Mixed-Motive Game," *Journal of Conflict Resolution*, Vol. 10, 1966, 211-20.

[51] Quandt, R.E., "On the Stability of Price Adjusting Oligopoly," *Southern Economic Journal*, Vol. 33, 1967, 332-6.

[52] Rapoport, A., and Chammah, A.M., *Prisoner's Dilemma*, Ann Arbor: The University of Michigan Press, 1965.

[53] Rapoport, A., and Orwant, C., "Experimental Games: A Review," *Behavioral Science*, Vol. 7, 1962, 1-37.

[54] Sato, R., and Nagatani, K., "The Stability of Oligopoly With Conjectoral Variation," *Review of Economic Studies*, Vol. 34, 1967, 409-16.

[55] Schelling, T.C., *The Strategy of Conflict*, New York: Oxford University Press, 1963.

[56] Schultz, D.P., "The Human Subject in Psychological Research," *Psychological Bulletin*, Vol. 72, 1969, 214-28.

[57] Scodel, A., Minas, J.S., Ratoosh, P., and Lipetz, M., "Some Descriptive Aspects of Two-Person, Non-Zero-Sum Games," *Journal of Conflict Resolution*, Vol. 3, 1959, 114-19.

[58] Sherman, R., "Individual Attitude Toward Risk and Choice Between Prisoner's Dilemma Games," *Journal of Psychology*, Vol. 66, 1967, 291-98.

[59] Sherman, R., "Personality and Strategic Choice," *Journal of Psychology*, Vol. 68, 1968, 191-8.

[60] Sherman, R., "Risk Attitude and Cost Variability in a Capacity Choice Experiment," *Review of Economic Studies*, Vol. 36, 1969, 453-66.

[61] Sherman, R., "Culture and Strategic Choice," *Journal of Psychology*, Vol. 75, 1970, 227-30.

[62] Sherman, R., and Willett, T.D., "Potential Entrants Discourage Entry," *Journal of Political Economy*, Vol. 75, August 1967, 400-403.

[63] Shubik, M., *Strategy and Market Structure*, New York: John Wiley & Sons, Inc., 1959.

[64] Siegel, S., and Fouraker, L.E., *Bargaining and Group Decision Making*, New York: McGraw-Hill, Inc., 1960.

[65] Simon, H.A., "A Comparison of Game Theory and Learning Theory," *Psychometrika*, Vol. 21, 1956 (reprinted in H.A. Simon, *Models of Man*, New York: John Wiley and Sons, Inc., 1957).

[66] Stackelberg, Heinrich, *Marketform and Gleichgewicht*, Wien and Berlin 1934.

[67] Stigler, G.J., *Five Lectures on Economic Problems*, London: Longmans, Green & Co., 1949.

[68] Stigler, G.J., "Notes on the Theory of Duopoly," *Journal of Political Economy*, Vol. 48, 1940, 521-41.

[69] Stigler, G.J., "The Economics of Information," *Journal of Political Economy*, Vol. 69, 1961, 213-25.

[70] Suppes, P., and Carlsmith, J.M., "Experimental Analysis of a Duopoly Situation from the Standpoint of Mathematical Learning Theory," *International Economic Review*, Vol. 3, 1962, 60-78.

[71] Sylos-Labini, P., *Oligopoly and Technical Progress*, Cambridge: Harvard University Press, 1962.

[72] Teger, A.I., Katkin, E.S., and Pruitt, D.G., "Effects of Alcoholic Beverages and Their Congener Content on Level and Style of Risk Taking," *Journal of Personality and Social Psychology*, Vol. 11, April 1969, 170-76.

[73] Theocaris, R.D., "On the Stability of the Cournot Oligopoly Solution of the Oligopoly Problem," *Review of Economic Studies*, Vol. 27, 1960, 133-34.

[74] Tiger, L., *Men in Groups*, New York: Random House, 1970.

[75] Tun Thin, *Theory of Markets*, Cambridge: Harvard University Press, 1960.

[76] Weiss, L., "Quantitative Studies of Industrial Organization," in Michael D.

Intriligator, ed., *Frontiers of Quantitative Economics*, Amsterdam: North Holland Publishing Co., 1971.

[77] Worcester, D.A., Jr., "Why 'Dominant Firms' Decline," *Journal of Political Economy*, Vol. 65, 1957, 338-46.

[78] Wrightsman, L.S., "Bibliography of Studies on Cooperation and Exploitation in Mixed Motive Games and Coalition Formation Situations," Mimeographed, August 1969, George Peabody College for Teachers, Nashville, Tennessee.

Part I:
Price Collusion in Oligopoly

Traditional price collusion (short-run collusion) is examined in Part I using laboratory experiments, and two main results are obtained. First, more price strategies are shown to make cooperation or collusion more difficult to reach. If firms in an oligopoly market followed a practice of pricing only at, say, $5.95 or $6.95, rather than all the prices in between, it would be easier for them to cooperate. Second, more firms in a market are shown to make cooperation less likely. An effort was made to control the structure of payoffs and hold it the same for each firm as the number of firms in an experimental market was changed, so that only number of firms, not number of firms plus payoff structure, would account for the observed differences in cooperation. The effect of the amount of information that is provided to firms in the experimental market is also examined.

2

Number of Strategies and Collusion[1]

Factors affecting collusion and competition in mixed-motive settings have been investigated extensively in recent years. Many experiments have dealt with the two-person, two-strategy prisoner's dilemma.[2] Other experiments have been modeled on real-world conflict situations, such as two competing firms whose decision sets include a large number of alternative prices (see [3, 5, 6, 7, 16]). The present study examines the effect of the number of strategy alternatives in an effort to integrate these two bodies of literature.

Many situations have a prisoner's dilemma embedded in a larger decision framework. For example, a firm in a market with a small number of other firms has a range of (low price) choices where it is to the advantage of each firm to price above average; a range (of moderate prices) where it is to the advantage of all firms to raise price together, but to the advantage of any individual firm to cut price—the prisoner's dilemma; and finally, a range (of high prices) where it is to no firm's advantage to increase all prices. The large experimental literature on the prisoner's dilemma would be relevant to investigating collusion in such markets if it could be established that behavior is "essentially the same" in the two-strategy game as in the multistrategy game.

While holding constant the number of decision-makers, we shall vary the number of choice alternatives. At the minimal choice extreme is the prisoner's dilemma. To contrast the behavior in that structure with behavior in a comparable but multistrategy situation, we construct two experimental games which offer the same points of "Cournot noncooperative maximization" and "joint maximization."

Price-Profit Games

Profit consequences for two firms in a duopoly market with only two price strategies are shown in Table 2-1.[3] Two players (acting as business firms), A and

Reprinted with permission from "Collusion in the Prisoner's Dilemma: Number of Strategies," by F.T. Dolbear, L.B. Lave, G. Bowman, A. Lieberman, E. Prescott, F. Rueter, and R. Sherman, in *Journal of Conflict Resolution*, 13 (June 1969), 252-61.

[1]This research was sponsored in part by a grant from the Ford Foundation.

[2]See [8, 10, 13, 14]. For experiments involving more than two strategies, see [9, 12].

[3]The model might be characterized as having differentiated products rather than a "low price sells all" situation.

Table 2-1
A Simple Price Setting Duopoly

		FIRM A	
		$p = 19$	$p = 23$
FIRM B	$p = 19$	19, 19	24, 13
	$p = 23$	13, 24	22, 22

B, must each choose a price of either 19 or 23. The combination of their choices determines the profit (in cents) accruing to each. (The structure of this matrix will be recognized as the prisoner's dilemma.[4]) A matrix which affords thirty alternative price choices is shown in Table 2-2. Notice that the two-strategy matrix of Table 2-1 is embedded in the larger matrix. The lower price of the small matrix (19) will be referred to as the noncooperative maximum (NCM) while the higher price (23) will be termed the joint maximum (JM). The latter point has the property that if the firms maximize their joint profit, they can do no better than a price of 23. Joint profit declines whenever price is raised above or lowered below 23. Any single firm can usually increase its profit by charging a price lower than the other firm whenever prices are above 19. But for prices below 19, the firm can usually increase its profit by charging a higher price than the other firm. A firm that acts independently (believing the other firm will not react to its moves) will thus be led to a price of 19.[5] Between these two prices lies a range where a firm can increase its profit by pricing below the other firm and both firms can increase their profit if both increase price cooperatively. This range (19-23) will be referred to as the prisoner's dilemma range.

Hypotheses

Hypothesis 1: *There will be more cooperation in the small matrix and more subjects at the JM.* This experiment was designed to relate behavior in two bargaining situations which differ only with respect to the number of strategy

---

[4]Numerous experiments have utilized this paradigm; their results provide an extensive set of predictions for behavior in such a simple compete-collude dilemma. Depending on the nature of the payoff structure and the conditions of the experiment, one can predict the frequency of cooperative behavior, the stability of collusion, etc. Experiments have reported on the affect of varying payoff structure, amount of information, amount of communication, number of trials, reward schemes, and equality of payoffs. They have also reported the effect of controlling personality variables, sex differences, and attitudes toward risk.

[5]Cournot assumed that a firm would attempt to maximize its profit believing that the rival firm would not react to price changes. [4] Two such firms would end up at the NCM. Cooperation of both firms would lead to the JM and maximum profit. Pareto formalized the idea that sellers would collude to maximize joint profit. [11]

Table 2-2
Thirty-Strategy Payoff Matrix

Player with lower price	Player with higher price																	
	6	7	8	9	10	11	12	13	14	15	16	17	18	19	20	21	22	23
6	-15,-15	-15,-11	-15,-8	-15,-5	-15,-2	-15,0	-15,1	-15,2	-15,2	-15,3	-15,3	-15,2	-15,1	-15,0	-15,-3	-15,-5	-15,-7	-15,-12
7		-11,-11	-11,-8	-11,-4	-11,-2	-11,0	-10,2	-10,3	-10,4	-10,5	-10,3	-10,3	-10,3	-10,0	-10,-1	-10,-2	-10,-7	-10,-9
8			-7,-7	-7,-4	-7,-2	-7,1	-7,2	-6,4	-6,5	-6,5	-5,5	-5,5	-5,3	-5,2	-5,1	-5,-2	-5,-4	-5,-6
9				-4,-4	-3,-1	-3,1	-3,3	-2,5	-2,5	-2,6	-1,7	-1,5	-1,5	0,5	0,1	0,0	0,-2	0,-6
10					-1,-1	0,2	0,4	0,5	1,6	2,8	2,7	2,7	3,7	3,5	4,4	4,3	4,-2	5,-4
11						3,3	3,4	3,6	4,8	4,8	5,8	6,9	6,7	7,7	8,6	8,3	8,1	9,-1
12							5,5	6,7	6,8	7,9	8,10	8,9	9,9	10,8	10,7	11,5	12,4	12,-1
13								7,7	8,9	9,10	10,10	11,11	12,11	12,9	13,8	14,8	14,5	15,2
14									10,10	10,11	12,12	13,13	13,11	14,11	16,11	16,8	17,6	18,5
15										12,12	14,13	14,13	15,13	17,13	17,11	18,10	20,9	20,6
16											15,15	16,15	17,15	17,13	18,13	20,13	20,9	22,8
17												16,16	16,15	18,15	20,15	20,13	22,12	23,9
18													17,17	19,18	20,15	21,15	23,13	23,12
19														19,19	20,18	22,17	23,15	24,13
20															20,20	20,18	23,17	25,16
21																20,20	23,19	23,18
22																	21,21	23,19
23																		22,22
24																		
25																		
26																		
27																		
28																		
29																		
30																		
31																		
32																		
33																		
34																		
35																		

profit of lower price player, profit of higher price player

Table 2-2 (cont.)

Player with higher price												Player with lower price
24	25	26	27	28	29	30	31	32	33	34	35	
-15,-15	-15,-15	-15,-15										6
-10,-12	-10,-15	-10,-15										7
-5,-12	-5,-15	-5,-15										8
0,-9	0,-12	0,-15										9
5,-6	5,-12	5,-15										10
9,-6	10,-9	10,-12	10,-15									11
13,-3	14,-5	14,-12	15,-15									12
17,0	17,-5	18,-8	19,-12	19,-15	20,-15		25,-15					13
18,2	20,-2	21,-5	21,-11	22,-15	24,-15	24,-15	29,-15	29,-15				14
21,3	23,1	23,-5	24,-8	26,-11	26,-15	27,-15	30,-15	32,-15	30,-15			15
23,6	23,1	25,-2	27,-6	27,-11	28,-15	30,-15	32,-15	34,-15	33,-15	33,-15	35,-15	16
23,7	25,4	27,0	27,-4	29,-8	31,-11	31,-15	35,-15	35,-15	34,-15	36,-15	38,-15	17
25,9	27,7	27,3	29,-1	31,-4	31,-11	33,-15	35,-15	37,-15	37,-15	39,-15	39,-15	18
26,12	26,8	28,5	31,3	31,-4	33,-7	35,-11	36,-15	39,-15	39,-15	39,-15	42,-15	19
25,13	27,10	29,8	30,3	32,0	34,-4	34,-11	38,-11	39,-15	39,-15	41,-15	43,-15	20
25,17	28,14	28,8	30,6	33,3	33,-3	35,-7	36,-8	38,-11	40,-15	43,-15	43,-15	21
25,19	25,18	28,14	30,10	30,6	33,3	36,-4	36,-7	38,-11	41,-15	41,-15	44,-15	22
23,19	25,18	28,15	28,13	30,7	33,4	33,0	36,-2	39,-11	39,-15	42,-15	45,-15	23
21,21	24,19	25,17	27,13	30,11	30,4	33,1	33,-2	39,-11	39,-11	42,-15	42,-15	24
	20,20	23,18	25,17	27,12	30,8	33,5	32,2	36,-6	39,-11	39,-15	42,-15	25
		20,20	22,18	25,14	27,12	30,7	29,6	35,-2	36,-10	38,-15	42,-15	26
			20,20	22,18	23,13	27,9	25,6	31,-2	34,-6	38,-10	38,-15	27
				18,18	22,16	23,13	21,7	29,2	31,-1	33,-10	36,-15	28
					18,18	20,14	23,10	25,6	27,-1	31,-6	33,-10	29
						17,17	20,14	21,7	25,3	27,-1	29,-10	30
							16,16	17,11	21,7	24,-1	27,-5	31
								15,15	17,8	20,4	24,-1	32
									14,14	17,8	19,0	33
										13,13	16,4	34
											9,9	35

alternatives. Previous results led us to predict that subjects using the small matrix will attempt cooperation (attempt to reach the joint maximum) but that this cooperation will be unstable.[6] In attempting to extrapolate these results to predict behavior in the large matrix, note that the large matrix provides more choices which might be used to signal or shade the payoff distribution. The small matrix offers only two alternatives: the NCM and the JM. Attempts to signal the desire to cooperate or to change the distribution of payoffs are limited by the existence of only two alternatives and by the general simplicity of the situation. In the small matrix the subjects must arrive at different payoff splits by changing their choices over time, rather than by choosing one pair of prices which would give them the desired payoff split. We hypothesize that the range of alternatives in the large matrix will be dysfunctional; it will lead subjects to be more demanding and so lead to less cooperation than in small matrix experiments.

Hypothesis 2: *There will be a more nearly equal division of payoffs between subjects in the small matrix.* In the small matrix unequal payoffs above the noncooperative level can be achieved only through complicated patterns of choices. The range of prices in the large matrix makes it possible to obtain unequal payoffs without sequential choice patterns. This hypothesis asserts that subjects will take advantage of the opportunity.

Hypothesis 3: *There will be more stable cooperation in the small matrix, once it is achieved.* Suppose, in the first few trials, subjects have reached the joint maximum. Subjects using the small matrix will probably tend to continue choosing the JM strategy on each trial; after all, in order to obtain a different payoff split, they must choose the noncooperative strategy—an act which might be perceived as a lack of desire to cooperate, not just an attempt to change the payoff split. In the large matrix more subtle behavior is possible. By lowering price one unit, a subject can attempt to gain a larger payoff without moving to the noncooperative price. It is the inability to be subtle in the small matrix which necessitates a narrowness in expectations and behavior and invites more stable cooperation.[7]

Hypothesis 4: *In the large matrix, subject pairs will be distributed across the range of prices between the NCM and JM.* This hypothesis implicitly asserts that few subjects will choose prices outside this range; further, there will not be a marked tendency to cluster at either of the two seemingly dominant points. One might expect that rational subjects would tend to converge on the JM if they found they could trust each other or on the NCM if they found they could not. This hypothesis asserts that such convergence will not occur. For some who tend to the cooperative strategies, the JM presents too large a temptation to double-cross. For some who tend to the noncooperative strategies, the NCM

---

[6]The former result is predicted by Lave (see [10]) and the latter result has been observed in payoff structures where defection is not prohibitively expensive to the other party.

[7]An effect similar to this hypothesis has been suggested by Carl Stevens in a proposal for "one-or-the-other" decisions in arbitrating labor-management disputes. [17]

might be regarded as having too low a payoff. The large matrix offers alternative choices which vary the degree of cooperation.

Method

Subjects were recruited from sophomore economics classes at the Carnegie-Mellon University. They were told they could volunteer for an experiment on market structure in which they might earn $2.00 or more. To mitigate the effects of information leakage, subjects were informed that a number of different experiments were being run and that telling a friend about the experiment could lead to confusion and loss of money for the friend. (Both statements were true.)

As he arrived, each subject was given an instruction sheet, the relevant payoff matrix, a decision sheet on which to record the price chosen (and on which the experimenter recorded the other subject's price and profit), and an explanation sheet on which to write the reasons for his choice. The game was described as a situation similar to a market in which two firms chose prices which determined profits. The instructions explained the operation of the matrix and noted that the subject would play opposite another person in the same room but would never learn the identity of this other person.

In addition to these sheets, the subject was given a tray containing $1.50 in change. He was told that this money represented a loan with which to begin the experiment; the loan was to be repaid at the end of the experiment. His pay would consist of his winnings in the game. As can be seen from the payoff matrices, earnings per trial and for the entire experiment were large. Earnings averaged $2.88 per subject for the ninety-minute experiment.

The game was begun by each subject choosing a price, recording this decision, and then writing a brief explanation for his choice while decision sheets were collected. The experimenter then filled in the other person's choice and profits for both players and returned the decision sheets. Subjects were paid their winnings and then a new trial was begun. The instructions noted that there would be a "large number of trials"; the decision sheet contained space for 32 trials.

Results

Three sessions were held involving a total of 46 subjects. Twenty-two participated in the first session where the small matrix (Table 2-1) was used. The second and third sessions consisted of ten and fourteen subjects respectively, all of whom were confronted with the large matrix (Table 2-2). There was a difference in the results of the latter two sessions which will be discussed below.

In addition to providing a point of comparison with the large matrix, the group using the small matrix is a control group that can be compared to previous experiments. Attempts at cooperation were found to be comparable to earlier results (see, e.g., [10]). Employing the context of a firm within an industry did not seem to have noticeable effects, aside from some written comments on the subjects' views of business behavior.

Hypothesis 1 conjectures that there will be more cooperation in the small matrix. Average payoff (for the pair) was used as an index of cooperation. (Payoffs rise as subjects jointly raise price, up to p = 23.) The average payoff under each matrix condition is presented in Table 2-3 along with a *t*-test for significant difference. The data were pooled in three ways: all of the trials were used, then the first five (learning) trials were eliminated, then the final (double-cross) trial was dropped. A one-tailed test shows significance in the first case, and comes close to significance in the others.

The hypothesis also asserts that there will be more subjects at the JM in the small matrix. Table 2-4 presents a comparison of the two matrices for (a) pairs who achieved the JM at least once and (b) pairs who stabilized in cooperation at the JM (i.e., stayed at the JM for a number of trials). In both cases, the small matrix predominates as predicted.

Hypothesis 2 asserts that there will be a more nearly equal division of payoffs in the small matrix. A comparison of payoffs within the pairs of each group is presented in Table 2-5. The average difference in payoff in both matrices is listed along with a *t*-test of differences. The results are in the predicted direction, but are not significant.

Difficulties in comparing equality of payoffs across the two matrices seemed biased against the hypothesis. In the small matrix, the first time one subject chooses a cooperative price in an attempt to signal, a difference of 11 cents in payoff will result. Thus, the mean difference of 19 cents is an indication that it took between one and two signals to induce cooperation or discourage the hope of obtaining it. The 19-cent mean difference therefore indicates considerable equality. In the large matrix, subjects could signal cooperation more subtly and incur only a slight difference in payoff. (Of course, it is possible that a more

Table 2-3
Effect of Small and Large Matrix Condition on Joint Payoff

Trials	Average joint payoff (in ¢)*		t-statistic for difference	Significance level
	Small matrix	Large matrix		
1–15	591.2	554.1	2.145	.05
6–15	399.4	370.4	1.801	.10
6–14	359.2	333.3	1.850	.10

* The average, across all firms in a particular treatment (either "small" or "large" matrix), of the payoff received by both subjects during the trials indicated.

Table 2-4
Collusion in the Two Matrices

	Small matrix (2 × 2)		Large matrix (30 × 30)	
Pairs arriving at:	No.	%	No.	%
JM at least once	7	63.6	2	16.7
JM and staying there	3	27.3	2	16.7

subtle signal would be missed.) The large difference noted must represent a prolonged effort at inducing cooperation, a prolonged effort to determine the division of payoffs, or changing perceptions regarding the value of cooperation.

Hypothesis 3 asserts that there will be more stability in the small matrix after cooperation is first achieved. Our measure of stability is the number of price changes made by each pair. After the initial trials, each price change is *prima facie* evidence of instability; one might get a more sensitive measure by weighting each change by the amount of movement. The former measure would be biased toward showing the small matrix to be more stable, since the minor price changes that constitute communication in the large matrix would be treated as equivalent to the large price changes necessary in the small matrix. The latter measure contains the opposite bias. These two measures (average number of price changes and average value of price changes) are both shown in Table 2-6.

The data are consistent with the hypothesis. The measure biased in favor of the hypothesis (showing that the small matrix is more stable) is significant; the other measure is in the right direction but lacks significance.

Hypothesis 4 states that pairs will be distributed across the range between NCM and JM in the large matrix. Pairs of subjects are distributed over a considerable range of payoffs. Many are distributed across the NCM-JM range as predicted by the hypothesis, but four of the twelve pairs are below this range. Thus, while the pair's tendency not to cluster at any point is consistent with *Hypothesis* 4, the failure of one-third of the pairs to settle in the range was not anticipated.

Table 2-5
Test of Equality of Within-Pair Payoffs

Average payoff differences:	
Small matrix	19.0¢
Large matrix	24.3¢
t-statistic for difference in payoff differences	.64
Significance level	.25

Table 2-6
Test of Stability From First Cooperative Trial Until Trial 15

Price changes	Small matrix	Large matrix	t-statistic for difference	Signifi-cance level
Average number	2.57	12.88	2.88	.01
Average value	10.29	26.75	1.71	.10

Rivalistic behavior of this sort has been observed in mixed-motive situations (see [7]). It is highly competitive behavior and unlike Cournot non-cooperative behavior inasmuch as it results when players try to maximize the difference in payoff. The two-strategy prisoner's dilemma affords no distinction between such rivalistic behavior and noncooperative (independent) behavior, as has been pointed out by Sermat. In the large matrix, rivalistic behavior would lead to a price of 15. Since no firms settled below this price, those below the NCM might be characterized as behaving rivalistically.

Before the data from the two sessions involving the large matrix were aggregated, a consistency test was performed on the difference in payoffs. The test showed that payoffs in the two groups differed significantly (they averaged $2.60 and $2.89). We attempted to isolate the cause of variation. One obvious hypothesis concerned the sex mix of the two groups, since the former group contained many girls while the latter group had none. Various studies have linked behavior to sex (see [8, 13]). Another possibility was that of difference in major field; we decided to classify on the basis of technical versus non-technical field.[8]

To see the role of sex and major field in these experiments, a regression analysis was performed with these two variables used to predict payoff. The results are shown in Table 2-7; major field is the stronger factor. In the first regression sex may have acted as a surrogate for major. (The correlation is 0.85.) A similar effect may have been present in previous studies.

The most unexpected result was the large number of pairs below the NCM-JM range in the large matrix. The choice of these low prices can be viewed as an integral part of the communication process. Subjects may have been threatening each other by their low price choices. Another explanation is offered by the concept of rivalistic behavior, where subjects attempt to maximize the difference between payoffs, rather than their own payoff.

---

[8]Technical majors consisted of all departments in the College of Engineering and Science plus graphic arts and architecture majors. Nontechnical majors were the remaining departments in the College of Fine Arts and Margaret Morrison Carnegie College (girls with liberal arts majors).

Table 2-7

Influence of Sex and Major Field on Payoff

Regression number	Intercept	Independent variables		
		Sex	Major field	R^2
1	271.7	16.9 ($t = 1.86$)		.073
2	267.4		22.4 ($t = 2.48$)*	.123*
3	267.8	−5.6 ($t = .33$)	27.27 ($t = 1.60$)	.125*

* Indicates significance at $\alpha = .05$.

Care must be taken before accepting the hypotheses put forth. While the results were in the predicted direction, the statistical tests were generally not significant at conventional levels. Perhaps the reason for the lack of significance is the small size of samples. If a confidence level of 0.90 had been used, all but one of the hypotheses would have been accepted.

Summary

The presence of a greater range of choices in a mixed-motive situation provided a mechanism for more subtle behavior. Joint maximum was harder to achieve and, if achieved, harder to maintain. Payoffs were more unequal. Furthermore, subjects used "irrationally" low price choices so often that many had average payoffs below the NCM.

The results permit a qualified interpretation that might be applied to the world. Apparently institutional arrangements that limit the number of possible prices firms consider will tend to facilitate cooperation and price stability.

References

[1] Bertrand, J., "Researches," *Journal des Savants*, 1883.

[2] Bishop, R., "Duopoly: Collusion or Warfare?" *American Economic Review*, 50 (1960).

[3] Chamberlin, E., "An Experimental Imperfect Market," *Journal of Political Economy*, 56 (1948).

[4] Cournot, A., *Researches in the Mathematical Principles of the Theory of Wealth.* New York: Macmillan, 1838 (1897 edition).

[5] Dolbear, F., L. Lave, G. Bowman, A. Lieberman, E. Prescott, F. Rueter, and R. Sherman, "Collusion in Oligopoly: An Experiment on the Effect of Numbers and Information," *Quarterly Journal of Economics*, 82 (May 1968).

[6] Friedman, J., "Individual Behavior in Oligopolistic Markets: An Experimental Study," *Yale Economic Essays*, No. 2, 3 (1963).

[7] Fouraker, L., and S. Siegel, *Bargaining Behavior*, New York: McGraw-Hill, 1963.

[8] Gallo, P., and C. McClintock, "Cooperative and Competitive Behavior in Mixed-Motive Games," *Journal of Conflict Resolution*, 9, 1 (March 1965).

[9] Komorita, S., "Cooperative Choice in a Prisoners' Dilemma Game," *Journal of Personality and Social Psychology*, 2 (1965).

[10] Lave, L., "Factors Affecting Cooperation in the Prisoners' Dilemma," *Behavioral Science*, 9 (1965).

[11] Pareto, V., *Manuel d'Economie Politique.* Paris, 1909.

[12] Pilisuk, M., P. Skolnick, K. Thomas, and R. Chapman, "Boredom vs. Cognitive Reappraisal in the Development of Cooperative Strategy," *Journal of Conflict Resolution*, 11, 1 (March 1967).

[13] Rapoport, A., and A. Chammah, *Prisoners' Dilemma.* Ann Arbor: University of Michigan Press, 1966.

[14] _____ and C. Orwant, "Experimental Games: A Review," *Behavioral Science*, 7 (1962).

[15] Sermat, V., "The Possibility of Influencing the Other's Behavior and Cooperation: Chicken versus Prisoner's Dilemma," *Canadian Journal of Psychology*, 21 (1967).

[16] Smith, V., "Effect of Market Organization on Competitive Equilibrium," *Quarterly Journal of Economics*, 78 (1964).

[17] Stevens, C., "Is Compulsory Arbitration Compatible with Bargaining?" *Industrial Relations*, 5 (1966).

3

Number of Firms and Collusion

Despite considerable scholarly effort, no theory has provided reliable predictions of price or output in oligopoly markets. Techniques have not been found which can unravel the complex interdependencies between firms. As long as the consequence of each firm's actions depend in large measure on the unknown reactions of other firms, rational behavior (for the firm) will be difficult to define. Since an analytic approach has not been fruitful, some researchers have turned to experiments on market behavior. Even under artificial conditions, experiments can provide insights into oligopoly markets. This paper reports an experiment designed to determine the effects of market characteristics on collusion.

Little is known about the quantitative way in which basic market characteristics affect the extent and kind of collusion. In this paper, the level, the dispersion, and the stability of prices and profits will be observed as two market characteristics are manipulated: the number of firms in the market and the amount of information available to each firm. The situation modeled is a price-setters' market in which cross-elasticities of demand are finite; each firm faces a downward sloping demand curve. The market might be regarded as one of firms selling slightly differentiated products or selling to spatially separated customers from different locations. The literature relevant to this type of market is reviewed first. The characteristics of the market are formalized in the following section. We then present the hypotheses to be tested and describe the experimental method. Results of the experiment and some implications are discussed. The final section presents a summary.

Price Variation Oligopoly

Bertrand[1] ridiculed Cournot's[2] choice of quantity as the firm's prime decision variable, claiming price to be more appropriate. However, in Bertrand's non-

Reprinted with permission from "Collusion in Oligopoly: An Experiment on the Effect of Numbers and Information," by F.T. Dolbear, L.B. Lave, G. Bowman, A. Lieberman, E. Prescott, F. Rueter, and R. Sherman, in *Quarterly Journal of Economics*, 82 (May 1968), 240-59. Copyright 1968 by Harvard University Press.

[1] J. Bertrand, "Review of Cournot's *Researches*," *Journal des Savants*, Sept. 1883.

[2] A Cournot, *Researches into the Mathematical Principles of the Theory of Wealth* (1838), trans. N. Bacon (New York: Macmillan, 1927).

cooperative price-setting model, violent shifts in quantity (sold by each firm) follow infinitesimal price changes (under the assumptions of homogeneous products, no spatial competition, and fully informed customers). This knife-edge instability is a result not observed in the world and so suggests a misspecification in the model. Further, it is a rather unfortunate complication for the analysis.

The instability disappears under conditions of (even slightly) differentiated products.[3] Instead of specific assumptions about the actions of other firms, Chamberlin and Robinson each constructed a one-firm versus the rest-of-the-market analysis. Each firm has a range of price choice where the violent quantity shifts of the Bertrand model are absent since the differentiated products in the industry dampen interactions between firms. Robinson offered a precise statement of an optimal price solution for the firm in such a market, utilizing monopoly analysis but drawing market resource allocation conclusions.

Chamberlin went further. In addition to the independent, monopolistic sort of solution available to each firm in such a market (even when the number of firms is large) Chamberlin added a solution which makes still greater profits available. The solution requires a degree of (possibly tacit) collusion among a few firms who come to recognize their interdependence in the market. Though rejected by Cournot, the tendency to seek maximum joint profit had been suggested earlier and can be expressed as a Pareto-optimal accommodation among sellers at the expense of unrepresented buyers (who will face higher prices). Chamberlin suggested that a small number of sellers could, without direct collusion, reach the higher price for a cooperative solution.[4]

This literature has led to two contending solutions for oligopoly markets. One is the result of independent, noncooperative maximizing behavior (called the NCM). Price will remain above the competitive level in a price setting market if products are differentiated. The other solution results from cooperative maximizing of joint seller's profit (called the CM). Between the two "solutions" there is a range of possible choices characterized by the fact that profit to an individual firm increases as all firms raise price in concert. This range has been called the "prisoner's dilemma" range since it is a generalization of that two-strategy situation.[5]

More recently, solutions have been proposed which stress the competitive nature of markets. Rather than focusing on their own profit, competitors might

---

[3]See J. Robinson, *The Economics of Imperfect Competition* (London: Macmillan, 1933), and E.H. Chamberlin, *The Theory of Monopolistic Competition* (8th ed.; Cambridge, Mass.: Harvard University Press, 1962).

[4]Also see W. Fellner, *Competition Among the Few* (New York: Knopf, 1949).

[5]For a summary of the literature on the prisoner's dilemma see L.B. Lave, "Factors Affecting Co-operation in the Prisoner's Dilemma," *Behavioral Science*, Vol. 10 (Jan. 1965), pp. 26-38, and A. Rapoport and C. Orwant, "Experimental Games: A Review" *Behavioral Science*, Vol. 7 (Jan. 1962), pp. 1-38. Definitions of the *n*-player *m*-strategy prisoner's dilemma appear in R. Weil, "A Systematic Look at the Prisoner's Dilemma," *Behavioral Science* Vol. 11 (May 1966), pp. 227-33.

become so embroiled in the competition that they strive to solidify their position vis-à-vis that of competitors; they might attempt to maximize the difference between their profit and that of their competitors. Fouraker and Siegel have termed this behavior "rivalistic."[6]

This more recent literature, based largely on experimentation, stresses the bargaining aspects of oligopoly. While jockeying for position, firms are seen to be willing to sustain losses. There is a presumption that these markets would settle down eventually to some more profitable accommodation, but the settling down might take an indefinitely long period of time.[7]

A Price-Profit Oligopoly Market

Controlled experimental settings, such as the prisoner's dilemma, offer a means of gaining insight into behavior in the collude-compete situations of oligopoly markets.[8] To enhance the relevance of these insights, it is necessary to design the experiment to reflect important features of real markets. Experiments have generally presented only two alternatives to subjects; the market presents many to the firm. Most experiments afford complete information, with consequences of actions already calculated for the decisionmaker; markets may provide a variety of information and calculation opportunities to its participants. Finally, experiments seldom involve more than two parties in the interaction, but markets usually comprise more than two parties. In extending experimental results along these lines, one must be sure that sufficient experimental control is retained.[9] We shall discuss the characteristics of real markets which we have attempted to reflect and shall present the market model which underlies this experiment.

In order to achieve cooperation all firms in an industry must realize that collusion is possible and be willing to take the risk inherent in attempting to collude. As the number of firms in a market increases, the probability that these conditions will be satisfied decreases. Two distinct effects might be seen. First, as a given market demand is divided among different numbers of firms, the

---

[6]L. Fouraker and S. Siegel, *Bargaining Behavior* (New York: McGraw-Hill, 1963).

[7]R. Bishop, "Duopoly: Collusion or Warfare?" *American Economic Review*, L (Dec. 1960), 933-67.

[8]R. Cyert and L. Lave, "Collusion, Conflict et Science Economique," *Economie Appliquée*, XVIII (July-Sept. 1965), 285-406, review some of the experimental results and their implications. See also Fouraker and Siegel, op cit.: J. Murphy, "Effects of the Threat of Losses on Duopoly Bargaining," *Quarterly Journal of Economics*, LXXX (May 1966), 296-313; and F.T. Dolbear and L.B. Lave, "Risk Orientation as a Predictor in the Prisoner's Dilemma," *Journal of Conflict Resolution*, X (Dec. 1966), 506-16.

[9]In the controlled experiment every effort is made to control characteristics that might affect the results. Gaming presents a less formal alternative where the richness of the environment might produce more realistic forms of behavior. However, richness and informality usually make the results difficult to analyze.

profit opportunities of each are changed; this is an effect on reward structure. Second, having more firms complicates bargaining and makes tacit agreement more difficult to achieve; this effect may be regarded as behavioral. We wish to examine the latter effect, and one way to do so is to maintain established reward structures.[10]

In their price-setting experiment, Fouraker and Siegel observed a decrease in collusion as the market was changed from duopoly to triopoly. However, their results could be attributed to structural as well as to behavioral differences in the modified Cournot model. The profit per firm resulting from collusion decreased as the number of firms increased. Also, the relative gains to a single firm from undercutting the market price increased as the number of firms increased. In our experimental design, the rewards for colluding and the inducement to undercut will be the same for all size markets.

Another influence on collusion is the information available to decision-makers. Most experiments have provided the decisionmaker with information of his profit possibilities; this information is not routinely available, at least explicitly, in industrial settings. Even further, most experiments present information on the profit consequences of actions of other firms—which suggests they were modeling industries where all cost and demand curves were fully and explicitly known.

In market experiments, making available the cost information within the firm as well as information on other firm's prices and sales seems a reasonable approximation of the information state of most industrial firms. Recent popular discussion of industrial espionage notwithstanding, most firms do not have specific knowledge of competitors' costs. A diversified, multi-product firm can comply fully with disclosure regulations, yet reveal almost nothing about the profit of individual products—the information of interest to competing decision-makers. There are exceptions. A number of important industries consist of essentially one product firms which all follow the same production and selling techniques and where trade associations provide up-to-date sales information. Here, more complete information may be assumed; each firm may at least proceed on the assumption that others are sufficiently well informed to draw inferences from what one firm does not do, as well as from what it does do. Such an information level may afford greater opportunities to bargain tacitly, and the effect on behavior of greater information is therefore worth examining.

The foregoing observations form the basis of the model to be investigated; they implicitly restrict the possible demand and cost curves and the information to be made available. Products are differentiated and price is the controlling decision variable. Quantity sold by an individual firm (q_i) will vary inversely

---

[10]We must point out that we do not minimize structural effects because we regard them as unimportant. Rather, we simply wish to separate those structural effects from the effects of a number of firms on bargaining behavior. Our attempt to minimize structural effects can be indicated best in the context of the specific model we employ.

with the firm's own price (p_i) and directly with the mean price of other firms (P^o_i) in the market. No measure of price dispersion is included in the model, although such a measure would probably be important in oligopoly markets. For simplicity, a linear construction is used.

These considerations give rise to a demand function for the ith firm of the following form:[11]

(1) $\qquad q_i = a + bP^o_i - cp_i \qquad\qquad a, b, c > 0, c > b.$

where

$$P^o_i = \sum_{j \neq i} \frac{P_j}{N-1}$$

and N is the number of firms in the industry. We require price and quantity to be nonnegative. For a solution on the firm's demand curve (1) this implies:

$$0 \leq p_i \leq \frac{a + bP^o_i}{c}.$$

Total market demand (Q) would then be:

(2) $\qquad Q = \sum_{i=1}^{N} q_i = N a + b \sum_{i=1}^{N} \left(\sum_{j \neq i} \frac{p_j}{N-1} \right) - c \sum_{i=1}^{N} p_i$

$\qquad\qquad Q = N [a + (b - c) P]$

where

$P = \sum_{i=1}^{N} \frac{p_i}{N}$. Note that $\sum_{i=1}^{N} \left(\sum_{j \neq 1} \frac{p_j}{N-1} \right) = \sum_{i=1}^{N} p_i = NP$.

Next, consider the effect of varying the number of firms (the effect of N).[12] Differences in results under varying N can be attributed to a pure behavioral interaction only if structural effects can be avoided. To isolate the behavioral effects, we keep the values of a, b, and c unaltered while changing N. Thus industry demand, Q, varies proportionately with the number of firms, N. Note that the demand curve faced by an individual firm (Equation (1)), is independent of N. Any action pursued by *all* other firms in the market will have the same

---

[11] This model is similar to one employed by J.W. Friedman, "Individual Behavior in Oligopolistic Markets," *Yale Economic Essays*, Vol. 3 (Fall 1963), pp. 359-417.

[12] By holding market demand constant and increasing the number of firms, Cournot showed in his original quantity variation model that although each firm would reduce quantity, aggregate output would increase, eventually reaching the competitive output. This result could be interpreted as a reduction in the size of each firm as N increases. H. Demsetz, "The Welfare and Empirical Implications of Monopolistic Competition," *Economic Journal*, LXXIV (Sept. 1964), has raised the question of a similar effect in the differentiated product model where results depend on the modification in the degree of differentiation of products which accompanies any change in the number of firms. Both of these effects due to N are structural inasmuch as the demand function faced by the individual firm depends on N.

effect on any individual firm for every N. It is not feasible to maintain also (for every N) the same effect on one firm of an action by *one* other firm.

We turn next to the specification of cost functions. Decreasing, constant, or increasing costs all raise different choice situations having different implications. We elected to study only constant marginal costs, since this is most consistent with the reports of businessmen,[13] and with empirical evidence.[14] Moreover, constant costs offer simplicity in experimentation. We further limited attention to cases where firms have the same cost function. Total cost, t_i, for the ith firm is shown in the equation:

(3) $\qquad t_i = F + v\,q_i$

where F is fixed cost and v is marginal cost. To avoid quantities of zero as a solution, the price intercept of the demand curve (with all firms setting identical prices) must be greater than marginal cost, namely

$$\frac{-a}{b-c} > \underline{v}.$$

Given the model specified in Equations (1) and (3), profit for the ith firm, π_i, is shown below:

(4) $\qquad \pi_i = p_i\,(a + bP^o_i - cp_i) - [F + v(a + bP^o_i - cp_i)]$, or
$\qquad \pi_i = (p_i - v)\,(a + bP^o_i - cp_i) - F$.

If the ith firm pursues an independent, or noncooperative profit maximizing strategy, given P^o_i, then by differentiating (4) with respect to p_i and setting it equal to zero we get:

(5) $\qquad p_i = \dfrac{1}{2c}\,(a + cv + bP^o_i)$

If *all* firms are noncooperative maximizers, an equilibrium will be achieved where $p_i = P^o_i$ for all i. Equation (5) then reduces to:

(6) $\qquad p_i = (a + cv)/(2c - b) = p^n$ (for all i) .

We call p^n the noncooperative maximum, or NCM.[15]

---

[13] *Cost Behavior and Price Policy*, National Bureau of Economic Research (New York: 1943).

[14] J. Johnston, *Statistical Cost Analysis* (New York: McGraw-Hill, 1960).

[15] That this equilibrium value will be approached from below can be seen if one assumes that the average price of other firms is below p^n, say $p^n - \epsilon$. Then the substitution of $p^n - \epsilon$ into (5) will produce

$$p_i = p^n - \frac{b}{2c} \cdot \epsilon \ .$$

Since $c > b > 0$, we know that $0 < \dfrac{b}{2c} < 1$, which means, in turn that $p_i > p^n - \epsilon$. But if each firm is motivated to price above the average price, $p^n - \epsilon$, while $\epsilon > 0$, we may expect convergence at p^n. A similar argument supports convergence from above as well.

By resisting independent profit maximizing behavior and cooperating instead at a price above p^n, higher profits for each firm can be obtained. To illustrate cooperative behavior, let the ith firm assume that all others will match its price. By substituting p_i for $P^o{}_i$ in Equation (4), the firm's profit becomes:

(7) $\qquad \pi_i = (p_i - v) \, [a + (b - c) \, p_i] - F$.

If *all* firms choose the cooperative strategy and maximize (7) with respect to price, then: the price each will use is:

(8) $\qquad p_i = \dfrac{a + v \, (c - b)}{2(c - b)} = p^c$ (for all i) .

Such a price will maximize joint profits and will be called the cooperative maximum, or CM. One of our main interests is to see whether firms tend to pursue either noncooperative *or* cooperative actions under different experimental conditions. Of course they might reach a compromise price between p^c and p^n.[16]

Independent profit maximizing firms are motivated to set price above the average if the average price lies below p^n (as defined in Equation (6). If firms act on the assumption that others will cooperate by matching their price increases, on the other hand, they are motivated to increase price only as long as their price is below p^c (as defined in Equation (8)). Observe that under either motivation, independent or cooperative profit maximizing, firms will never be motivated to price below p^n or above p^c. For this reason, we regard the price range between p^n and p^c as the "rational" price range.

Enthusiastic bargaining, however, might cause firms to focus on their relative position and give little attention to their current level of profit. Fouraker and Siegel argue that such firms attempt to maximize the difference between their profit and the profits of the rest of the market; firms pursuing this strategy are termed "rivalistic." If other firms all charge the same price, $P^o{}_i$, the rivalistic firm will set its price p_i to maximize:

---

[16]It should be clear that the noncooperative maximum p^n is below the cooperative maximum p^c. This can be shown formally by comparing equations (6) and (8). Remembering that $c > b$ and $a > v \, (c - b)$ we can substitute $c = b + \delta_1$, and $a = v\delta_1 + \delta_2$, where δ_1 and δ_2 are positive real numbers, into equations (6) and (8). This yields:

$$p^n = \frac{(v\delta_1 + \delta_2) + (b + \delta_1)v}{2(b + \delta_1) - b} \text{ and}$$
$$p^c \frac{(v\delta_1 + \delta_2) + v(b + \delta_1 - b)}{2 \, (b + \delta_1 - b)} \; .$$

Simplifying we get:

$$p^n = v + \frac{\delta_2}{2\delta_1 + b} \text{ and } p^c = v + \frac{\delta_2}{2\delta_1} \; .$$

Since all parameters are positive, p^c is greater than p^n.

(9) $\qquad \pi_i - \pi^o_i = \{(p_i - v)\ (a + b\,P^o_i - c\,p_i) - F\}$
$\qquad\qquad - \{(N-1)\ [(P^o_i - v)\ (a + b\,P^o_j - c\,P^o_i) - F]\}$

where π^o_i is the total profit of the $N-1$ other firms and

$$P^o_j = \frac{(N-2)P^o_i + p_i}{N-1}$$

is the average "other price" for the other firms.

Maximization of (9) with respect to p_i yields:

(10) $\qquad p_i = \dfrac{a + cv + bv}{2c} = p^r$

Since p^r is below p^n,[17] the rivalistic motive would lead to prices below the rational range.

In summary, Equation (4) represents profit for each firm in a market model which minimizes structural effects of variations in the number of producing firms in an oligopoly market. It therefore permits study of *behavioral* effects of changes in N apart from the *structural* effects on profit consequences which changes in N had in the Cournot model. The model assumes constant costs for producers over the available output range, consistent with businessmen's views of their cost circumstances. Our objective is to explore by controlled experimentation the effects that N and information conditions have on behavior in such a market model. But before describing the experimental procedures and the results, we enumerate the hypotheses which we shall test.

Hypotheses

Hypothesis 1: The equilibrium market price for all markets will be in the range between the noncooperative profit maximum (NCM) and the cooperative profit maximum (CM) prices.

We expect for all information states and market sizes that bargaining and learning will be completed in the course of the experiment and that "rationality" will prevail. In the discussion of the experimental design in the previous section, it was argued that a profit maximizing firm would select a price above the average market price if the average market price is below NCM. If all firms behave in this way, the average market price must increase at least to the NCM. Similarly, a colluding industry (cartel) would not select a joint price above CM, since the cooperative maximum offers maximum joint profit. Thus, equilibrium prices should fall into the range NCM through CM.

---

[17]The equilibrium NCM price, p^n, is $\dfrac{a+cv}{2c-b}p^r$ is obtained by adding bv to the numerator and b to the denominator; thus, it is immediately apparent (since p^n exceeds v) that p^r will be below p^n.

Hypothesis 2: *Equilibrium prices and profits will be inversely related to the number of firms in an industry and directly related to the amount of information.*

As N increases, effective bargaining becomes more difficult. For large N, one firm's price change will have little effect upon the average market price and (by Equation (1)) upon the competitors' sales. Thus, punishing a competitor for not colluding, or rewarding a competitor for colluding is more difficult, which makes bargaining more difficult as the number of firms in an industry increases. The second factor, information, should facilitate bargaining by making more apparent both the opportunities to collude and the resulting rewards.

Hypothesis 3: *The dispersion of average market price and profits will be directly related to the amount of information and inversely related to the number of firms in the industry.*

As hypothesized in 2, more bargaining and attempts at collusion are expected as N decreases and information increases. In addition to increasing the probability of effective collusion, increased bargaining should tend to increase the dispersion of average market prices and profits over the NCM-CM range. With fewer attempts at collusion, on the other hand, average market prices and profits should be more concentrated at the NCM.

Hypothesis 4: *Stability of market prices will increase with the number of firms in an industry.*

The previous hypotheses have identified the market conditions where collusion is to be expected. Collusion is generally unstable in these circumstances. But if subjects reject collusion as being unattractive or unattainable, they would settle at the NCM and the market would become quite stable. Thus, we conjecture that given the same information, the effect of increasing market size (number of firms) would be to increase the stability of market prices (because of the decreasing tendency to collude).

It is more difficult to predict the effect of information on stability. As with market size, one might expect the relation between information and stability to be the reverse of the information-collusion relation. The experiment encompasses only a small number of trials, however, and other effects might intrude. For example, under conditions of limited information, subjects will be attempting to learn more about the underlying structure of demand; they might experiment more in order to learn. As a result, markets with incomplete information might be less stable than markets of the same size with more information. Because of such conflicting effects, no hypothesis is offered about the effect of information on stability.

Method

The subjects were recruited from sophomore economics classes at the Carnegie Institute of Technology. They were told they could volunteer for an experiment on market structure in which they might earn $2.00 or more. To mitigate the effects of information leakage, a number of different experiments were run at about the same time. Subjects were informed that a number of different experiments were being run and that telling friends about their experiment could lead to confusion and loss of money for the friend. There was no evidence that a subject knew about an experiment before he participated.

As each subject arrived, he was given an instruction sheet, the profit matrix which was relevant to his particular experiment, a decision sheet on which to record the prices which he chose and an explanation sheet on which to record the reasons for his choice. Subjects were assigned to industries at random.

Incomplete information: For this information state the relevant profit matrix, which relates price and quantity sold to profit, is shown in Table 3-1. Note that the table embodies a cost curve and simply relates the profit to be gained by selling a particular quantity (determined by the experimenter) when a particular price is chosen (by the subject). The subject was told that, for any period, the lower his price and the higher his competitors' prices, the more he would sell. Thus, in effect, the subject knew his own cost functions, that the cross-elasticity of demand was finite, and that his demand curve was downward sloping.

Complete information: In this case the subject was given the matrix shown in Table 3-2 which relates profits to his price and the average price of the competitors. The subject was told that his competitor(s) had the same profit matrix. Thus, in effect, the subjects knew the precise structure of the industry demand and the competitor(s) cost function. For any set of prices, they were able to compute the profits for each firm in the industry.

Table 3-1 was derived from Equation (3) which specified the cost curve of the firm. To construct the table, fixed cost was taken to be 15 and marginal cost was taken to be 6. Table 3-2 is derived from Equation (4) which specifies the profit of the firm. The parameters used for derivation of the table were $a = 42/9$, $b = 1/9$, $c = 2/9$, $f = 15$ and $v = 6$ (note that the table is in 1/6 units). Since both tables were expressed in integers, rounding was necessary. In deriving the tables, an (only partially successful) attempt was made to preserve the underlying structure of the equations in spite of the rounding. Using the parameters specified, $p^c = 24$, $p^n = 18$, and $p^r = 15$. Due to rounding, the table reflects values of $p^c = 23$, $p^n = 18$, and $p^r = 16$.

The instruction sheet explained how to use the profit table (Table 3-1 or 3-2) and noted that the subject was playing opposite another person (or persons) in the room, although he would never learn the identity of his competitor(s). In all experiments he was told the number of competitors in his market.

In addition to these sheets, the subject was given a tray containing $1.50 in change. He was told that this money represented a loan from the bank with which to begin the experiment; the loan was to be repaid at the end of the experiment. His remuneration would consist of his profits in the game. As can be

Table 3-1
Profit Matrix for Incomplete Information Experiment

QUANTITY (measured in 1/6 units)

P_i (PRICE)	1	2	3	4	5	6	7	8	9	10	11	12	13	14	15	16	17	18	19	20	21	22	23	24	25	26	27	28	29	30
6	-15	-15	-15	-15	-15	-15	-15	-15	-15	-15	-15	-15	-15	-15	-15	-15	-15	-15	-15	-15	-15	-15	-15	-15	-15	-15	-15	-15	-15	-15
7	-15	-15	-14	-14	-14	-14	-14	-14	-13	-13	-13	-13	-13	-13	-12	-12	-12	-12	-12	-12	-11	-11	-11	-11	-11	-11	-10	-10	-10	-10
8	-15	-14	-14	-14	-13	-13	-13	-12	-12	-12	-11	-11	-11	-10	-10	-10	-9	-9	-9	-8	-8	-8	-7	-7	-7	-6	-6	-6	-5	-5
9	-14	-14	-13	-13	-12	-12	-11	-11	-10	-10	-9	-9	-8	-8	-7	-7	-6	-6	-5	-5	-4	-4	-3	-3	-2	-2	-1	-1	0	0
10	-14	-14	-13	-12	-12	-11	-10	-10	-9	-8	-8	-7	-6	-6	-5	-4	-4	-3	-2	-2	-1	0	0	1	2	2	3	4	4	5
11	-14	-13	-12	-12	-11	-10	-9	-8	-7	-7	-6	-5	-4	-3	-2	-2	-1	0	1	2	3	3	4	5	6	7	8	8	9	10
12	-14	-13	-12	-11	-10	-9	-8	-7	-6	-5	-4	-3	-2	-1	0	1	2	3	4	5	6	7	8	9	10	11	12	13	14	15
13	-14	-13	-11	-10	-9	-8	-7	-6	-4	-3	-2	-1	0	1	3	4	5	6	7	8	10	11	12	13	14	15	17	18	19	20
14	-14	-12	-11	-10	-8	-7	-6	-4	-3	-2	0	1	2	4	5	6	8	9	10	12	13	14	16	17	18	20	21	22	24	25
15	-13	-12	-10	-9	-7	-6	-4	-3	-1	0	2	3	5	6	8	9	11	12	14	15	17	18	20	21	23	24	26	27	29	30
16	-13	-12	-10	-8	-7	-5	-3	-2	0	2	3	5	7	8	10	12	13	15	17	18	20	22	23	25	27	28	30	32	33	35
17	-13	-11	-9	-8	-6	-4	-2	0	2	3	5	7	9	11	13	14	16	18	20	22	24	25	27	29	31	33	35	36	38	40
18	-13	-11	-9	-7	-5	-3	-1	1	3	5	7	9	11	13	15	17	19	21	23	25	27	29	31	33	35	37	39	41	43	45
19	-13	-11	-8	-6	-4	-2	0	2	5	7	9	11	13	15	18	20	22	24	26	28	31	33	35	37	39	41	44	46	48	50
20	-13	-10	-8	-6	-3	-1	1	4	6	8	11	13	15	18	20	22	25	27	29	32	34	36	39	41	43	46	48	50	53	55
21	-12	-10	-7	-5	-2	0	3	5	8	10	13	15	18	20	23	25	28	30	33	35	38	40	43	45	48	50	53	55	58	60
22	-12	-10	-7	-4	-2	1	4	6	9	12	14	17	20	22	25	28	30	33	36	38	41	44	46	49	52	54	57	60	62	65
23	-12	-9	-6	-4	-1	2	5	8	11	13	16	19	22	25	28	30	33	36	39	42	45	47	50	53	56	59	62	64	67	70
24	-12	-9	-6	-3	0	3	6	9	12	15	18	21	24	27	30	33	36	39	42	45	48	51	54	57	60	63	66	69	72	75
25	-12	-9	-5	-2	1	4	7	10	14	17	20	23	26	29	33	36	39	42	45	48	52	55	58	61	64	67	71	74	77	80
26	-12	-8	-5	-2	2	5	8	12	15	18	22	25	28	32	35	38	42	45	48	52	55	58	62	65	68	72	75	78	82	85
27	-11	-8	-4	-1	3	6	10	13	17	20	24	27	31	34	38	41	45	48	52	55	59	62	66	69	73	76	80	83	87	90
28	-11	-8	-4	0	3	7	11	14	18	22	25	29	33	36	40	44	47	51	55	58	62	66	69	73	77	80	84	88	91	95
29	-11	-7	-3	0	4	8	12	16	20	23	27	31	35	39	43	46	50	54	58	62	66	69	73	77	81	85	89	92	96	100
30	-11	-7	-3	1	5	9	13	17	21	25	29	33	37	41	45	49	53	57	61	65	69	73	77	81	85	89	93	97	101	105
31	-11	-7	-2	2	6	10	14	18	23	27	31	35	39	43	48	52	56	60	64	68	73	77	81	85	89	93	98	102	106	110
32	-11	-6	-2	2	7	11	15	20	24	28	33	37	41	46	50	54	59	63	67	72	76	80	85	89	93	98	102	106	111	115
33	-10	-6	-1	3	8	12	17	21	26	30	35	39	44	48	53	57	62	66	71	75	80	84	89	93	98	102	107	111	116	120
34	-10	-6	-1	4	8	13	18	22	27	32	36	41	46	50	55	60	64	69	74	78	83	88	92	97	102	106	111	116	120	125
35	-10	-5	0	4	9	14	19	24	29	33	38	43	48	53	58	62	67	72	77	82	87	91	96	101	106	111	116	120	125	130

Table 3-2
Profit Matrix for Complete Information Experiment

PRICE P_i	AVERAGE PRICE OF COMPETITORS: P°. 6	7	8	9	10	11	12	13	14	15	16	17	18	19	20	21	22	23	24	25	26	27	28	29	30	31	32	33	34	35
6	-15	-15	-15	-15	-15	-15	-15	-15	-15	-15	-15	-15	-15	-15	-15	-15	-15	-15	-15	-15	-15	-15	-15	-15	-15	-15	-15	-15	-15	-15
7	-11	-11	-11	-11	-11	-11	-10	-10	-10	-10	-10	-10	-10	-10	-10	-10	-10	-10	-10	-10	-10	-10	-10	-10	-10	-10	-10	-10	-10	-10
8	-8	-8	-7	-7	-7	-7	-6	-6	-6	-6	-6	-5	-5	-5	-5	-5	-5	-5	-5	-5	-5	-5	-5	-5	-5	-5	-5	-5	-5	-5
9	-5	-4	-4	-4	-3	-3	-3	-2	-2	-2	-1	-1	-1	0	0	0	0	0	0	0	0	0	0	0	0	0	0	0	0	0
10	-3	-2	-2	-1	-1	0	0	1	1	2	2	2	3	4	4	4	5	5	5	5	5	5	5	5	5	5	5	5	5	5
11	-1	0	0	1	2	3	3	3	4	5	5	6	7	7	8	8	9	9	10	10	10	10	10	10	10	10	10	10	10	10
12	1	1	2	3	4	4	5	6	6	7	8	9	9	10	11	11	12	13	14	14	15	15	15	15	15	15	15	15	15	15
13	1	3	4	4	5	6	7	7	8	10	11	11	12	13	13	14	15	17	17	18	19	19	20	20	20	20	20	20	20	20
14	2	4	4	5	6	8	8	9	10	10	12	13	14	14	16	17	17	18	20	21	21	22	24	25	25	25	25	25	25	25
15	3	3	5	6	6	8	9	11	11	12	12	14	15	17	18	18	20	21	21	23	24	26	26	27	29	30	30	30	30	30
16	2	3	5	5	7	8	10	12	12	13	13	15	15	18	18	20	22	22	23	25	27	27	28	30	30	32	33	35	35	35
17	2	2	3	5	7	7	9	11	13	13	14	16	16	18	20	22	22	23	25	27	27	29	31	31	32	34	34	36	38	40
18	-1	1	3	5	5	7	9	9	11	13	15	15	17	19	21	23	23	25	25	27	27	29	31	33	35	35	37	39	41	41
19	-2	0	0	2	5	7	7	9	11	11	13	15	16	18	20	22	24	26	26	28	28	31	33	35	35	37	39	39	42	42
20	-3	-3	-1	1	1	4	6	8	8	11	13	15	15	18	20	20	22	25	27	29	29	32	34	36	36	39	39	41	43	43
21	-7	-5	-2	-2	0	3	5	5	8	10	10	13	15	18	18	20	20	23	25	28	30	30	33	35	38	40	40	43	43	45
22	-10	-7	-7	-4	-2	-2	1	4	6	6	9	12	12	14	17	20	20	22	25	28	28	30	33	33	36	38	41	44	44	46
23	-15	-12	-9	-6	-6	-4	-1	-1	2	5	8	8	11	13	16	16	19	22	22	25	28	30	30	33	36	36	39	42	45	50
24	-15	-15	-12	-12	-9	-6	-6	-3	0	3	3	6	9	9	12	15	18	18	21	24	24	27	30	33	33	36	39	39	42	45
25	-15	-15	-15	-15	-12	-12	-12	-5	-5	-2	1	4	4	7	10	10	14	17	20	20	23	26	29	29	33	36	36	39	42	45
26	-15	-15	-15	-15	-15	-15	-15	-8	-8	-5	-2	2	2	5	8	8	12	15	18	18	22	25	25	28	32	35	35	38	42	45
27	-15	-15	-15	-15	-15	-15	-15	-15	-11	-11	-8	-4	-1	-1	3	6	6	10	13	17	17	20	23	23	27	31	34	34	38	41
28	-15	-15	-15	-15	-15	-15	-15	-15	-15	-15	-11	-11	-8	-4	0	0	3	7	7	11	14	18	18	22	25	29	29	33	35	36
29	-15	-15	-15	-15	-15	-15	-15	-15	-15	-15	-15	-15	-11	-11	-7	-3	0	0	4	8	12	12	16	16	20	23	27	31	31	35
30	-15	-15	-15	-15	-15	-15	-15	-15	-15	-15	-15	-15	-15	-15	-11	-7	-7	-3	1	1	5	9	13	13	17	21	21	25	29	33
31	-15	-15	-15	-15	-15	-15	-15	-15	-15	-15	-15	-15	-15	-15	-15	-15	-11	-7	-7	-2	2	2	6	10	14	14	18	23	27	27
32	-15	-15	-15	-15	-15	-15	-15	-15	-15	-15	-15	-15	-15	-15	-15	-15	-15	-15	-11	-6	-6	-2	2	7	7	11	15	15	20	24
33	-15	-15	-15	-15	-15	-15	-15	-15	-15	-15	-15	-15	-15	-15	-15	-15	-15	-15	-15	-15	-10	-6	-6	-1	3	8	8	12	17	17
34	-15	-15	-15	-15	-15	-15	-15	-15	-15	-15	-15	-15	-15	-15	-15	-15	-15	-15	-15	-15	-15	-15	-10	-6	-6	-1	4	8	8	13
35	-15	-15	-15	-15	-15	-15	-15	-15	-15	-15	-15	-15	-15	-15	-15	-15	-15	-15	-15	-15	-15	-15	-15	-15	-10	-5	0	0	4	4

seen from the profit matrixes, earnings could be quite large and subjects seemed to be well motivated by the earnings per trial period. Earnings averaged $2.73 per subject.

All experiments (whether information was complete or incomplete) were conducted with the same procedure. Initially, each subject chose a price, recorded this price on the decision sheet, and then wrote a brief explanation while the decision sheets were collected. The experimenters entered the quantity sold, the resulting profits, and the price(s) of the other firm(s) in the industry on the decision sheet before returning it to the subject.[18] Each subsequent trial was conducted in the same way.

In all, a total of ninety subjects participated in the experiments. There were six industries with two firms, three with four firms and one with sixteen firms, all with incomplete information.[19] There were also twelve markets with two firms and six with four firms, all with complete information. (The number of markets in each category may be seen in Table 3-3.) The instructions noted that there would be a large number of trials and the decision sheet contained space for thirty-two trial periods. In each case, fifteen trials were conducted. (The experiments lasted about ninety minutes.)

Results

Market conditions rarely allow oligopolies long periods of stability which would allow convergence to a stable equilibrium. Instead, one might imagine firms having enough information to predict the general reactions of their competitors and having enough time before some shift (such as a change in demand, a new product or technological change) to establish a tendency toward competition or collusion. Thus, one might argue that experiments should not be so long that equilibrium is obtained. Moreover, experiments must come to an end, and subjects generally perceive about when the end will occur. As a result, behavior sometimes changes during the final trials. This behavior was corroborated in a pilot run where subjects guessed the experiment was about to end (since the alloted ninety minutes were almost over). Similarly, in the first trials there is a process of learning about the situation and the other participants. A number of trials are required for the subject to familiarize himself with the procedures and learn about the general cooperativeness or competitiveness of his opponents.[20]

---

[18]For the industry with the sixteen firms, only the average market price was recorded—not the entire set of fifteen prices of the competitors.

[19]Actually there were seven markets with two firms and incomplete information. The comments of one subject indicated he had misunderstood the experiment, so his market was deleted.

[20]These data were analyzed for the speed with which they came to equilibrium. It was concluded that almost all of them had come to equilibrium by trial 8. Note that equilibrium is not taken to mean "static equilibrium" with market price settling to some level and staying there. Rather, the concept is one of a "stochastic equilibrium" with fluctuations about a mean price.

Table 3-3
Equilibrium Prices

Number of Firms in an Industry	Complete Information		Incomplete Information
	16.2*	19.7	18.3
	16.8*	19.8	18.9
2	18.4	20.0	19.4
	18.9	20.4	19.4
	19.1	22.4	19.7
	19.4	23.0	20.0
	16.1*		17.2*
4	17.2*	18.2	18.1
	17.5*	20.8	18.4
	17.9*		
16			16.9*

* Indicates prices outside of the cooperative-noncooperative range.

While there are cases where a market must be started or where a market is going to end, these cases are not of direct interest in this experiment. To control (at least crudely) for beginning and end effects, the first seven and last three trials were excluded from the analysis. The price choices seemed generally consistent and stable within each market over the included trials.

The equilibrium price and profit were taken to be the average (within a market) over trials 8 through 12. This average price, classified by the number of firms in the market and by the information state is displayed in Table 3-3.

Hypothesis 1 asserts that the equilibrium market price will be in the range between the points representing the noncooperative maximum and the cooperative maximum (18 to 23 cents here). Of the twenty-six markets, eighteen had average prices in this range. However, the deviants did not range more than 1.9 cents below the NCM in average price and so were well above p^r. These deviations will be discussed at greater length in the next section.

Hypothesis 2 predicts that equilibrium prices and profits (per firm) will be directly related to the completeness of information and inversely related to the number of firms in the market. Table 3-4 displays the price and profit averages within the several markets.[21]

Of the five pairwise comparisons in each table, only one is not in the predicted direction: the information effect for the four-firm markets; the

---

[21] Actually there was a change in procedure between the markets with four firms and the one with sixteen firms. In the latter case it was decided *not* to record the fifteen "other prices" on the decision sheet of the firm; instead only the mean price was recorded. While this simplication means that the sixteen-firm market received less information than other markets, we do not feel this effect was very significant.

Table 3-4
Average Equilibrium Prices and Profits

Number of Firms in an Industry	Complete Information Prices	Profits	Incomplete Information Prices	Profits
2	19.5	18.5	19.3	17.6
4	17.8	16.0	17.9	16.1
16			16.9	14.1

difference amounts to only 0.1 cents. Thus, the data are basically consistent with the hypothesis.

In testing for significance of difference in the means, a student t-test is not appropriate since the variances are not equal. However, using a generalization of the t-test[22] and a 95 per cent significance level, all three pairwise comparisons involving N, the number of firms in the market, were found to be significant (both under conditions of complete and incomplete information).[23] However, the effect of information was not found to be significant in any comparison. (The comparison across the two-firm market for average profit indicated a t that would be exceeded less than 0.1 times by chance.)

Hypothesis 3 asserts that the dispersion of equilibrium prices and profits (per firm) will be directly related to the amount of information and inversely related to N. Dispersion of market equilibria, under a given condition, might be measured by the variance of the population. The larger the variance, the greater is the dispersion. The sample variances are shown in Table 3-5.

Inspection of the table reveals that all four pairwise comparisons are in the hypothesized order. Using an F-test, no comparison with respect to N was found to be significant. (Both would have been significant at a 90 percent level of significance.) In testing for difference with respect to information, the two-firm markets were significantly different, while the four-firm markets were not.

Table 3-5
Sample Variances of Equilibrium Prices and Profits

Number of Firms in an Industry	Complete Information Prices	Profits	Incomplete Information Prices	Profits
2	2.9	2.0	0.4+	1.0
4	2.0	1.1	0.4	0.7

[22]B.L. Welch, "The Generalization of 'Student's' Problem When Several Different Population Variances Are Involved," *Biometrika*, XXXIV (Jan. 1947), 28-35.
[23]In comparing sixteen-firm with four-firm markets, we assumed the variances were equal since only a single observation was available for the former case.

Hypothesis 4 asserts that stability will increase as N becomes larger. Stability is measured by the variance (within a market) of average market price over periods 8 through 12. The smaller the variance, the greater the stability is said to be. As a crude summary, the mean of these variances is shown for each treatment in Table 3-6.

Of the three possible pairwise comparisons across N (holding information constant), two are in the predicted direction. The exception occurs under full information for the comparison of two-firm and four-firm markets. The comparison indicates that the two-firm markets were more stable in their collusion.

The Wilcoxon-Mann-Whitney rank test was used to test the null hypothesis that one population is stochastically larger than another versus the hypothesis that the two populations are stochastically equal.[24] The t-test is not appropriate here since the distribution of stability measures does not approach normality and the sample sizes are not sufficiently large to invoke large sample theory. Of the three pairwise comparisons across N (holding information constant), one was statistically significant (the comparison of two- and four-firm markets under incomplete information).

No hypothesis was offered as to the direction of effect of complete

Table 3-6

Variance (Within a Market) of Average Market Price

Number of Firms in an Industry	Complete Information		Incomplete Information
2	0	1.7	2.7
	0	1.8	4.8
	0.2	2.7	5.7
	0.2	2.8	8.5
	1.2	3.8	14.5
	1.3	6.2	23.0
	mean variance = 1.83		mean variance = 9.86
4	0.7	1.5	0.5
	1.1	2.4	1.3
	1.3	7.7	5.6
	mean variance = 2.45		mean variance = 2.47
16			1.2
			mean variance = 1.2

[24]The random variable X is stochastically larger than Y if the distribution function $F_x(C) \leqslant F_y(C)$ for all C. Stochastically equal implies equality of the distribution functions. If X is stochastically larger than Y, then the mean of X is greater than the mean of Y.

information. Both pairwise comparisons show that full information led to more stability than did incomplete information. The order of the data would tend to support the explanation of firms groping for more information about demand in the incomplete information markets.

Discussion

Ten of the twelve conjectured pairwise comparisons were in the predicted direction. However, only about half of these comparisons were statistically significant at conventional levels. Perhaps the primary reason for the lack of significance was the combination of small sample size and nonparametric tests: any comparison across the four firm markets had to rely on six and three observations, and any comparison involving the sixteen-firm market had only a single observation. This lack of significance might be used to make a more general point. In an experiment of this sort, the results must be viewed as suggestive rather than as a conclusive test of the hypotheses.

Eight of the markets had average prices below the NCM-CM range. One might conclude that these markets contained one or more rivalistic firms and tended toward *the rivalistic point of p = 16*. A second explanation is possible for the markets operating under incomplete information. Firms may have been groping for more understanding of the demand situation even at the end of the experiment. A third possible explanation is that the prices were in integer values and so the profit table did not always reflect precisely the structure of Equation (4).

The third reason for prices below p^n cannot be evaluated further. The second conjecture might be explored by noting that six of the deviants were provided with complete information. This fact seems to rule out the possibility that they were groping for information about the demand structure of the market. It seems likely that these six firms engaged in intensive bargaining, i.e., they were groping for information about rivals and attempting to give information about their own demands. Further support for this conjecture comes from an examination of the relation between number of firms in the market and speed of bargaining. We would expect that, as the number of firms in the market increased, the time taken to complete bargaining would increase. Five of the markets with prices below the NCM contained four firms and a sixth was the market with sixteen firms. (Of the eighteen markets with two firms, only two were below the NCM; of the nine markets with four firms, five were below the NCM; and the one market with 16 firms was below the NCM.) Apparently, it takes longer than seven trials to reach equilibrium in these markets.

Results of other experiments suggest directions in which these results might be generalized. Similar results have come from experiments with a population of business executives (used instead of college students). Equilibrium price levels have been found to be invariant to cues which serve as opening prices; markets which were opened at high price levels were found to reach the same equilibrium as markets opened at low price levels. Under incomplete information, equilibrium seemed to occur a number of trials later than under complete information.

In the experiment reported here, a small number of alternative prices (six) span the entire NCM-CM range. Real markets involve many more price choices.[25] In Chapter 2, cooperation has been shown to be more difficult to establish as the number of alternative price choices is increased. A greater range of alternative choices led to a greater variety of actions, which impeded cooperation.

Another dimension of interest concerns the effect of asymmetry between firms. In particular, price leadership behavior might be studied under varying conditions of firm dominance by establishing unequal market shares. Unequal cost conditions are also a possibility worth exploring. Firms could be differentiated with respect to either marginal or fixed costs.

Summary

Experimental oligopoly markets have been investigated here in a controlled setting modeled after a price-setters' oligopoly market. Special care was taken to minimize structural effects due to change in N, the number of firms in the industry, in order to separate structural from behavioral effects. A stronger conclusion may be drawn than that reported by Siegel and Fouraker: a decrease in the number of firms in a market produces less competition which cannot be attributed to differences in the structure of the profit functions. These results suggest that tacit collusion is possible and more likely to occur in an oligopoly market with a small number of firms.

All of the markets converged to prices in or just below the cooperative-non-cooperative range. The number of firms in the market had a significant effect upon average profit and price under both information states. Although information did not affect mean price and profit significantly, it did have a significant effect upon the variances of price and profit, while N did not. Finally, stability increased as N decreased; and as information increased. Information seems to induce bargaining attempts that tend to result in price war or collusion. Thus, information is likely to increase the variability among markets, but should reduce the variability within one market over time.

---

[25]Of course, such choice limitations might be encountered in real markets. For examples of industry practices which limit the number of price choices, see R. Cyert and J. March, *A Behavioral Theory of the Firm* (Englewood Cliffs, N.J.: Prentice-Hall, 1964), Chap. 7.

Part II:
Capacity Choice and the
Persistence of Price Collusion

The analysis of capacity choice is developed here in Part II. First, previous empirical studies of industrial firms' cost functions are discussed. The prevailing pattern of constant long-run average cost beyond a minimum efficient size is used as support for the existence of a choice by the firm of its own size, via its capacity decision. The effect on reward structure of economic variables, such as market share and cost function properties, is set out with a capacity choice included, and the effect of risk attitude on capacity choice also is examined in experimental games. Persons who are more averse to risk prefer smaller capacities, and with smaller capacities price cooperation is easier to achieve. Despite many efforts to do so, predictions of behavior based on psychological attitudes had not been possible before in prisoner's dilemma games, so it is especially interesting that here, with a longer-run capacity choice option added, risk attitude serves to predict behavior. The variability of total cost with short-run output influences the degree of cooperation, too, and is shown able to intervene in the effect that number of firms has on the likelihood of cooperation.

4

Cost Functions of Industrial Firms

The payoffs for alternative actions by firms in oligopolistic markets can depend very much on properties of the firms' cost functions. Gains available for cooperation at higher prices in the market game of Chapter 3 obviously depended in part on the specific cost function parameters chosen for that experiment. Differences by industry in cost function properties can be expected to have comparable effects on rewards for alternative pricing actions by real-world firms. But the form of the cost functions also can affect the scope of firms' actions in oligopolistic industries. For empirical studies of industrial firms' cost functions show them to have constant long-run average cost, which means that such firms have no unique optimal size. So when new entry is barred their capacity expansion decisions also can become a subject for tacit agreement, and cost function parameters can affect rewards in that choice, too.

Of course the cost functions of industrial firms admittedly are hard to identify. Estimates must rely on imperfect accounting approximations, and then are carried out in settings where the effects of one firm's output adjustments on its own cost can seldom be separated from a host of other effects. Here we shall review briefly the results of empirical investigations of cost functions, and we shall note also major difficulties in their interpretation. In the end we find a particularly simple cost function that has survived empirical tests contains a substantial range of constant long-run average cost, and yields a short-run function in which marginal cost most often lies below average cost. We shall characterize cost functions of this type according to the variability (or fixity) of total cost with respect to short-run output changes, and introduce the term "cost variability" (or "cost fixity") for that purpose. This property of cost functions and its effect on choice opportunity and payoff structure will play an important role in the chapters that follow.

Estimates of Cost Functions

In 1936, Joel Dean carried out the first serious effort at statistical estimation of cost functions. [5] He found total cost to be a simple linear function of output in the belting industry, and in other industries as well. [6] His results suggested that average cost would be decreasing with output in the short-run, when some costs were fixed and independent of output. In a survey of English businessmen in 1939, Sir Robert L. Hall and Charles J. Hitch found the businessman thought marginal cost was below average cost in the short-run, so average cost would be decreasing. [9] A National Bureau of Economic Research conference also heard evidence of short-run decreasing average cost for large U.S. firms in heavy manufacturing industries and retailing. [15] W.J. Eiteman and G.E. Guthrie surveyed American businessmen and their results, reported in 1952, showed marginal cost below average cost through most of the output range, too, although about one third of the respondents (113 of 354) felt there was a small range very close to maximum full capacity output where average cost was rising because marginal cost was higher than average cost. [7] Soon after that, in a careful investigation based on engineering and other data from two to five firms in each of 20 industries, Joe Bain examined more general longer-run cost functions. [2][1] He found decreasing long-run average cost in varying degrees at smaller output levels, and constant long-run average cost beyond some particular level of output for each industry. All of these characterizations are reasonably consistent with one another, and when shorn of extreme claims (including one of generality), they still remain plausible today.

Much debate over cost functions and the behavior of firms in concentrated,[2] or oligopolistic, industries occurred in the 1950's. Another National Bureau of Economic Research conference was held and raised criticism of cost function studies. [16][3] But later alternative approaches did not turn up results that ran counter to previous findings. For instance, George Stigler focused on the issue of an optimal firm size, which would not exist uniquely if firms experienced constant long-run average costs. Introducing what has come to be called the survival technique, he observed changes in shares of industry output coming from different size classes of firms, and found no tendency for firms to converge on a unique "best" size. [23] Applying the same technique, investigators have found evidence in a few industries of economies at small scales and of diseconomies at very large scales, but a wide range of outputs with apparently equal average cost still has been found. [19, 26] Studies of firm growth also tend to support the eventually constant long-run average cost hypothesis, because when firms beyond some minimal efficient size are studied, no clear connection has emerged between firm size and rate of growth.[4] If long-run average cost depended on firm scale, more systematic effects of firm size on growth would probably have been detected.

---

[1]Reprinted as Chapter 8 in [3].

[2]Concentration is an operational measure of the extent to which the sales, employment, or other activity in an industry is concentrated in only a small number of firms. The simplest and most common measure is the top-4 concentration ratio, which takes the activity (usually sales) accounted for by the largest four firms and divides it by the total activity for the industry. For a discussion of this and other measures see [17].

[3]See in particular [8] and [22].

[4]For examples, see [10, 14, 18 and 21]. A link between size and growth was claimed in [11], but see also [20].

A very thorough statistical estimation of cost functions for electricity generation, road transportation, food processing, coal mining, building association, and life insurance firms was undertaken by J. Johnston and published in 1960. [12] In his own estimates and in other studies he reviewed, the predominant finding for the short-run was decreasing average cost and constant, lower, marginal cost. For the long-run, there was evidence of decreasing average cost at small outputs but beyond some output level average cost was constant. An exhaustive review of statistical cost function estimates was provided in 1963 by Alan Walters. [25] It shows counter arguments and problems of interpretation as well as evidence in favor of the simple linear total cost function for manufacturing firms.

The main handicap in statistical estimates of cost functions is their reliance on accounting data. Accounting data may approximate genuine economic costs, but they do not reflect them with precision. For instance, total accounting costs are gathered over substantial time periods of at least a month and often longer, and are divided by output for that same period to obtain unit costs. Such averaging obviously will eliminate extremely high and extremely low output conditions, and thereby will prevent observation of the most revealing cases. In one way or another, accounting practices also categorize costs either as depending on output or not. This tends to create a category of fixed costs that helps to make short-run average cost appear to decrease with output, because that particular collection of costs typically includes arbitrary imputations of equal amounts to each time period. Making "fixed" costs equal in each time period will tend to make average cost appear to decrease, because the same cost amount divided by greater output quantities will tend to lower average cost then. Other accounting practices may cause biases too, as when equipment is depreciated in proportion to output so it automatically will make average cost constant. Such consequences of accounting practices can be traced primarily to the uncertainty that invites use of arbitrary rules.

A subtle bias that Friedman noted [8] follows also from such accounting practices. If output varies randomly from short-run period to short-run period, uniform fixed costs will make average cost appear to be lower for a firm when it happens to have high output, and higher when it happens to have low output. This result is no different from the effect of uniform fixed cost already noted, but it shows how it can create the appearance of decreasing average cost merely from randomness in output, without any true relation between output and total cost.

There are additional problems in the identification of cost functions, and we can sketch only some of them here. One firm's cost and output experience may be different if industry output also is adjusted. The main reason for a difference is that industry adjustments can be so large that they affect input prices, whereas single firm adjustments will not. While some techniques can discount for changes in input prices, they are difficult to apply and imperfect as well. Consequently, the separation of firm and industry output effects on the average cost of firms is difficult to accomplish, and so some statistical studies of firm cost functions might actually capture effects of industry output adjustments as well.

Efforts to estimate cost functions also focus on only two variables. The studies seek a relationship between rate of output and total cost, when other variables that are not taken into account may also be affecting cost. Armen Alchian has shown how the total volume of an order or the lead time before delivery could affect cost, yet not be accounted for in cost function estimates. [1] A.C. Charnes and W.W. Cooper drew attention to a similar problem caused by costs associated with the rate of expansion of a firm, but not traced to their proper source in cost function estimates. [4] Variables such as these that affect costs but are not allowed for in cost estimates might bias estimates either in favor of or against the finding of a linear relation between total cost and output.

Thus empirical estimates of firms' cost functions are subject to criticism. But they repeatedly have revealed decreasing average cost for the short-run, and constant average cost for the long-run beyond some particular output level in each industry. More subtle curvature in the cost function has not typically been revealed. Moreover, the region of constant long-run average cost is the only cost condition consistent with the wide range of sizes of successful surviving firms that we observe in many manufacturing industries. And decreasing short-run average cost is clearly believed by businessmen to exist, so such a cost relation probably will influence their actions.

The main implication of constant long-run average cost is that firm size is indeterminate. Firms can expand and change their sizes if profit opportunities seem to warrant it. This possibility is very important, for it complicates the maintenance of tacit collusion by a few oligopolistic firms, even though they may be protected from new entry by barriers to entry. If the firms are able to set a high price, some firm (or firms) among them may be tempted to expand and then will have an incentive to win more business, possibly by advertising more or by cutting price. Thus constant long-run average cost enlarges the scope of firm interdependence in oligopoly, and it makes capacity as well as price decisions crucial to the persistence of collusion in oligopoly.

Total Cost Variability

Let us turn to more subtle effects of cost function properties on choices by the firm. We have seen that constant long-run average cost affords the firm a capacity choice, but we have not considered how properties of the cost function might affect rewards for alternative actions. We shall take up that task for the case of two firms in the chapter to follow. Here we wish to define a property of the cost function that will be useful when we attempt to link cost function properties to firm behavior.

The cost function property we shall emphasize is *total cost variability*, a term intended to represent the extent to which total cost varies with changes in short-run output. Although we shall refer to this property later simply as cost variability, we must point out that we do not refer to the variability of *average* cost or *marginal* cost with output.[5] Indeed, as average cost tends to be constant in the short-run, total cost might be most variable. Marginal cost determines how much total cost will vary with output. It will contribute most to changes in total cost when it is high. Since empirical studies seldom have found marginal cost above average cost, we might expect marginal cost to be high when it equals average cost; but then of course average cost would be constant. And as marginal cost was farther below average cost, average cost would vary more with output, yet total cost would vary less.

The linear cost function that emerges from empirical studies offers a particularly simple way to characterize cost variability. It possesses a fixed portion of total cost in the short-run and a variable portion that is the product of quantity times a constant parameter representing short-run marginal cost. As the constant level of short-run marginal cost is higher, relative to price or average cost, total cost will vary more as output varies. Obviously, the level of short-run marginal cost plays a crucial role in determining the degree to which total cost varies with output. The convenient outcome of empirical cost function studies is that this short-run marginal cost can be approximated by a constant parameter, and thus it can be represented in a very simple way.

We still shall need a basis for normalizing short-run marginal cost so comparisons can be made across industries. In Part III, where we examine industry data, we shall look at marginal cost in relation to price in order to characterize total cost variability. We shall find convenient and operational the price minus marginal cost all divided by price measure that was introduced by Lerner as the "measure of monopoly power." [13] We shall relate this measure also to advertising and to profit risk, both theoretically and empirically.

Here in Part II our main interest is in the influence of total cost variability on capacity choice by the firm. We have a constant short-run marginal cost which determines the portion of total cost that varies with output. We also relate the portion of total cost that does not vary with short-run output, the "fixed" cost, to the level of capacity chosen by a firm. The capacity decision is a long-run decision that will influence the reward structure for price and output decisions in future short-run periods. Separated in this way between short-run cost effects due to output, and long-run cost effects due to capacity, the cost function can influence the extent to which oligopolistic firms might be concerned about short-run cooperation at a higher price, or long-run cooperation at smaller capacities (and a higher price).

---

[5]The variability of marginal cost with short-run output has also been emphasized. [24] Though changes in marginal cost admittedly are difficult to detect, we assume that, short of full capacity, large changes in marginal cost do not occur.

Summary

Empirical estimates of firms' cost functions inherently are subject to many problems. Despite these difficulties, accumulated evidence suggests that a simple linear total cost function will serve as a reasonable approximation for the cost function of firms beyond a so-called minimum efficient size in many manufacturing industries. The function comprises a fixed cost and a variable cost that is the product of output quantity times a constant marginal cost. To be sure, this cost function is a crude approximation to reality. It reflects accounting approximations to economic costs, and it may fail to reflect important differences in cost functions from firm to firm and industry to industry. But empirical analysis has not uncovered those differences and business managers do not believe they exist, so firm behavior probably is based on the linear total cost function that is so apparent from analysis of accounting data.

The constant short-run marginal cost that emerges from empirical cost function studies affords a particularly simple way to represent the extent to which total cost varies with output, or the degree of *total cost variability*. This property of cost functions will vary by industry and perhaps by firm, and will be linked in Part III to several aspects of firms' behavior in oligopolistic industries. Here in Part II we shall emphasize its influence on capacity choice, and on the extent to which few firms that are protected from new entry will cooperate or compete in short-run price or in long-run capacity decisions.

References

[1] A.A. Alchian, "Costs and Outputs," in Moses Abramovitz, *et al., The Allocation of Economic Resources* (Stanford, Cal.: Stanford University Press, 1959).

[2] J.S. Bain, "Economies of Scale, Concentration, and the Condition of Entry in Twenty Manufacturing Industries," *American Economic Review*, 44 (March 1954), 15-39.

[3] _____, *Essays on Price Theory and Industrial Organization* (Boston, Mass.: Little, Brown and Company, 1972).

[4] A.C. Charnes and W.W. Cooper, "Silhouette Functions of Short-Run Cost Behavior," *Quarterly Journal of Economics*, 68 (February 1954), 131-50.

[5] Joel Dean, *Journal of Business Studies in Business Administration, Vol. 7* (Chicago, Ill.: University of Chicago Press, 1936).

[6] _____, *Journal of Business Studies in Business Administration, Vol. 14* (Chicago, Ill.: University of Chicago Press, 1941).

[7] W.J. Eiteman and G.E. Guthrie, "The Shape of Average Cost Curves," *American Economic Review*, 42 (December 1952), 823-28.

[8] M. Friedman, "Comment," in [16].

[9] R.L. Hall and C.J. Hitch, "Price Theory and Economic Behavior," *Oxford Economic Papers*, 1 (No. 2, 1939), 12-45.

[10] P.E. Hart and S.J. Prais, "The Analysis of Business Concentration: A Statistical Approach," *Journal of The Royal Statistical Society*, Ser. A (1956), 150-81.

[11] S. Hymer and P. Pashigian, "Firm Size and Rate of Growth," *Journal of Political Economy*, 70 (December 1962), 556-67.

[12] J. Johnston, *Statistical Cost Analysis* (New York: McGraw-Hill, Inc., 1960).

[13] A.P. Lerner, "The Concept of Monopoly and the Measurement of Monopoly Power," *Review of Economic Studies*, 1 (June 1934), 157-75.

[14] E. Mansfield, "Entry, Gibrat's Law, Innovation, and the Growth of Firms," *American Economic Review*, 52 (December 1962), 1021-51.

[15] National Bureau of Economic Research, *Cost Behavior and Price Policy* (New York: Columbia University Press, 1943).

[16] National Bureau of Economic Research, *Business Concentration and Price Policy* (Princeton, N.J.: Princeton University Press, 1955).

[17] G.W. Nutter, "Concentration," *International Encyclopedia of the Social Sciences* (New York: Crowell-Collier and Macmillan, Inc., 1968), Vol. 3, pp. 218-22.

[18] R.E. Quandt, "On the Size Distribution of Firms," *American Economic Review*, 56 (June 1966), 416-32.

[19] T.R. Saving, "The Four-Parameter Log-normal, Diseconomies of Scale, and

the Size Distribution of Manufacturing Establishments," *International Economic Review*, (January 1965), 105-14.

[20] H.A. Simon, "Comment: Firm Size and Rate of Growth," *Journal of Political Economy*, 72 (February 1964), 81-2.

[21] _____ and C.P. Bonini, "The Size Distribution of Business Firms," *American Economic Review*, 48 (September 1958), 608-17.

[22] C. Smith, "Survey of Empirical Evidence on Economies of Scale," in [16].

[23] G.J. Stigler, "The Economies of Scale," *Journal of Law and Economics*, 1 (October 1958), 54-71.

[24] _____, "Production and Distribution in the Short-Run," *Journal of Political Economy*, 47 (June 1939).

[25] A.A. Walters, "Production Functions: An Econometric Survey," *Econometrica*, 31 (January-April 1963), 1-67.

[26] L.W. Weiss, "The Survival Technique and the Extent of Suboptimal Capacity," *Journal of Political Economy*, 72 (June 1964), 246-61.

5

Economics and Capacity Choice

Firms face a capacity choice whenever their unit costs are constant, for then a given market price no longer implies a unique best capacity level for each firm.[1] If in addition there are only two firms and entry is difficult, capacity can join price as a subject for tacit negotiation by the firms. Our purpose is to identify a reward structure that reflects interdependence between firms in their capacity choices as well as in their price choices. Then the structure of profit consequences for these decisions can be examined, together with effects of cost variability. Properties of the entire structure of rewards for alternative actions have been found to be an important determinant of cooperation in laboratory experiments with interdependent decision makers [6, 8].

Price actions that are available to each firm in a duopoly market in the short-run, when capacity is fixed, can be compared with the choices within an experimental prisoner's dilemma (P.D.) game matrix (see Table 5-1 below). Whether to cut price calls for comparing the gain from cutting price against the possible loss arising from the fact that the other firm may match the price out, thus making both prices lower, and less profitable, than before. Whether to raise price depends on a similar comparison. Raising price unilaterally will involve a sacrifice which can be compared with the possible gain available when (if) the other firm raises his price to the same level. In prisoner's dilemma experiments, Lave found that a comparison such as the latter (expressed as a ratio of payoffs) was related to the attempts that subjects would make toward cooperation. [6]

Without capacity limits, the very competitive experimental price variation market results found by Fouraker and Siegel are to be expected. [4] Having the lower price is handsomely rewarded, more handsomely as the number of firms is larger. But the reward for cutting price will be modified when capacity limits are introduced. By cutting price, one firm can only win a quantity up to his capacity limit, not the whole market. Capacity is also an important influence on the attractiveness of attempting cooperation, for each firm's loss upon raising price is reduced because the other firm has reduced its capacity.

The capacity choice for a firm in a duopoly market is similar to a choice of one P.D. matrix in which to make short-run choices rather than another P.D.

Reprinted with permission from *Rivista Internazionale di Scienze Economiche e Commerciali*, 15 (July 1968), 685-98. I am indebted to Professors R.M. Cyert, O.A. Davis, F.T. Dolbear, and Richard Schramm for advice and criticism.
[1] Much evidence suggests that unit costs are constant over wide output ranges in many industries. See [1, 7] and Chapter 4.

Table 5-1
Payoffs to Firm One

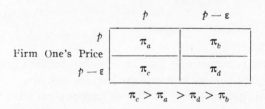

Firm Two's Price

	p	$p - \varepsilon$
p	π_a	π_b
$p - \varepsilon$	π_c	π_d

Firm One's Price

$$\pi_c > \pi_a > \pi_d > \pi_b$$

matrix. Assuming that behavior is influenced by the payoff consequences for alternative actions, even when interdependence produces analytic indeterminacy, the effect of economic variables on the structure of payoff consequences deserves attention. Price interdependence has been investigated extensively, but other economic variables also affect the reward structure, and cannot be ignored when each firm is aware of its dependence on others. This is especially so if individuals' risk attitudes can predict behavior in the choice of a variable corresponding to capacity, but not one corresponding to price. In particular, fixed costs, which do not enter in the short-run decision calculus of competitive firms, will play an important role in the structure of payoffs for interdependent firms. Thus their importance to business firms, indicated by business literature, [11] may reflect rational behavior despite its apparent lack of consistency with standard marginal analysis.

Cost variability and other economic variables will be examined for their effect on the reward structure faced by duopoly firms using a market model that is general in some respects but limited in others. It is general in that it can accommodate constant costs regardless of the cross-elasticity of demand condition among firms' products, and it makes explicit provision for capacity limits. The model is limited, however, to one specific method of allocating market demand between firms and to constant cost functions, and its usefulness is confined to local rather than global search behavior.[2]

Demand will be allocated using a form of Shubik's contingent demand. [10] We first specify the contingent demand function and define a constant cost function to determine a reward structure for duopoly. Then we examine the effect that capacity, price, and cost variables have on profit consequences and, by implication, on the behavior of duopoly firms. Results are summarized in a final section.

---

[2] A market model with discrete short-run capacity limits is not a convenient one, for discontinuities from fixed capacities restrict mathematical manipulation. Such limits might be criticized as unrealistic because in the real world they could be modified by order backlogs and inventories. But consideration of these buffer devices would take us far afield without apparent changes in firms' motives to alter price or capacity.

The Duopoly Reward Structure

Several issues that could have been raised by Edgeworth's introduction of capacity limits into oligopoly models [3] remained hidden for some time. For example, Nichol pointed out that Edgeworth awarded unsatisfied demand to the duopolist having a higher price without asking what proportion of consumers were willing to pay more than the lower price. [7] Shubik has made such matters explicit, and has offered a formulation of contingent demand that is more sparing than Edgeworth's model in its assumptions. [10, Chaps. 5 and 7] Under Shubik's reasonable compromise convention, consumers are chosen randomly to buy from a low-price firm whenever its output is limited by its capacity. Then an expected demand can be defined for firms whose prices are higher. The convention is symmetric and avoids specialized assumptions of less generality. [10, pp. 86-87]

In order to identify rewards for alternative actions, both in the short-run and in the long-run, we can apply Shubik's contingent demand to capacity limited duopoly. Rather than simultaneous price and quantity choices, however, we have a capacity choice that must be made earlier than price and will then limit current output. A price choice can always be made in view of known capacity levels of all firms. This does not mean that the capacity choice is not influenced by price; it merely means that more time is required to alter capacity than to alter price.

A rule must be specified for distributing market quantity among firms when their prices are equal. In such cases we shall distribute quantity among firms in the same proportions that their capacities are of the total market capacity. In addition to its plausibility, this rule offers an equilibrium point whether firm capacities are equal or not.[3] Let a linear market demand function, to be aggregated following Shubik's convention, be $Q = a - b \cdot p \cdot Q$ is total market quantity demanded at any price, p. For simplicity it is assumed that each consumer will purchase (or not purchase) one unit of the good over the time period of analysis. Let the minimal effective price change (the interval separating discrete prices) be ϵ. Then two firms with prices p_1 and p_2 and capacities k_1 and k_2 receive market shares q_1 and q_2 according to the following rules:

(1)   If $p_1 = p_2$

$$q_1 \begin{cases} = [k_1/(k_1 + k_2)] (a - b \cdot p_1) \text{ if } < k_1 \\ = k_1 \text{ otherwise} \end{cases}$$

q_2 by same procedure with subscripts reversed

(2)   If $p_1 = p_2 - \epsilon < p_2$ (same for $p_1 > p_2$ but subscripts reversed)

$$q_1 \begin{cases} = k_1 \text{ if } k_1 \leq a - b \cdot p_1 \\ = a - b \cdot p_1 \text{ otherwise} \end{cases}$$

[3]See [10, pp. 92-109].

$$q_2 \begin{cases} = [1 - k_1/(a - b \cdot p_1)] (a - b \cdot p_2) \text{ if } k_1 < a - b \cdot p_1 \\ = 0 \text{ otherwise.} \end{cases}$$

The expression (1) for distributing market quantity between firms when their prices are equal follows the rule that such a distribution be based on the capacities of the firms. When prices differ we follow Shubik's contingent demand convention in expression (2). The firm with the lower price, p_1, attracts the total market quantity up to its capacity limit, k_1. It is assumed that some of the consumers who bought a unit of the good from firm I were willing to pay a higher price. More specifically, at every price level the same proportion, $k_1/(a-bp_1)$, of the consumers who are willing to buy are assumed to have made their purchases from firm 1. This makes it possible to estimate the remaining quantity demanded at any higher price by multiplying the remaining proportion, $[1-k_1/(a-bp_1)]$, times the market demand at the higher price, $(a-bp_2)$. If the firm with the lower price can absorb the total market quantity, no quantity will remain for the firm with the higher price.

Constant long-run average cost is consistent with the existence of a capacity cost. In the long-run, as capacity is varied (beyond some minimum size), average cost is constant. If there is a capacity cost it must be part of that long-run average cost, adding to total cost as capacity is increased. By definition, capacity cannot be changed in the short-run so capacity costs will be fixed, unaffected by quantity. As a result, short-run average cost decreases as output increases up to the capacity limit. If we let f equal the cost per unit of capacity, k, and v equal the variable cost per unit of a firm's output, q, we have total cost, C:

(3) $\qquad C = f \cdot k + v \cdot q$

This cost function assumes a single cost per unit of capacity (f), and is consistent with Johnston's findings for firms beyond a minimal size. [5]

We now wish to combine contingent demand and constant costs for capacity limited firms, so that we may examine profit consequences of alternative actions in the resulting market structure. The interdependence of two firms leads to four possible short-run profit outcomes, comparable to a P.D. matrix, when only local choices between two prices are considered: a) both firms' prices are high, b) firm one has a higher price, c) firm two has a higher price, or d) both firms' prices are low. Profit outcomes for firm one under the four possible duopoly price combinations, based on Equations (1), (2) and (3) above, are:

a) Profit for firm one when both prices are high:

(4a) $\qquad \pi_a = \dfrac{k_1}{\Sigma k} (a - bp) (p - v) - f \cdot k_1$

b) Profit for firm one when it has a higher price than firm two:

$$(4b) \qquad \pi_b = \left[1 - \frac{k_2}{a - b \, (p - \varepsilon)} \right] (a - bp) \, (p - v) - f \cdot k_1$$

c) Profit for firm one when it has a lower price than firm two:

$$(4c) \qquad \pi_c = (p - \varepsilon - v) \, k_1 - f \cdot k_1$$

d) Profit for firm one when both prices are low:

$$(4d) \qquad \pi_d = \frac{k_1}{\Sigma k} \left[a - b \, (p - \varepsilon) \right] (p - \varepsilon - v) - f \cdot k_1$$

For all combinations of p and $p-\epsilon$, Equations (4) show how profits depend on economic variables. Profit values π_a and π_d depend on market shares defined in Equation (1). Quantities for π_b and π_c follow from Equation (2) when p and $p-\epsilon$ are substituted for p_1 and p_2. In all cases, costs for both firms are defined by Equation (3).

The profit values provided by Equations (4) correspond to payoff entries in the prisoner's dilemma of Table 5-1; π_a corresponds to (4a), π_b to (4b), etc. Among these values, three differences can be given special meaning. The difference, $\pi_c-\pi_a$, represents the gain in profit that one firm may achieve by lowering price from the more cooperative price, p, to $p-\epsilon$. The gain from cooperating when both firms raise price is $\pi_a-\pi_d$. And the difference, $\pi_d-\pi_b$, represents the relative loss consequent on attempting to cooperate by raising price unilaterally. These profit differences are all positive in the prisoner's dilemma context, where $\pi_c > \pi_a > \pi_d > \pi_b$. They will also be positive here with the constraints we are about to introduce.

Whether to raise price depends on a comparison of the cost of attempting cooperation, $\pi_d-\pi_b$, with the advantage of achieving cooperation at a higher price, $\pi_a-\pi_d$. A measure of the attractiveness of cooperation, C, will be defined as $(\pi_a-\pi_d)/(\pi_d-\pi_b)$. Similarly, whether to lower price depends on a comparison of the gain from unilateral defection, $\pi_c-\pi_a$ with the value of cooperation, $\pi_a-\pi_d$. A measure of attractiveness of defection, D, is thus $(\pi_c-\pi_a)/(\pi_a-\pi_d)$. These are types of reward structure measures that have been linked to cooperative behavior within P.D. experiments [6, 8] and to choices *between* P.D. matrix games in which to play. [9] We therefore wish to trace the effects that economic variables have on these measures.

The Effect of Economic Variables On
Reward Structure and Behavior

We are interested in the effects that changes in economic variables will have on measures of the attractiveness of cooperation and defection in the duopoly setting. Constraints on values of the variables can be adduced from the market setting in order to determine qualitative effects on C and D measures (and also to ensure continuity of functions). We confine our attention to that price range in which independent and cooperative motivations conflict, the prisoner's dilemma price range.[4] The range can be given an upper bound by noting that at the joint profit maximum, collective marginal revenue will equal marginal cost. We shall be interested in prices below the joint maximum, where marginal joint revenue is positive and exceeds marginal cost. Since joint profit is $(a-bp)$ $(p-v)-f\Sigma k$, marginal joint profit will be positive when $a-2bp+bv > 0$.

We consider only those cases in which a firm with a lower price is unable to satisfy the total market demand ($a-bp > k_1, k_2$). This is a plausible limitation on price and capacity which enables us to rely on a single continuous demand relation for each profit outcome in (4). For the same reason (and also to make $\pi_d-\pi_b > 0$), we consider only those cases in which the combined capacities of both firms exceeds the total market quantity ($a-b(p-\epsilon) > \Sigma k$). This means that there will be some excess capacity in the industry.[5] Finally, an independent profit maximizing firm is never motivated to price below marginal cost,

$$p - \varepsilon \geq v$$

All variables and the demand curve parameters, a and b, are positive.

With these constraints, the Equation (4) values serve to determine effects of important economic variables on measures of the attractiveness of cooperation and competition. The effects are summarized in Table 5-2.

Increasing the price-level alone indicates diminishing returns to collusion. Notice in Table 5-2 that as price increases, the attractiveness of cooperation decreases while that of defection increases. It is also evident, however, that capacity *reductions* might offset that effect. Indeed, by reducing their capacities, duopoly firms can preserve a situation in which cooperation is attractive and defection is not attractive, even though price is increased substantially. Of course this situation could persist only if entry were difficult for other firms.

To pinpoint specifically the firms' motivations to alter capacity, assume they agree (tacitly) to forego competition in price, and examine $\partial\pi_a/\partial k_1$ (or $\partial\pi_d/\partial k_1$, where prices are also equal) for one firm:

(5) $\qquad \partial\pi_a/\partial k_1 = (k_2/(\Sigma k)^2)(a - bp)(p - v) - f$

When $\partial\pi_a/\partial k_1$ is greater than zero, the firm will wish to expand capacity even without cutting price; when it is less than zero, the firm will prefer to reduce capacity instead. By itself, even with the constraints imposed above, Equation (5) is ambiguous in sign.

---

[4]Bargaining behavior is not always confined to this range. See Chapter 2. But the P.D. range is most relevant for establishing collusion.

[5]Excess capacity at a lower bound non-cooperative price is shown to exist, when prices are discrete, in [9].

Table 5-2
Effects of Economic Variables on Cooperation and Defection Measures

		Variable or Parameter Increased					
		p	ε	k_1	k_2	f	v
Cooperation	$\left(\dfrac{\pi_a - \pi_d}{\pi_d - \pi_b}\right)$	—	+	—	—	o	+
Defection	$\left(\dfrac{\pi_c - \pi_a}{\pi_a - \pi_d}\right)$	+	—	+	+	o	—

But the circumstances that would make Equation (5) negative are easy to trace; since $(a-bp)\,\Sigma k$ measures the utilization of industry capacity, $\partial\pi_a/\partial k_1$ is negative when the following inequality is satisfied:

$$(k_2/\Sigma k)\ x\ (\Sigma k\ \text{utilized}) < f\ /\ (p - v)$$

Four factors will determine whether the inequality is satisfied. First, lower utilization of industry capacity will tend to satisfy the inequality. So will a lower price, for as price rises, each firm will be more likely to find capacity expansion attractive even without a cut in price. It is particularly interesting to note that firm one's gain from capacity expansion is greater as his share of present industry capacity is smaller; or, put another way, the firm with the larger market share is more apt to cooperate by constraining its capacity. Finally, cost variability will affect $\partial\pi_a/\partial k_1$. As a greater portion of unit costs are variable with output (as $v/(f+v)$ is greater), $\partial\pi_a/\partial k_1$ tends to become positive and firms' tendencies to constrain capacity at a cooperative price will decline.

If no aggreement on price is achieved, capacity decisions may depend on each firm's preference for cooperation and defection opportunities. Then managements that have a higher tolerance for risk would be more apt to expand, for they prefer the higher defection and lower cooperation rewards that accompany larger capacities. Two duopolists less tolerant of risk would tend to constrain their capacities, however, since that makes a higher profit tacit agreement on price easier to reach.

Returning once again to Table 5-2, notice that as variable costs increase, price cooperation is made more attractive and defection less attractive in the short-run (with capacities fixed). Longer-run cooperation may involve capacity choices, however, either as a first step to price cooperation or after price cooperation is already established and less capacity is needed. To the extent that cooperation is associated with capacity choice, given a tacit price agreement, Equation (5) shows that a greater fixed capacity cost would tend to encourage cooperation. As the cost of a capacity unit, f increases, the likelihood also increases that $\partial \pi_a / \partial \pi_1 < 0$, inviting smaller capacities.

Where the magnitude of the minimal effective price change, ϵ, is large, either because of very low prices per unit, where even the smallest currency unit comprises a significant fraction of price, or because of industry practices which lead to the use of large discrete price intervals, the reward for cooperation is enhanced.[6] This effect is consistent with the experimental finding in Chapter 3, that when fewer price strategy alternatives are available at larger intervals, more cooperation is achieved.

Summary

Constant cost functions, which have been found empirically in studies of industrial firms, leave firm size indeterminate on economic grounds. As a result, capacity can become a topic for tacit negotiation in duopoly markets, where reward structure can influence price and capacity choices. If firms fail to cooperate with respect to capacity, a non-cooperative solution can result, not because of physical entry into the market by new firms, but simply because existing firms expand. Our objective here has been to relate economic variables to a reward structure which, in turn, should influence behavior. A homogeneous product duopoly market model in which firms have constant costs and capacity limits was formulated. Profit relations in such a model indicate the atractiveness and thus suggest the likelihood of cooperation, based on behavior observed in experimental settings. The model used here distributed market quantity in proportion to firm's capacities when their prices were the same, and according to Shubik's contingent demand function when their prices differed.

At given capacity levels, the attractiveness of price cooperation or defection is influenced by costs. Short-run price cooperation is more attractive and defection less so as a greater proportion of unit cost varies with output. When a smaller portion of cost is variable, on the other hand, price cooperation is less attractive and defection becomes more attractive. The size of typical price changes also affects cooperation. As this is larger (e.g., price at \$5.95 or \$6.95, rather than \$5.95 or \$6.00), cooperation tends to be more attractive and competition less attractive.

Having capacity as a variable enables each firm, over time, to influence the situation in which both firms will later choose prices, particularly if there are only two firms and if barriers to entry exist. Even if capacity is free, limiting it may offer advantages. Enormous gains from price cutting are lost, but so are large losses if the other firm also limits its capacity, and risk-averse managements

---

[6]For an example of such firm and industry practices, see [2, ch. 7].

may pursue as an objective a smaller profit variance. Managements more tolerant of risk are more likely to expand capacity, for they prefer the relatively greater gains from competition that larger capacities offer. But if firms forego price competition, they can be independently motivated to constrain capacity. One firm's motivation to limit its capacity was shown to be greater as the utilization of industry capacity is lower, as industry price is lower, as the firm's share of total industry is greater, and as the fixed cost of capacity accounts for a greater portion of unit cost.

References

[1] Bain, J.S., *Barriers to New Competition*, Cambridge: Harvard University Press, 1956.

[2] Cyert, R.M. and March, J.G., *A Behavioral Theory of the Firm*, Englewood Cliffs: Prentice-Hall, 1964.

[3] Edgeworth, F.Y., *Papers Relating to Political Economy*, Vol. I, London: Macmillan & Co., Ltd., 1925.

[4] Fouraker, L.E. and Siegel, S., *Bargaining Behavior*, New York: McGraw-Hill, Inc., 1963.

[5] Johnston, J., *Statistical Cost Analysis*, New York: McGraw-Hill, 1960.

[6] Lave, L.B., "Factors Affecting Cooperation in the Prisoner's Dilemma," *Behavioral Science*, Vol. 10, (1965), pp. 26-38.

[7] Nichol, A.J., "Edgeworth's Theory of Duopoly Price," *Economic Journal*, Vol. 45 (1935), pp. 51-66.

[8] Rapoport, A. and Chammah, A.M., *Prisoner's Dilemma*, Ann Arbor: The University of Michigan Press, 1965.

[9] Sherman, R., "Capacity Choice in Duopoly," unpublished Ph.D. thesis, Carnegie-Mellon University, 1966.

[10] Shubik, M., *Strategy and Market Structure*, New York: John Wiley & Sons, Inc., 1959.

[11] Smith, R.A., "The Incredible Electrical Conspiracy," *Fortune* (April and May, 1961).

6

Psychology and Capacity Choice

When firms in an industry face constant long-run average cost they are able to make capacity choices, and how they make those choices can be as important for the establishment and persistence of collusion in the industry as new entry. In their capacity choices the firms are interdependent when they are few in number, and the outcome of their actions is indeterminant on analytical grounds. We therefore shall make a brief investigation of the psychology of capacity choice, to see what role personality variables might play in it. Capacity decisions alter payoffs in the reward structure faced by firms. So we shall look at choices between prisoner's dilemma games as an analogue for capacity choice.

The prisoner's dilemma is a mixed-motive two-person game that offers each person a choice of cooperative or competitive action. Studies of American college students in experimental prisoner's dilemma games have revealed no personality measure that reliably predicts individual choice. The importance of mutual trust for cooperation has been established, [2, 10] and over many trials male subject-pairs have been shown to cooperate more than female pairs. [9] But more subtle personality measures have failed as predictors of cooperation. [3, 7] The failure of personality variables to predict behavior may be due to the narrow range of choice afforded by the dilemma. In many conflict situations, over longer time periods, each party can influence the nature of the dilemma he faces.

Extension of the prisoner's dilemma to provide a matrix choice affords a model of increased relevancy for those situations that contain long-run as well as short-run actions. Moreover, the matrix choice permits a motivation distinction that the prisoner's dilemma does not afford. Within a given prisoner's dilemma, a subject might make a cooperative choice either because he regarded the gain from cooperating as high or the gain from defecting (competing) as low; there is no way to distinguish one motivation from the other. Individual preference for cooperation or defection opportunities can be revealed, however, through matrix choice. The present study investigates individuals' preferences to play in certain matrices rather than others, on the basis of definitions of cooperation and defection opportunities; a measure of preference for cooperative game matrices will then be compared with the individual's attitude toward social risk.

Most of this chapter is drawn from my article, "Individual Attitude Toward Risk and Choice Between Prisoner's Dilemma Games," with permission from *Journal of Psychology* 66 (July 1967), 291-98. Some latter excerpts are taken from "Personality and Strategic Choice," *Journal of Psychology*, 70 (November 1968), 191-97, also with permission.

The relations among all the payoffs in any one prisoner's dilemma can be represented, up to a linear transformation, by two ratios of payoff differences. [9] The prisoner's dilemma offers four different payoffs to one person from the four possible outcomes: (a) both cooperate, (b) one person cooperates but the other does not, (c) one person does not cooperate but the other person does, and (d) both persons choose noncooperative actions. If we call these payoffs to person one a, b, c, and d, then his gain from cooperation may be represented by the payoff difference, $a-d$; his cost of attempting cooperation by the difference $d-b$; and his gain for breaking away from a cooperative agreement by the difference, $c-a$. Ratios of payoff differences such as these have been shown to influence behavior in prisoner's dilemma games. One such ratio, which has been linked to individual attempts at cooperation by Lave, [6] compares the gain available from cooperation, $a-d$, with the cost of attempting cooperation, $d-b$. We can consider this ratio as a measure of the attractiveness of cooperation, $C = (a-d)/(d-b)$. A measure of the attractiveness of defecting from a cooperative solution can be represented by the ratio, $D = (c-a)/(a-d)$, which compares the gain for breaking away from a cooperative agreement, $c-a$, with the gain for cooperating, $a-d$. Either a greater value of C or a smaller value of D in any matrix would invite a greater number of cooperative choices because a high C value reflects a high gain for cooperation relative to the cost of attempting it, while a low D value reflects a small gain for defecting relative to the gain for cooperating.

A choice between two different prisoner's dilemma games can also be influenced by the C and D ratio values of the matrices. One individual may prefer to play in a game where C is higher in the hope that he can achieve a cooperative solution; another may prefer a game where D is higher, however, for he is attracted more by competitive rewards. If one game matrix dominates another because its payoff values equal or exceed those of the other, that will, of course, provide an easier basis for choice; if the a payoffs are equal in the two matrices and the d payoffs are also equal, the dominant matrix will offer equal or higher C and D ratios.

The longer-run matrix choices can be interrelated in complicated ways. This is so in real-world choices under conflict. In a market setting, for example, where a firm's price action may be cooperative or not cooperative (competitive), a game matrix choice corresponds to the firm's longer-run choice of its capacity. And each firm's choice affects the payoffs of both firms.[1] A similar analogy can be made for the decision to harden missile sites as a cold-war strategy. In some cases, the longer-run or matrix choice can lead to what could be called a strategist's dilemma because preferred independent long-run choices, if followed, will make cooperation still harder to achieve. Thus a dilemma can exist in long-run as well as short-run choice.

Risk-taking has traditionally played an important role in strategic behavior.

[1] See Chapter 5 for analysis of these payoff relationships in the market setting.

Although risk attitude measures have not been found related to choices within a prisoner's dilemma, they may be reflected in preferences between alternative prisoner's dilemma games. We should expect that persons who have a preference for less risky alternative actions are apt to seek a game where cooperation is easy to establish. Conversely, those fond of risk would be attracted by opportunities for large gains through defection from cooperative solutions.

A Method of Examining Capacity Choice

To investigate game matrix preference, ten pairs of prisoner's dilemma games were prepared and presented to subjects. The ten pairs are shown in Figure 6-1. To facilitate comparisons within each matrix pair, two of the four payoffs to each player were kept the same in the two matrices; payoffs for coincident actions on the part of the players in the upper left and lower right hand cells (payoffs *a* and *d*) were kept the same. Dichotomous choices of the games they would prefer to play repeatedly were offered to 44 undergraduate males at the University of Virginia in two different groups of 22 students each. Two different forms were used within each group to reduce position bias.

Iterated (simultaneous choice) prisoner's dilemma games were explained to the subjects before they made their choices. One half of the subjects were in a group about to participate in prisoner's dilemma game experiments, while the remaining 22 were students in an intermediate economics course. Subjects for the game experiments had been recruited to work in an economics research project for which they were to be compensated. These subjects were allowed to think that their choices would influence the experimental games they would later participate in. In the economics class group, students' choices were solicited as part of a study which, they were assured, would have no effect on them.

Measures of the attractiveness of cooperation and defection are given in Table 6-1 for the ten matrices shown in Figure 6-1. Pairs *1* through *5* present choices in which Matrix B dominates Matrix A. In Pairs *6* through *9*, Matrix A offered a higher value for ratio *C* than did Matrix B, but Matrix B offered a higher value for ratio *D*. Thus, in these four pairs, Matrix A offered a more attractive opportunity to cooperate than did Matrix B; and Matrix B offered a more rewarding defection opportunity than did Matrix A. *Pair 10* offered no difference in either the *C* or the *D* ratio. This assortment of game matrix choices allows investigation of two bases for game preference. First, we can see whether most subjects prefer dominant game matrices. Second, we can distinguish persons who prefer cooperative matrices from those who prefer ones with defection opportunities. Then, to determine whether matrix game choices are related to attitude toward risk, individuals' cooperative matrix choices can be compared with the Kogan and Wallach measure of their social risk preference (SRP). [5] The Kogan and Wallach social risk measure was chosen because it

Figure 6-1
Ten Matrix Pairs Used to Solicit Subject Choices

The number to the left in each cell is payment to the player who chooses a row in the prisoner's dilemma matrix; the number to the right goes to the player who chooses a column. Of the row and column choices within a matrix, Choice 1 is cooperative, Choice 2 is competitive. Of the A or B matrix choices, Choice A offers greater opportunity to cooperate, Choice B offers greater reward for competition.

Table 6-1
Cooperation and Defection Ratios of Figure 6-1 Matrix Pairs

Matrix pair	Matrix A		Matrix B	
	C	*D*	*C*	*D*
1	1.0	1.0	1.0	2.0
2	.5	1.0	.5	2.0
3	3.0	.7	3.0	2.0
4	.6	.7	1.0	1.3
5	.5	1.0	1.0	2.0
6	1.0	1.0	.5	2.0
7	1.0	1.0	.5	2.0
8	3.0	.7	1.0	1.3
9	1.0	1.0	.5	2.0
10	.5	2.0	.5	2.0

would yield a validated measure of attitude toward risk and it is economical to administer. It presents 12 social situations in which a subject has an opportunity to choose a risky alternative action. The subject is asked to estimate a minimum probability of success that the more risky action would have to possess in order for him to choose it.

The Effect of Risk Attitude on Choice

From the first five matrix-pairs, dominant matrices were chosen by 88 per cent of the subjects. Thus, where dominance is present, it provides a strong basis for overall preference between games. If Matrix *Pair 10* is excluded, the remaining pairs offer an opportunity to distinguish players who seek cooperative opportunities from those who prefer competitive ones. Persons who choose Matrix A either pass up an opportunity to take a dominate game-matrix (*Pairs 1 to 5*), or they select a matrix for which the *C* ratio is larger and the *D* ratio is smaller (*Pairs 6-9*). The total number of Matrix A choices is shown by subject in Table 6-2, together with the subject's SRP score.

We wish to test the null hypothesis that there is no relation between the cooperative game choice and aversion to risk measures against an alternative hypothesis that there is a positive relationship (one-tailed test). The measures with which we deal possess no genuine cardinal meaning, only an ordinal one. Each measure can be used to rank subjects, however, and the ranks can then be tested by the Spearman rank correlation method. Adjusted for tied ranks, the Spearman rank correlation coefficient for these data is .404, which is significant ($p < .01$) and leads to rejection of the hypothesis that there is no relation between the ranks. Persons who rank high in the above matrix-choice test of preference for competitive opportunities also tend to rank high in the Kogan and Wallach test of their preference for situations involving risk. Separate Spearman rank correlation coefficients calculated for the 22 subjects who were about to

Table 6-2
Matrix A Choices and Social Risk Preference Score by Subject

Subject*	SRP score	Matrix A choices	Subject*	SRP score	Matrix A choices
7-1	84	4	13-1	64	4
7-2	68	3	13-2	76	4
7-3	76	3	13-3	76	0
7-4	60	0	13-4	80	5
7-5	50	4	13-5	66	5
7-6	63	2	13-6	73	4
7-7	57	0	13-7	84	5
7-8	85	2	13-8	60	3
7-9	76	0	13-9	60	3
7-10	94	5	13-10	67	4
9-1	83	4	13-11	68	1
9-2	64	0	13-12	61	0
9-3	84	5	13-13	86	6
9-4	92	4	13-14	79	3
9-5	65	3	13-15	67	0
9-6	69	4	13-16	60	0
9-7	48	0	13-17	74	1
9-8	78	0	13-18	80	6
9-9	62	3	13-19	66	4
9-10	54	4	13-20	62	2
9-11	82	2	13-21	68	0
9-12	80	3	13-22	82	2

participate in prisoner's dilemma experiments and the 22 subjects from an economics class were each significant at the .05 level. Coefficients were .42 and .41 (adjusted for tied ranks), and the criterion at the .05 level in each of these cases is .36. The strength of the relationship thus seems uniform across these two groups of subjects, even though their motivation might have been different.

After these tests were completed, an effort was made to distinguish high and low SRP subjects, to examine separately their effectiveness in predicting matrix choices. The SRP score and matrix choice data in Table 6-2 were divided into two halves by high and low SRP scores, and ranks of corresponding matrix choices were then reassigned within each smaller sample. The high SRP score group produced a Spearman rank correlation coefficient of .443 (adjusted for tied ranks), which exceeded the criterion value of .36 at the .05 level of significance (one-tailed test). Among low SRP scores, however, the Spearman rank correlation coefficient was only .125 (adjusted for tied ranks), a value that is not significant. This result indicates that the relation between SRP score and tendency to cooperate is stronger among those persons who avoid risky situations.

Thus a strategic dilemma can arise in long-run choice that seems amenable to experimental investigation along the lines of prisoner's dilemma games. The connection of risk attitude with matrix choice suggests that the force of a strategist's dilemma will vary with the individual players. Two risk-averse persons may observe no real choice dilemma because both prefer a setting that facilitates cooperation. But facing the same situation, two persons more tolerant of risk may each prefer long-run actions that make cooperation difficult, and so are in conflict with their collective interests. Thus, risk attitudes not only affect individual choice of long-run alternatives, they can also determine the extent to which a long-run dilemma is perceived.

The separation of long-run and short-run choice that is suggested here may help to reconcile prior results regarding risk attitudes and cooperation. Groups have been found to accept more risk than individuals in the Wallach and Kogan test of risk preference, [1, pp. 656-708, 3] yet in prisoner's dilemma games, pairs of persons acting as one decision unit cooperated more than individuals. [8] The results reported here suggest that groups would tend to select games that offered more competitive opportunities, since groups are more willing to accept risk than are individuals. Once in any particular game, however, groups could still achieve a higher degree of cooperation than individuals.

Other Psychological Effects

A choice between two prisoner's dilemma games, as a measure of individual preference for games with high rewards for competition, has been found related to social risk attitude. The same risk attitude has also been found related to success in a bilateral monopoly bargaining situation with incomplete information. [4] Let us replicate the risk attitude and strategic choice relation and investigate also the influence on strategic choice of internationalist attitude and tolerance for ambiguity.

Three personality scales to be administered are (a) the Kogan and Wallach test of social risk preference, [5] (b) the Sampson and Smith scale of worldminded (internationalist) attitude, [11] and (c) a tolerance for ambiguity measure as modified by Pilisuk, *et al.* [7] The Kogan and Wallach test has already been introduced, but now will be given a minus sign, so higher scores denote fondness for risk. The internationalist and tolerance for ambiguity scales each present a series of statements with which the subject expresses degree of agreement (or disagreement) on a six-point scale.

Preference for social risk and tolerance for ambiguity are both expected to correlate with competitive strategy choice. So is internationalism, based on the negative (but not significant) relationship between internationalism and cooperation found by Pilisuk, *et al.* Each of the measures was administered to 78 undergraduate male subjects in three different economics classes at the University of Virginia. In one of the groups (Group 3) all measures were obtained in one class period, while in the other two groups the scales were administered at several different class meetings.

Each independent personality measure was correlated with matrix choice by the Spearman coefficient of rank correlation (adjusted for tied ranks), and the degree of association of all four measures was determined by the Kendall coefficient of concordance. All coefficients are shown in Table 6-3 for each of the three subject groups and for all groups combined.

Table 6-3
Summary of Association Measures

Group	Risk pref.	Toler. ambig.	World-minded	Coefficient of concordance for all four measures
1	.30**	.16	.39**	.43***
2	.28*	.59**	.13	.49***
3	.17	.02	.14	.37*
All	.19**	.17*	.09	.37***

  * $p < .10$.
 ** $p < .05$.
*** $p < .01$.

The Kendall coefficient of concordance reveals an association among all four of the measures; the coefficient is significant overall ($p < .01$). Risk attitude is significantly related to matrix choice ($p < .05$) over all of the groups, but significant at that level for only one of the subgroups. Tolerance for ambiguity is associated with selection of competitive matrices, being significant in one of the subgroups ($p < .05$), but overall only marginally significant ($p < .10$). While internationalism is significant ($p < .05$) in one of the subgroups, it is not significant overall. Thus, although the three measures do appear as correlates of one another and each is somewhat related to strategic choice, neither tolerance for ambiguity nor internationalism affords as strong a relationship as risk preference with strategic choice. We may expect some marginal improvement in strategic choice predictability as a result of tolerance for ambiguity and internationalist score information, but neither appears as effective as attitude toward social risk.

To the extent internationalism is at all correlated with strategic choice, highly internationalist subjects choose more competitive opportunities, not less. This is consistent with the findings of Pilisuk *et al.* that internationalism, while not significant, was negatively related to cooperation. It suggests that the survey scale for worldminded attitude may find as internationalist those persons more willing to place themselves in risky situations where competitive opportunities are high. Possibly such persons may be willing to adopt the worldminded outlook because they are successfull in competitive situations rather than innately internationalistic. The survey technique may therefore fail to identify genuine internationalism.[2]

―――――――――――

[2]Comparison of a small sample of British university students with a small sample of American university students showed the British sample to have a greater preference for those matrix games in which competitive opportunities were greater. See [14].

Sermat has emphasized that rivalistic behavior, in which one person attempts to win more than his opponent, can be examined in the chicken game, but cannot be distinguished from independent maximizing behavior in the prisoner's dilemma game. [12] Another possible difference is that the chicken game can be used to represent long-run strategic choices, [15] whereas actions within a prisoner's dilemma can only be short-run actions. Then the longer run, strategic choices, either between prisoner's dilemma games in which to play or within a chicken game, would seem to correlate with personality measures. Additional correlates with strategic choice may further reduce unexplained variance in mixed-motive conflict situations, which serve as a test of validity in predicting strategic choice behavior.

Summary

Prisoner's dilemma experiments usually preclude long-run, strategic choices of game matrices; they only permit a choice of action within a given matrix. So confined, the experiments have not revealed any reliable connection between personality measures and cooperative behavior. Here, a basis for game-matrix preference has been examined as an analogue to long-run choice, and found related to individual risk attitude. Two structural influences on game-matrix choices were distinguished. Dominance in payoff comparisons was found to lead to strong preferences. More subtle distinctions were also made, with the use of cooperation and defection measures that reflect relations among different payoffs in each prisoner's dilemma game matrix. Based on these latter distinctions some individuals indicated an interest in matrices that offered higher cooperation but lower defection measures, while others tended to prefer matrices with higher defection but lower cooperation measures. Those who preferred cooperative matrices tended to be more averse to social risk than those who preferred matrices with higher defection measures.

The relation between risk avoidance and preference for cooperative games was stronger than that associating high tolerance for risk with preference for competitive games, where the relation was positive but not signficant. The relationship between SRP score and matrix choice was equally strong among subjects, however, whether they expected that their choices would influence which matrix game they would later play in or they were simply expressing choices that had no future consequences for them. Internationalist or world-minded subjects tended if anything to make more competitive matrix choices, as did subjects with high tolerance for ambiguity. But neither of these personality traits was as strongly or as consistently related to matrix choices as risk attitude.

References

[1] Brown, R., *Social Psychology*, New York: Free Press, 1965.

[2] Deutsch, M., "Trust and Suspicion," *Journal of Conflict Resolution*, 2 (1958), 265-79.

[3] Dolbear, F.T., Jr., & Lave, L.B., "Risk Orientation as a Predictor in the Prisoner's Dilemma," *Journal of Conflict Resolution*, 10 (1966), 506-15.

[4] Harnett, D.L., Cummings, L.L., & Hughes, G.D., "The Influence of Risk-Taking Propensity on Bargaining Behavior," *Behavioral Science*, 13 (1968), 91-101.

[5] Kogan, N., & Wallach, M.A., *Risk Taking: A Study in Cognition and Personality*, New York: Holt, Rinehart & Winston, 1964.

[6] Lave, L.B., "An Empirical Approach to the Prisoner's Dilemma Game," *Quarterly Journal of Economics*, 76 (1962), 242-36.

[7] Pilisuk, M., Potter, P., Rapoport, A., & Winter, J.A., "War Hawks and Peace Doves," *Journal of Conflict Resolution*, 9 (1965), 491-508.

[8] Pylyshyn, Z., Aghew, N., & Illingworth, J., "Comparison of Individuals and Pairs as Participants in a Mixed-Motive Game," *Journal of Conflict Resolution*, 10 (1966), 211-20.

[9] Rapoport, A., & Chammah, A.M., *Prisoner's Dilemma*, Ann Arbor, Mich.: Univ. Michigan Press, 1965.

[10] Rekosh, J.H., & Feigenbaum, K.D., "The Necessity of Mutual Trust for Cooperative Behavior in a Two Person Games," *Journal of Social Psychology*, 69 (1961), 149-54.

[11] Sampson, D.L., & Smith, H.P., "A Scale to Measure World-Minded Attitudes," *Journal of Social Psychology*, 45 (1957), 99-106.

[12] Sermat, V., "The Possibility of Influencing the Other's Behavior and Cooperation: Chicken versus Prisoner's Dilemma," *Canadian Journal of Psychology*, 21 (1967), 204-19.

[13] Stoner, J.A.F., "A Comparison of Individual and Group Decisions Including Risk," Unpublished Master's thesis, Massachusetts Institute of Technology, Cambridge, Massachusetts, 1961.

[14] Sherman, R., "Culture and Strategic Choice," *Journal of Psychology*, 75 (July 1970), 227-30.

[15] Sherman, R., & Willett, T.D., "Potential Entrants Discourage Entry," *Journal of Political Economy*, 75, (1967), 400-403.

7

Risk Attitude, Cost Variability, and Collusion[1]

Firms in many industries experience constant long-run average cost over wide ranges of output. [1, 9, 21] A competitive market can still provide a solution when constant cost makes individual firm size indeterminate, for each firm will simply expand or contract as price rises above or falls below its average cost. But among a few firms the implications of a capacity choice are less clear. Ever since Cournot, [4] most formulations of oligopoly models have emphasized short-run behaviour.[2] Assuming barriers to new entry, the models deal with tacit collusion at a price higher than the competitive one, and only after that is achieved do the firms choose a size or level of capacity, usually one that is optimal for that price.

Entry barriers afford less protection when capacity expansion can come from within an industry, so oligopolists should find collusion more difficult. But if there are barriers to new entry, existing firms may observe how the level of industry capacity will affect their future price-setting motives. Any tacit agreement among them could then take account of both capacity and price. This does not mean that capacity must replace price as the crucial variable in tacit collusion, but rather that the causal priority of price over capacity in competition need not represent the ordering of decisions in oligopoly. Oligopolists may emphasize their capacity choices instead, for those choices influence the environment in which they will later take price decisions.[3] The presence of a capacity choice thus affects the form of the cooperate-or-compete dilemma that characterizes oligopoly.

Experimental market and prisoner's dilemma game investigations of behaviour in oligopoly have also been confined to short-run price or output choice. These experiments have revealed structural factors that can influence the behaviour of decision makers in such mixed-motive (cooperate-or-compete)

Reprinted with permission from "Risk Attitude and Cost Variability in a Capacity Choice Experiment," *The Review of Economic Studies*, 36 (October 1969), 453-66.

[1]I am grateful to Professors J.A. Carlson, R.M. Cyert, O.A. Davis, F.T. Dolbear, L.B. Lave, and V.H. Vroom for advice and criticism, and to Evelyn Glazier and Howard Schneider for help in carrying out experiments.

[2]Chamberlin considered entry but the entry decision was based on a prevailing price which followed a short-run adjustment process. [3, pp. 81-109] The main other exception to such short-run emphasis is Bronfenbrenner's argument that a long-run time horizon will normally determine price, which is then rigid over short-run periods. [2]

[3]In the context of a ruin-game, Shubik made clear the importance of asset position as a determinant of price behavior. [20] Also, his contingent demand revealed how important capacity limits can be in determining the structure of each firm's short-run decision.

settings. [6, 7, 11, 16] But personality variables in general, and risk attitudes in particular, have not been linked reliably to cooperation in these
experiments.[4] [5, 8, 14]

Here we expand the prisoner's dilemma setting to include a choice between prisoner's dilemma game matrices as well as a choice of action within a
particular game matrix. First we describe the strategist's dilemma that results.
The method is then set out for an experiment which uses this choice setting to
represent the bare essentials of a duopolist's capacity choice. Hypotheses are
stated formally and results are presented. The results are summarized and
discussed in a final section.

Capacity Choice as a Strategist's Dilemma

To investigate capacity choice behaviour under controlled conditions we need a
simple paradigm that can characterize the decision situation. Much as a choice of
action within a prisoner's dilemma can be related to a firm's market decision
regarding price or output, a choice of prisoner's dilemma matrix will be used to
represent the firm's capacity choice. But first let us illustrate the structural
influences on cooperation that have been found in prisoner's dilemma game
experiments, and trace them to economic variables. Lave chose a ratio of payoff
differences to measure the attractiveness of cooperation in a game. [11] The
ratio is shown in Figure 7-1 as C which compares the gain available by moving to
a cooperative solution, $a-d$, with the cost of unilaterally attempting cooperation, $d-b$. Lave found that a higher value of C tended to elicit more cooperative

Figure 7-1
Prisoner's Dilemma

Player 2

		1	2
	1	a	b
Player 1	2	c	d

$$c > a > d > b$$

$$C = \frac{a-d}{d-b} \qquad D = \frac{c-a}{a-d}$$

---

[4]Internationalism has been linked to cooperative behaviour in a mixed motive game called
chicken, which differs from the standard prisoner's dilemma game. [12, 13] The chicken
game has been applied to a long-run economic choice setting, the entry decision, in [19].
Male subject pairs have been found to cooperate more than female pairs in repeated play of
prisioner's dilemma games. [15]

behaviour. A similar ratio that measures the attractiveness of defection, D is also indicated in Figure 7-1. It compares the gain from leaving a cooperative agreement, $c-a$, with the gain from cooperation that may thereby be foregone, $a-d$; a higher value of D can be expected to invite more competitive behaviour.[5]

The C and D values for a prisoner's dilemma game matrix can be related to total cost variability in a corresponding market choice of price or quantity.[6] Consider in particular the effect on total cost of short-run output changes, when the capacity choice determines a maximum output level and a level of fixed costs as well. *Ceteris paribus*, if a large fraction of total cost is associated with the capacity decision, raising market price will be less attractive than if only a small fraction of total cost is associated with capacity. The reason is that less cost can be saved immediately on reducing output when a large portion of total cost is associated with capacity (more of total cost is fixed in the short run). In the prisoner's dilemma matrix representation of price choices in Figure 7-1, greater capacity cost would therefore cause $a-d$ to be relatively smaller, and that, in turn, would make C smaller and D larger.

Subjects can also be afforded a choice of payoff matrix in which to play. And if their matrix choices are interdependent the subjects can together determine the setting for their later short-run actions. Such a matrix choice can then be analogous to the long-run capacity choice of a duopoly firm. When one firm increases its capacity it incurs added capacity costs, which are greater as total cost depends more on capacity, and it can also produce a larger output. We assume that when firms have the same price, capacity expansion sufficiently increases market share for the expanding firm to offset added capacity costs, and so we maintain the same a and d values in Figure 7-1.[7] The main effects of increasing capacity will then occur in the b and c payoffs, which are effective when prices differ. Payoff c will increase relative to the a and d values in Figure 7-1 because the expanded firm can produce more output and thereby take fuller advantage of a price cut. As a result, $c-a$ would be larger after expansion and so, as a consequence, would D. Payoff b could decrease, relative to a and d, because when undercut in price, the expanded firm will be left with the same output yet capacity costs could be higher than before expansion. So $d-b$ could be larger as a result of expansion, making C smaller.

Choices by individuals between alternative matrices have indicated that some

[5]Two ratios such as C and D can describe all the payoffs in a prisoner's dilemma up to a linear transformation. See [15].

[6]The price or quantity choices must be assumed to lie in the prisoner's dilemma range between cooperative (joint profit maximizing) and independent, or non-cooperative, solutions. Market demand elasticity will also affect payoff values, of course, but it is assumed to be given and unchanged in comparisons here. For an elaboration of these effects of economic variables on prisoner's dilemma payoffs, see [18].

[7]There exist several equally plausible assumptions regarding the effect that capacity decisions can have on market shares. We deliberately choose one that makes capacity expansion attractive (by increasing market share) so that any tendency to constrain capacity will then be due only to capacity cost.

persons prefer matrices where cooperation can be more readily established (higher value of the ratio, C), while others are attracted by an opportunity to make gains from competitive behaviour (higher value of D). Moreover, an individual's preference for matrices in which the opportunity for cooperation is greater was found to be positively related to his aversion for risky actions. [17] These preferences were obtained without any subject interaction, but they indicate that with interaction, personality variables may affect long-run cooperation even though they have failed as predictors in short-run choice.

Bringing together a choice *between* prisoner's dilemma game matrices and a choice *within* a game matrix can produce a double dilemma. Within any particular game matrix, the well-known prisoner's dilemma obtains. But a second dilemma, which will be called a strategist's dilemma, may also exist because independent game matrix choices can lead two subjects to a prisoner's dilemma game in which cooperation is difficult. Yet if they were to act collectively, they could choose a different game matrix that would make cooperation easier. In the corresponding price and capacity choice market setting, the force of this strategist's dilemma will be greater as a larger fraction of total cost varies with short-run output, because capacity costs are less important then and do not discourage the firms from the capacity expansion which makes cooperation harder to sustain. The strategist's dilemma should also be stronger for persons more tolerant of risk, who prefer game matrices that reward competiton. Such matrices correspond to larger capacities in the market setting.

Method

The experiment is an extension of prisoner's dilemma experimental games. Each of two subjects faces a payoff table which shows monetary rewards to both subjects as an outcome for every possible combination of their choices. Subjects cannot communicate with each other and do not know the identity of the person with whom they play; they choose simultaneously, so that each is unsure of the other's current choice; and the subjects are paid the monetary outcomes corresponding to their choices.

The main difference between this experiment and earlier prisoner's dilemma experiments lies in the reward structure. We use Payoff Tables (I through V) shown in Figures 7-2 and 7-3. Each of these payoff tables requires two choices, one intended as a long-run choice and the other as a short-run choice. Each subject must select an action, 1 or 2, within a given prisoner's dilemma, but he must also make a matrix choice, A or B, which, together with the other person's, determines the prisoner's dilemma game matrix in which the two subjects will next play. That is, the choice sequence is arranged to make the choice of matrix precede the choice of action within the matrix. In period 2, for example, a subject will choose a number strategy (1 or 2) for that period but he will choose

Figure 7-2
Payoff Tables I, II, III

Payoff tables used in differential competitiveness experiments. The left-hand figure in each cell is the payoff to Player 1, the right-hand figure to Player 2.

PAYOFF TABLE I

Player 2

			A		B	
		1	2	1	2
A	1	20, 20	0, 25	20, 20	−10, 35
	2	25, 0	5, 5	25, 0	5, 5
B	1	20, 20	0, 25	20, 20	−10, 35
	2	35, −10	5, 5	35, −10	5, 5

Player 1 (rows)

PAYOFF TABLE II

Player 2

		A		B	
		1	2	1	2
A	1	15, 15	−5, 25	15, 15	−15, 35
	2	25, −5	5, 5	25, −5	5, 5
B	1	15, 15	−5, 25	15, 15	−15, 35
	2	35, −15	5, 5	35, −15	5, 5

Player 1 (rows)

PAYOFF TABLE III

Player 2

		A		B	
		1	2	1	2
A	1	20, 20	0, 30	20, 20	−20, 50
	2	30, 0	10, 10	30, 0	10, 10
B	1	20, 20	0, 30	20, 20	−20, 50
	2	50, −20	10, 10	50, −20	10, 10

Player 1 (rows)

Figure 7-3
Payoff Tables IV, V

Payoff tables used in joint cooperation experiment. The left-hand figure in each cell is the payoff to Player 1, the right-hand figure to Player 2.

PAYOFF TABLE IV

Player 2

			A		B	
			1	2	1	2
Player 1	A	1	15, 15	0, 20	15, 15	−10, 30
		2	20, 0	5, 5	20, 0	5, 5
	B	1	15, 15	0, 20	15, 15	−10, 30
		2	30, −10	5, 5	30, −10	5, 5

PAYOFF TABLE V

Player 2

			A		B	
			1	2	1	2
Player 1	A	1	15, 15	−5, 20	10, 15	−15, 30
		2	20, −5	10, 10	20, −10	5, 10
	B	1	15, 10	−10, 20	10, 10	−20, 30
		2	30, −15	10, 5	30, −20	5, 5

a game matrix (A or B) for period 3. Then when he reaches period 3 he will know the other person's matrix choice as well as his own for that period, so that he will know exactly which prisoner's dilemma matrix he is playing in. He can choose a number action for that prisoner's dilemma game matrix and must also make his letter, or game matrix, choice for the following period. The choice of a game in which to play corresponds to a long-run decision, while the choice of an action within one matrix is a short-run action, taken in a framework produced by earlier long-run choices.[8]

---

[8] The experimental setting requires that time as well as payoff relations be specified explicitly. Each prisoner's dilemma matrix should be relevant for the time period required for one party to respond to an action by the other. Several such periods of time might pass before long-run adjustments could be made. Also, adjustments in one direction might take longer than adjustments in the other direction. We only consider a case in which long-run adjustments require one more period than short-run actions.

Of the two game matrix alternatives, action B always represents the larger capacity, and the effect of capacity size is reflected in all payoff values. Table 7-1 gives values of C and D ratios (see Figure 7-1) for the four prisoner's dilemma games embedded in each payoff table in Figure 7-3. Notice that as a player moves from matrix A to matrix B in each payoff table, the D ratio or attractiveness of defection always increases. In Payoff Table IV, matrix B can be said to dominate matrix A, because all payoffs for Player 1 in matrix B are equal to or greater than those in matrix A; the C ratio is the same in both matrices and the D ratio is always greater in matrix B. There is a "strategist's dilemma" in Payoff Table IV because matrix B dominates matrix A regardless of the other's choice of matrix, and yet cooperation is more difficult to sustain when both players choose matrix B because the attractiveness of defection is then greater. Payoff Table IV represents a case in which all costs vary with short-run output.

Dominance does not arise in the matrix choice in Payoff Table V. Notice that for Player 1, one payoff is higher in the B matrix and one is lower; the value of D is greater in the B matrix but C is lower. Without dominance, the force of the strategist's dilemma will depend more on the attitudes of individual players. For those who tend to avoid risk, a strategist's dilemma may not hold, for they could choose matrix A and face only a prisoner's dilemma in which cooperation is relatively easy to achieve. Payoff Table V represents a case in which a significant portion of total cost varies with capacity rather than short-run output. All other payoff tables represent costs that are highly variable with output, as Payoff Table IV does.

Table 7-1
Cooperation and Defection Ratios for Matrices in Payoff Tables IV and V

Matrix choice		Payoff Table IV		Payoff Table V	
Own	Other's	C	D	C	D
A	A	2	$\frac{1}{2}$	$\frac{1}{3}$	1
B	A	2	$1\frac{1}{2}$	$\frac{1}{4}$	3
A	B	$\frac{2}{3}$	$\frac{1}{2}$	$\frac{1}{4}$	2
B	B	$\frac{2}{3}$	$1\frac{1}{2}$	$\frac{1}{5}$	4

Subjects are stratified into three categories for the experiment according to their scores in the Kogan and Wallach measure of Social Risk Preference (SRP).[9] Persons from different SRP score classes are joined as subject pairs and their relative competitiveness is examined by contrasting behaviour within the subject

[9]The Kogan and Wallach social risk preference measure is described in [10]. It presents a series of twelve decision situations in which one alternative is riskier than the other. Subjects must estimate the minimum probability of success that the riskier alternative would have to possess in each situation before they would choose it. For other measures of risk attitude, see [5] and [14].

pairs. Relative competitiveness within subject pairs is observed in a mixture of the payoff tables shown in Figure 7-2. Persons from the same SRP score class are also joined as subject pairs, and their degree of joint cooperation is examined by contrasting the behaviour of groups of subject pairs by SRP class. When joint cooperation is examined, the effect of cost variability is also considered, in the form of a contrast between behaviour in Payoff Table IV and Payoff Table V, which are shown in Figure 7-3. The same persons play together in both of these payoff tables, and by controlling for the order in which they play, balanced reward structure and risk attitude effects on cooperation can be examined. Procedures for administering the experiments are described in the Appendix.

Hypotheses

We distinguish three classes of risk attitude, by high (risk averse), medium, and low SRP scores.[10] In view of the previously observed tendency of individuals more tolerant of risk to prefer matrices with greater competitive opportunities (high D or low C ratio), we should expect the subject in a lower SRP score class to compete more. Within each subject pair, one subject can earn more money than the other only by behaving more competitively, so we can examine differential earnings as a measure of competitiveness. If we denote earnings of a high SRP subject by F_h, earnings of a medium SRP subject by F_m, and earnings of a low SRP subject by F_l, then we wish to test the null hypothesis that within subject pairs, $p(F_h < F_m) = p(F_h < F_l) = p(F_m < F_l) = \frac{1}{2}$, against the alternative hypotheses that

Hypothesis

$$(1a) \quad p(F_h < F_m) > \tfrac{1}{2},$$
$$(1b) \quad p(F_h < F_l) > \tfrac{1}{2},$$
$$(1c) \quad p(F_m < F_l) > \tfrac{1}{2}.$$

The union of these alternative hypotheses is: (1) *within any subject pair, the subject with the higher SRP score class will tend to compete less and will experience stochastically lower earnings than the subject with the lower SRP score class.*

When subjects who fall in the same SRP score class are joined in pairs, we can expect the SRP score of both persons to influence the amount of their joint cooperation and thus their joint earnings.[11] Pairs of individuals with high SRP

---

[10] High scores are those above 70, medium scores 60 to 70, and low scores below 60 in the Kogan and Wallach test. Higher scores indicate more aversion to social risk and lower scores indicate greater tolerance.

[11] Joint earnings of a subject-pair will reflect their degree of joint cooperation whenever $2a \geq c + b$ in Figure 7-1. This constraint on the payoff relations is usually imposed in prisoner's dilemma experiments, and it is observed here. The same relation between cooperation and the profit of firms exists over the relevant price range in a duopoly market.

scores should more often prefer the greater cooperative opportunities of the A matrices and cooperate more than medium or low SRP score subject pairs. If we denote the joint earnings of a high SRP subject pair by F_{hh}, of a medium SRP subject pair by F_{mm}, and of a low SRP subject pair by F_{ll}, then we wish to test the null hypothesis that

$$p(F_{hh} > F_{mm}) = p(F_{hh} > F_{ll}) = p(F_{mm} > F_{ll}) = \tfrac{1}{2}$$

against the alternative hypotheses that

Hypothesis   (2a) $p(F_{hh} > F_{mm}) > \tfrac{1}{2}$,

                    (2b) $p(F_{hh} > F_{ll}) > \tfrac{1}{2}$,

                    (2c) $p(F_{mm} > F_{ll}) > \tfrac{1}{2}$.

In order to form more powerful Mann-Whitney U tests using all data, these alternative hypotheses are also combined. *Hypotheses* (2a) and (2b) together imply

$$p(F_{hh} > F_{mm+ll}) > \tfrac{1}{2},$$

where F_{mm+ll} represents joint earnings of a subject pair from the medium and low SRP subject pairs combined, and hypotheses (2b) and (2c) together imply $p(F_{hh+mm} > F_{ll}) > \frac{1}{2}$, where F_{hh+mm} represents joint earnings of a subject pair from high and medium SRP subject pairs combined.

Two other hypotheses compare the effects of structural contrasts in this joint cooperation experiment. The structural contrasts are related to total cost variability, and their effects are based on behavior that has been observed separately in prisoner's dilemma and matrix choice situations. In Payoff Table IV, which is intended to reflect costs highly variable with short-run output, matrix B always dominates matrix A. (All payoffs to one person in B are equal to or better than his payoffs in A.) Dominant matrices have been shown to be strongly preferred when they were available in matrix choices. [17] Because such dominance is not present in Payoff Table V, the independent preference for matrix B should be less strong there, and so we may expect stochastically more matrix A choices in Payoff Table V. We test the null hypotheses that the A matrix will be chosen equally often in either payoff table against the alternative that

Hypothesis (3) *Subjects will choose the A matrix more often in Payoff Table V than in Payoff Table IV.*

In economic terms this means firms will prefer smaller capacities in a strategic situation as capacity cost, which is fixed in the short-run, accounts for a larger portion of total cost.

Compared with Payoff Table V, every prisoner's dilemma in Payoff Table IV offers a higher value of C, the cooperative measure, and a lower value of D, the defection measure. From results of prisoner's dilemma experiments, we could expect cooperation within each matrix (that is, choosing number 1) to occur more often in Payoff Table IV than in Payoff Table V. *Hypothesis* (3) predicts more A choices in Table V than in Table IV, however, and since the attractiveness of cooperation relative to defection is always greater in A matrices than in B matrices in both IV and V, *Hypothesis* (3) alone would lead to the opposite result: more 1 choices in Payoff Table V. To separate these conflicting effects we qualify our fourth hypothesis so that 1 choices are compared separately for each matrix actually chosen. We test the null hypothesis that the number of 1 choices will be no greater, *per trial in the A matrix game*, in one payoff table than another, against the alternative that

Hypothesis (4a) *A greater number of 1 choices can be expected* per trial in the A matrix game *in Payoff Table IV than in Payoff Table V.*

And we test the null hypothesis that the number of 1 choices will be no greater, *per trial in the B matrix game*, in one payoff table than another, against the alternative that

Hypothesis (4b) *A greater number of 1 choices can be expected* per trial in the B matrix game *in Payoff Table IV than in Payoff Table V.*

Results

Hypotheses were subjected to one-tail non-parametric statistical tests. A level of significance was chosen at 0.05, but the actual probability of the observed result or a more extreme one is reported for each test assuming the null hypotheses true. This probability information affords interpretation beyond an accept or reject decision, which seems appropriate in view of the small samples and the limited power of non-parametric tests.

For experiments with paired subjects having different risk attitudes, the earnings of each subject over 15 trials in Payoff Matrix I, II or III are shown in Table 7-2. Subjects with lower SRP scores more often earned more. But as shown in Table 7-3, only in the high versus medium SRP subject contrast did the difference in earnings occur often enough to approach significance at the 0.05 level. Over all combinations, the null hypothesis cannot strictly be rejected at the 0.05 level in favour of *Hypothesis* (1) that the higher SRP score (risk averse) class subject will tend to earn less, but the result (or a more extreme one) would occur only with probability 0.06 and so *Hypothesis* (1) would still seem to have considerable promise.

We examine next the effect of SRP class on joint cooperation, through joint earnings. The combined profits of each pair of subjects over their last ten trials in both Payoff Tables IV and V are shown by SRP class in Table 7-4. Results of the Mann-Whitney-U Test are summarized in Table 7-5. *Hypothesis* (2*a*), which claims it is more probable that high SRP subject pairs earn more than medium SRP subject pairs, can be accepted over the corresponding null hypothesis. There is some support for *Hypothesis* (2*b*) that high SRP subject pairs are likely to earn more than low SRP subject pairs, but not enough to be significant, and there is no support for *Hypothesis* (2*c*). The combination of *Hypotheses* (2*a*) and (2*b*) into one that has high SRP subject pairs likely to earn more than all others can be accepted in preference to the corresponding null hypothesis, but the related hypothesis that low SRP subject pairs are likely to earn less than all other subject pairs cannot be accepted.

Both the differences in earnings within pairs of subjects that have different

Table 7-2
Earnings of Each Subject by SRP Score Class

Payoff Table	High	Medium	High	Low	Medium	Low
I	2·45	2·95	2·55	0·55	2·15	2·20
I	2·40	1·50	3·00	2·75	0·65	1·35
I	2·25	2·70	0·65	2·30	1·90	1·40
I	0·60	2·55	0·95	2·25	1·00	1·50
I	1·35	1·65	0·95	0·75	2·25	0·15
II	0·85	1·65	1·75	1·05	1·15	1·35
III	2·60	0·80	1·50	1·80	2·00	1·70
III	1·50	3·10	0·90	2·30	1·00	2·60
III	0·80	2·50	...	...	1·40	1·80
III	1·80	2·10	...	...	...	...

Table 7-3
Contrast of Earnings Within Subject Pairs

Hypothesis	Agree (+) or disagree (−)		
	(+)	(−)	p
(1*a*) $p(F_h < F_m) > \frac{1}{2}$	8	2	0·06
(1*b*) $p(F_h < F_l) > \frac{1}{2}$	4	4	0·64
(1*c*) $p(F_m < F_l) > \frac{1}{2}$	6	3	0·25
(1) Lower earnings for higher SRP class subject	18	9	0·06

Table 7-4

Joint Earnings of Subject Pairs by SRP Score Class

Order of Payoff Tables	High	Medium	Low
IV-V	3·45	2·80	2·75
IV-V	5·60	3·00	3·70
IV-V	6·00	4·40	3·90
V-IV	3·30	2·50	2·80
V-IV	4·25	2·70	3·20
V-IV	6·00	2·70 ·	6·00

Table 7-5

Contrast of Joint Earnings by SRP Classes

Hypothesis	Mann-Whitney U	p
(2a) $p(F_{hh} > F_{mm}) > \frac{1}{2}$	3	0·01
(2b) $p(F_{hh} > F_{ll}) > \frac{1}{2}$	9	0·09
(2c) $p(F_{mm} > F_{ll}) > \frac{1}{2}$	27	0·91
(2a) and (2b) Higher joint earnings for HH than all other subject-pairs	12	0·02
(2b) and (2c) Lower joint earnings for LL than all other subject-pairs	36	0·50

risk attitudes, and the differences in joint earnings between pairs of matched risk attitude subjects suggest that the high SRP or risk averse subjects differ most markedly from others in their behavior.[12] It is worth noting that for individual matrix preferences the correlation between SRP score and preference for cooperative matrices was stronger among high SRP subjects. [17] Moreover, learning in the experiments reported here with matched risk attitude subject pairs would tend to disconfirm hypotheses involving low SRP subjects, for when they are paired with one another their jointly competitive behavior would be least reinforcing. Lack of reward for jointly competitive behavior could lead low SRP subject pairs to change from their normal behavior, and that is a possible explanation for their more often earning more than the medium SRP subject-pairs.

---

[12] Responses to an end-of-experiment questionnaire also suggest that high SRP subjects play differently. Among the low and medium SRP classes, only about half of the subjects said they paid attention to signals from the other player. In the high SRP class, on the other hand, ten out of 12 reported that they attended to the other player's signals. Whether the subject took a long or short view also differed. Three low SRP subjects and five medium SRP subjects said they tried to achieve a maximum gain each trial. Only one high SRP subject expressed such an interest. And the high SRP subjects confesses a greater interest in punishing (teaching) the person with whom they played whenever his actions were harmful. Eight high SRP subjects reported that they had done so, compared with six in the medium and four in the low SRP classes.

Table 7-6
Contrasts of Letter and Number Choices by Payoff Table

Hypothesis	Agree (+) or disagree (−)		
	(+)	(−)	p
(3) More A's chosen in Payoff Table V	10	6	0·23
More A's in Payoff Table V, given High SRP	6	0	0·02
More A's in Payoff Table V, given Medium SRP	2	3	0·81
More A's in Payoff Table V, given Low SRP	2	3	0·81
(4a) More 1's in Payoff Table IV, given A	6	7	0·71
(4b) More 1's in Payoff Table IV, given B	9	2	0·03

It remains to consider whether reward structure effects in this game agree with those observed separately in prisoner's dilemma and matrix choice situations. Table VI shows probabilities, based on the binomial distribution, of each result or a more extreme one under the null hypothesis that agreement (a plus) or disagreement (a minus) with *Hypothesis* (3), (4a), and (4b) is equally likely. Overall, the matrix *A* choices would not reject a null hypothesis of no relation between reward structure and matrix choice. Simple effects are included in Table VI for *Hypothesis* (3), however, because they indicate that the structure had an effect on matrix choices of high SRP subject-pairs but not for others.[13] High SRP subject-pairs always chose more *A* matrices in Payoff Table V, as *Hypothesis* (3) predicts. This suggests that low and medium SRP subjects may continue to face a strategist's dilemma even when dominance is not present, but that high SRP subjects avoid it because of their preference for *A* matrices.

Hypothesis (4b) receives support but (4a) does not. When choosing from matrix *B*, subjects did make significantly more number 1 choices from Payoff Table IV than from Payoff Table V. When choosing from matrix *A*, however, no difference in number 1 choices could be traced to either structure.[14] One reason

[13]This result is equivalent to SRP-class by payoff-table interaction. The effect of payoff structure differs within each SRP class, and so the classes need to be investigated separately. It should be noted that no such interaction is visible in connection with the order effect. Parametric tests for interaction, as well as main hypotheses, were not planned or carried out because the data do not satisfy assumptions of the analysis of variance model, [22, pp. 369-374] and were not expected to satisfy them.

[14]For *Hypotheses* (3) and (4) it is also possible to compare the choices of each group of subject-pairs after they have played in only one payoff table, rather than repeated measures of the same subject-pairs in each payoff table. A more powerful test can be applied but to a sample only half as large. The comparison involves two independent samples of only nine subject-pairs each, one having played in Payoff Table IV, the other in V. For this comparison, all subject pairs were ranked based on total choices of matrix *A* games, and also based on number of action 1 choices, and the sum of ranks under Payoff Table IV versus V conditions were then used to determine Mann-Whitney *U* values. The value of *U* was 20 for the matrix *A* choice comparison against *Hypothesis* (3) and 23 for the action 1 choice comparison called for by *Hupothesis* (4). Each was in the predicted direction. The criterion value of *U* in both cases at the 0.05 level is 21 or less. The independent measure comparison definitely supports *Hypothesis* (3). The measures are not independent in the sense of being separate from the relative measures made above, of course, since the data are not separate, nor are they free of the interaction with risk attitude noted in note 13.

for this failure could be that subjects move to matrix A because it makes cooperation at 1, 1 more attractive, and the effect of that motivation is stronger than the structural difference. Or, once in matrix A, the threat of going back to B might constrain subjects' behavior and override the structural effect. But number choice cooperation in matrix B would be affected by payoff structure more directly without these intervening considerations.

Summary

The prisoner's dilemma poses a cooperate-or-compete conflict analogous to price or output choice in duopoly. Behavior in the dilemma has been investigated by social psychologists, who have found that reward structure can influence the degree of cooperation but that personality variables do not serve as reliable predictors of behavior. Here the prisoner's dilemma has been extended to a strategist's dilemma which includes a choice of prisoner's dilemma matrix as well as a choice of action within a prisoner's dilemma. Subjects' attitudes toward risk were found related to behavior in this game. There appears a tendency for persons more tolerant of social risk to compete more than opponents more averse to risk. On the other hand, when risk averse subjects play together they tend to cooperate more than other pairs, in part because their shared preference for matrices where cooperation is easier to achieve diminishes conflict in the strategist's dilemma.

These results come from a small sample of American college students and they emphasize initial tendencies, before subjects have long experience together in the game. But they indicate that the longer-run strategist's dilemma may reflect the personalities of decision makers more fully than does the more severely constrained prisoner's dilemma. It is appropriate that attitude toward risk influence choice in this setting, for risk has played an important role in long-run choices in economic theory.

The motivation for this extension of the prisoner's dilemma comes from the presence of a capacity choice in oligopoly markets for firms that experience constant average cost. Even with entry barred, tacit price agreement is no longer sufficient to establish persistent collusion, for expansion can come from within the industry to undermine a price agreement. Yet agreement on capacities can make agreement on price easier to achieve and to sustain. The same effects arise in the strategist's dilemma investigated here, in which the B matrices correspond to larger capacities.

Short-run cost variability influences the reward for short-run (price) relative to long-run (capacity) cooperation. As total cost depends more on the level of capacity than on short-run output, the force of the strategist's dilemma is reduced, for the advantage of having a large capacity is offset by its greater cost. The effect of capacity cost was investigated by a contrast of payoff tables in the joint cooperation experiment. Evidence of an interaction effect between payoff table and risk attitude indicates that pairs of subjects who share the same risk attitude will respond differently to the payoff tables, depending on their risk-attitude. Lack of dominance in the matrix choice, which reflects a market situation where cost depends more on capacity, could cause two risk-averse subjects to observe no matrix-choice strategist's dilemma; both would select small capacities. Yet two persons more tolerant of risk would be apt to expand capacities independently, actions that would continue to be in conflict with their collective interests. Thus cost variability can influence behavior in the strategist's dilemma, but its influence varies with the risk attitudes of participants.

It should be noted that although preliminary games were played to reduce its effect in the joint cooperation experiment, learning is apt to have greater effect in some conditions than in others. In the joint cooperation experiment, risk averse subjects are often reinforced in their behavior because they are always paired with subjects who also tend to cooperate. Risk tolerant subjects find their competitive behavior unrewarded, because they are paired with other risk tolerant subjects. Thus, the design of the joint cooperation experiment gives risk tolerant subjects more motivation to depart, based on experience, from the behavior expected of them. The departure would tend, however, to confirm the null hypothesis rather than a proposed alternative hypothesis. A similar effect of learning is present in the differential competition experiments, but there is no reason for it to be more important in one comparison than another.

Appendix 7-A: Procedures

Subjects were male undergraduates recruited "to earn money in a research project" at the University of Virginia. From eight to 12 subjects participated in each of seven sessions. All of the matched SRP class, joint cooperation experiments took place over a period of eight days, but the others were as much as a year apart. Each session lasted from one to two and one-half hours. An attempt to assign subjects randomly to sessions was only modified slightly by occasional conflicts in subject's schedules. In each session, the SRP test was carried out first; then subjects read instructions explaining the number and letter choice matrix-game. They are situated so that none could see another's work space, payoff tables, decisions, or earnings.

Thirty-six subjects were formed into subject-pairs from the same SRP class for the joint cooperation experiment. To minimize the learning that might occur, similar (letter and number choice) games were played first, before Payoff Tables IV and V were used for the joint cooperation experiment. Assignments of subjects to pairs were made randomly for the preliminary games, and fifteen of these pairs involved differential SRP score classes, which were used in the examination of differential earnings within pairs. Twelve other differential SRP class pairs were observed at other sessions solely for this purpose. A total of 60 subjects participated in the experiments.

When the joint cooperation experiment was begun subjects were told that the other persons with whom they were matched would definitely be different than in the preliminary game. Subject pairs were then drawn from identical risk classes. Half of the subject-pairs within each SRP class started the experiment in Payoff Table IV, the other half in V.[15] About midway in the joint cooperation experiment, payoff tables were changed from IV to V and from V to IV. At the time of this change, subjects were told that they might be assigned to play with a different person, but that a change would not be guaranteed in every case as it had been before. No changes were actually made.

The length of the experimental games was not announced. Anticipation of endings did not induce noticeable end-play, however, possibly because cooperation, if it was considered, was attractive even if only two or three plays could be expected. Decision sheets were collected each trial, and experimenters recorded the other's decisions in each case before returning decision sheets. Subjects then entered their own profit and were paid by experimenters (who checked the profit entries) as the next trial began.

---

[15] The joint cooperation experimental design considers an order factor in addition to reward structure and Social Risk Preference (SRP) score class for each subject-pair. These three factors are combined in a $3 \times 2 \times 2$ factorial experiment with repeated measures on the payoff-table factor. (Each subject pair plays in both Payoff Tables, IV and V.)

References

[1] Bain, J.S. *Barriers to New Competition* (Cambridge, Harvard University Press, 1956).

[2] Bronfenbrenner, M. "Imperfect Competition on a Long-Run Basis," *Journal of Business*, 23 (1950) 81-93.

[3] Chamberlin, E.H. *The Theory of Monopolistic Competition*, 8th ed. (Cambridge, Harvard University Press, 1962).

[4] Cournot, A. *Researches into the Mathematical Principles of the Theory of Wealth*, Translated by N.T. Bacon and Irving Fisher (New York, Macmillan Co., 1927).

[5] Dolbear, F.T., Jr., and Lave, L.B. "Risk Orientation as a Predictor in the Prisoner's Dilemma," *Journal of Conflict Resolution*, 10 (1966), 506-515.

[6] Dolbear, F.T., Jr., et al. "Collusion in Oligopoly: An Experiment on the Effect of Numbers and Information," *Quarterly Journal of Economics*, 82 (1968), 240-259.

[7] Fouraker, L.E., and Siegel, S. *Bargaining Behaviour* (New York, McGraw-Hill. Book Co., Inc., 1963).

[8] Gallo, P.S., Jr., and McClintock, C.G. "Cooperative Behavior in Mixed-Motive Games," *Journal of Conflict Resolution*, 9 (1965), 68-78.

[9] Johnston, J. *Statistical Cost Analysis* (New York, McGraw-Hill Book Co., Inc., 1960).

[10] Kogan, N., and Wallach, M.A. "Aspects of Judgment and Decision Making: Interrelationships and Changes with Age," *Behavioral Science*, 6 (1961), 23-26.

[11] Lave, L.B. "Factors Affecting Cooperation in the Prisoner's Dilemma," *Behavioral Science*, 10 (1965), 26-38.

[12] Lutzker, D.R. "Internationalism as a Predictor of Cooperative Behavior," *Journal of Conflict Resolution*, 4 (1960), 426-430.

[13] McClintock, C.G., Harrison, A.A., Strand, Susan, and Gallo, P. "Internationalism-Isolationism, Strategy of the Other Player, and Two-Person Game Behavior," *Journal of Abnormal and Social Psychology*, 67 (1963), 63-66.

[14] Pilisuk, M., Potter, P., Rapoport, A., and Winter, J.A. "War Hawks and Peace Doves," *Journal of Conflict Resolution*, 9 (1965), 491-508.

[15] Rapoport, A., and Chammah, A.M. *Prisoner's Dilemma* (Ann Arbor: The University of Michigan Press, 1965).

[16] Rapoport, A., and Orwant, C. "Experimental Games: A Review," *Behavioral Science*, 7 (1962), 1-37.

[17] Sherman, R. "Individual Attitude Toward Risk and Choice Between Prisoner's Dilemma Games," *Journal of Psychology*, 66 (1967), 291-298.

[18] Sherman, R. "Capacity Choice in Duopoly," unpublished Ph.D. thesis, Carnegie-Mellon University, Pittsburgh, 1966.

[19] Sherman, R., and Willett, T.D. "Potential Entrants Discourage Entry," *Journal of Political Economy*, 75 (1967), 400-403.

[20] Shubik, M. *Strategy and Market Structure* (New York, John Wiley and Sons, Inc., 1959).

[21] Stigler, G.J. "The Economics of Scale," *Journal of Law and Economics*, 1 (1958), 54-71.

[22] Winer, B.J. *Statistical Principles in Experiment Design* (New York, McGraw-Hill Book Co., Inc., 1962).

8 Cost Variability, Number of Firms, and the Persistence of Collusion

A tacit price agreement among a few firms need not persist, even when new entry is barred. For if average cost is constant, [1, 7] some existing firms may expand their capacities and then find adherence to the price agreement less attractive than before.[1] So it is important to know whether firms in industries with entry barriers might *independently* restrain capacity expansion, and thereby preserve the benefits of their agreement on price. In particular, does the number of firms, already well established as a factor affecting price (or quantity) collusion, [2, 3, 5] play an equally important role in determining the *persistence* of collusion?

Edgeworth first emphasized the effects of capacity limits on the behavior of duopolists, [4] noting in particular that when other industry capacity was filled, one firm could have an incentive to raise its price. When capacity is already scarce, price cuts are not motivated; the price cutter will not gain and other firms will not be harmed. Capacity was not a variable of choice for Edgeworth's firms. But from what we now know about cost functions in manufacturing industries it is clear that capacity adjustment is a choice for the firm, and because capacity limits can be so important in influencing short-run cooperation or competition, it is natural to ask what determines this longer run capacity adjustment. Assuming constant costs, and in the presence of uncertainty, it is possible to argue that the relative cost of capacity, not surprisingly, is an important determinant. What is of interest is that relative cost also can determine the importance of the number of firms in enforcing competition. Relatively high costs of productive capacity not only can make new entry to an industry more difficult, as is well known, but it also can encourage cooperation by existing firms at higher than competitive prices.

Here we examine factors affecting a firm's capacity expansion decision when ordinary price competition can be replaced by a tacit agreement on price because no entry is expected. Assuming the maximization of expected profit as the firm's goal, we show capacity expansion related to the fraction of total cost that varies with capacity rather than short-run output. This effect of capacity cost is tested in a classroom game where demand and cost conditions, plus the

Reprinted with permission from "An Experiment on the Persistence of Price Collusion," *Southern Economic Journal*, 37 (April 1971), 489-95. I am grateful to Bennett T. McCallum, Richard Schramm, and Thomas D. Willett for helpful discussions and comments, and to the Wilson Gee Institute for Research in the Social Sciences for financial support.

[1]Case studies of oligopolistic industries have traced price competition to excess capacity. For an illustration of how capacity will affect price-cutting incentives, see [11] and [12].

number of firms, can be controlled. The cost conditions affect collusion and determine when the number of firms (or average firm size) will affect the degree of collusion.

The model of individual firm capacity adjustment under no entry and rigid price conventions is developed first. Evidence of firm size and cost condition interaction in a classroom game is then presented. Results are summarized in a final section.

Restraint in Capacity Expansion

Assuming constant costs, and that greater capacity will bring greater market share whenever prices are equal, the attractiveness of price collusion has been shown to depend on cost variability. [11] When more costs vary with short-run output (we shall call this circumstance high cost variability), price collusion is more attractive, while the attractiveness of cooperating by restraining capacities is greater when costs vary more with capacity level and less with short-run output. This effect of the relative magnitude of variable and capacity costs in determining whether price or capacity collusion might develop has also been demonstrated in an experimental setting, together with effects of individual risk attitudes. [12] The question remains how capacity cost might alter the effect that the number of firms has on collusion, an effect which dominated classical treatments of oligopoly [2] and also has been confirmed when tested experimentally. [3, 5, 6, 13] In particular, can high capacity cost foster collusion via capacity restraint, even as the number of firms increases?[2]

Special problems arise in an experimental investigation of effects of capacity choice. First, including capacity as a variable complicates experimental control, since variations in firm size could confound one of the conditions to be investigated, the number of firms. Such confounding can be minimized if the market is divided equally among firms that have the same price (capacities permitting), because that will tend to keep the firms equal in size and thereby eliminate possible effects of differences in firm sizes within a market.[3] A related problem concerns the payoff structure, or profit consequences of various combinations of price and capacity choices. In the simple Cournot model, the number of firms would affect the payoff structure for each firm, and such structural effects accounted for changes with N in Cournot's solution. However, even when structural effects are minimized so that individual firms face roughly

---

[2]The two person experiments in [12] posed a "strategist's dilemma" for capacity choice analogous to the prisoner's dilemma for price choice. The strategist's dilemma was less strong when capacity cost was high, because the temptation to expand was then reduced. Experimental approaches to the study of oligopoly are described in [13].

[3]This convention lacks convenient stability properties that some other rules offer [15, p. 100]. Such properties are less important, however, when capacity cannot be adjusted as quickly as price.

the same payoff consequences regardless of N, N can still affect outcomes (e.g., [3]). The number of firms in a market affects the behavior of each. And the behavioral, as opposed to what may be called structural effects of N deserve emphasis in experiments that examine behavior in conflict situations. The structural effects can be minimized, even with capacity as a variable, if market size is increased whenever N is increased. We shall elaborate a capacity choice model that possesses such properties, and can thus be used as a basis for experimental market games.

Consider a simple model in which the ith firm's current profit is

$$\pi_i = (p - v) \ q_i - fk_i \qquad (1)$$

where p is market price, v is variable cost, q_i is the firm's current quantity, f is fixed cost per unit of capacity, and k_i is the firm's capacity. When all firms have the same price, and if capacities permit $(q_i \leqslant k_i)$, we have $q_i = Q/N$, where Q is the market demand function, $Q(p)$, and N is the number of firms. If the ith firm lowers its price below that of other firms to p_1, it will enjoy profits of $(p_1 - v - f)k_i$, provided only that k_i is less than the total market quantity at that price, $Q(p_1)$. The fraction of consumers not satisfied at p_1 (assuming $k_i < Q$) remain for the other firms that kept their prices at p, so they will divide the quantity $(1 - k_i/Q(p_1))Q(p)$. Thus, a firm need not lose all its sales when its price is above that of others, but the odds of high sales become less favorable, and sales then depend on others' capacities. Total sales for each firm can be determined in any period by beginning with the lowest price firm (or firms), permitting it (them) full capacity sales, and moving up to higher prices, dividing quantities equally unless capacity limits interfere, until demand is exhausted.

Any firm in such a market has to speculate about the gain from expanding its capacity, since it cannot be certain about the behavior of other firms, to say nothing of consumers. We shall concentrate on a manageable case, presupposing equal market shares, and consider the gain to be made from one more unit of capacity. Assume a price is given, p, that causes Q to equal Σk, at least roughly. If the firm already has a share of industry capacity, $k_i/\Sigma k$, that exceeds $1/N$, it is likely to gain nothing from adding a capacity unit, and instead lose the cost of a unit of capacity, f. On the other hand, if the firm has a share of industry capacity less than $1/N$ it may expect an increment in profit, $p - v - f$, on adding one more unit of capacity. To make this speculation concrete, we specify the expected increase in profit, $\Delta \pi$, from an additional unit of capacity as

$$E(\Delta \pi) = w_i(-f) \\ + (1 - w_i)(p - v - f) \qquad (2)$$

where w_i is the probability that the capacity will not be used. Let us specify further that

$$w_i = \frac{k_i}{(\Sigma k/N) + k_i}. \qquad (3)$$

A host of probability representations are conceivable to make w_i go up as k_i/Σ_k goes up relative to $1/N$, but this one has the added desirable attribute that $0 < w_i < 1$.[4] Any similar representation will also make a firm more willing to tolerate excess capacity as capacity is less costly, which is the plausible and important characteristic we wish to reflect. We assume the firm will resist expansion; i.e., restrain its capacity, whenever $E(\Delta \pi) < 0$.

Substituting (3) into (2) and simplifying, we find capacity restraint motivated whenever:

$$\left(\frac{\Sigma k}{\Sigma k + Nk_i}\right)\left(\frac{p - v}{f}\right) < 1.$$

Letting a_i represent the ith firm's share in industry capacity, $k_i/\Sigma k$, this reduces to

$$\left(\frac{1}{1 + N\alpha_i}\right) < \frac{f}{p - v}. \qquad (4)$$

For given N, (4) shows how $f/(p - v)$ can influence α_i. Such a result is more general than our specific example might suggest. Ignoring interdependence and instead simply introducing a random variable into the demand function faced by the firm, it is possible to show that

$$\frac{1}{Pr(q_i \leq k_i)} < \frac{f}{p - v}$$

where $Pr(q_i \leq k_i)$ is the probability that quantity demanded will not exceed capacity.[5] This probability moves with k_i roughly as $1 + Na_i$ moves with k_i, reflecting the same qualitative influence of $f/(p - v)$.

Condition (4) may be solved as an equality for any given level of p and costs, v and f, to find the crucial capacity share, a^*, above which capacity restraint will be motivated. Such minimum capacity shares are given in Table 8-1 for price levels 10%, 30%, and 50% above $v + f$, and for cost conditions representing ratios of v to f of 3.5 and 0.6. Costs vary more with output when the ratio of v to f is 3.5, and they depend more on capacity level when the ratio is only 0.6. Minimum capacity shares are represented as fractions of the equal share, $1/N$,

---

[4]Of course these w_i's may not add to one.

[5]This claim is demonstrated in the Appendix, which is a modification of [10] to treat capacity rather than inventory cost.

since they are always the same fraction of $1/N$ no matter what the value of N is, and can thus be interpreted without specifying any particular value for N. In this form, when the minimum share is below 1 capacity restraint can be expected of firms, while they may be expected to expand capacity when the minimum share is above 1.

Specific values in Table 8-1 are only relative and suggestive; they are based on a crude characterization of capacity expansion prospects. Nevertheless, they show that as price rises above $v + f$ in the more variable cost condition ($v/f =$ 3.5), expansion becomes attractive for firms individually, and any price collusion can persist only if the firms together resist these incentives. Presumably, two firms can tacitly agree to resist expansion more easily than can three, or four, or more firms. Such agreement may not be needed in the high capacity cost condition ($v/f = 0.6$). Even when price is 50% above $v + f$, capacity restraint is still indicated for individual firms. Thus high capacity costs can support persistent price collusion, by causing firms to resist the sort of capacity expansion that would work against continuation of any price agreement.

Table 8-1
Price Level and Capacity Restraint

Ratio of Price to Cost	$\alpha*N$: Minimum Share to Induce Capacity Restraint, as Fraction of Average Share	
$(v + f)$	$v/f = 3.5$	$v/f = 0.6$
1.10	0.45	0.16
1.30	1.35	0.48
1.50	2.25	0.80

Capacity Choice in a Market Game with Entry Barred

Here we describe a market game, with student participants, that was based on the relationships illustrated in Table 8-1. Each student acted as one firm in a market with a total of two, three, four or six firms and under cost conditions that made total cost either quite variable with output ($v = 7, f = 2$ and $v/f = 3.5$; see Table 8-1) or related more to capacity ($v = 3, f = 5$ and $v/f = 0.6$; see Table 8-1). There were five markets at each of four different number of firm conditions and under each of the two cost conditions. The market demand function was $Q = N(17-p)$, where N represents the number of firms in the market. Expanding the total market demand in proportion to N in this way has the advantage noted above of giving each firm the same relative rewards from competing or cooperating, regardless of N. That is, effects of N on the profit prospects, so important in the Cournot model, are avoided here. This by no means prevents N from having an important effect on results, as experiments have already shown. [3, 6, 13] But it helps to confine the observed effects of N more to the behavioral differences it causes. This demand curve does not yield a profit maximizing price that is ever more than 50% above $v + f$, and capacity restraint should be expected over all reasonable prices under the $v/f = 0.6$ cost condition. As price rises under the $v/f = 3.5$ cost condition, however, expansion will become attractive, and coordination among firms will be needed to make any tacit price agreement persist. Thus, markets with fewer firms should tend to reach smaller capacities and greater profits under the high variable cost, $v/f = 3.5$, condition, whereas the number of firms should not be a decisive determinant of collusion under the high capacity cost, $v/f = 0.6$, condition.

Firms divided the market quantity equally when their prices were the same (capacities permitting), and when prices were not the same, the firm with the lowest price filled his capacity, then the firm with the next lowest price filled his, and so on (firms with high prices could receive zero quantity). This determination of market and firm quantities when prices were not the same followed Shubik's contingent demand function. [15, pp. 86-87] The market was divided equally when prices were the same, to keep the firms within each market equal in size and thus make capacity shares negatively correlated with the number of firms.

Each period, the firm (subject) would choose a current price and also a capacity for two periods in the future, so price actions were always taken under current capacity conditions that had been chosen earlier. Price and capacity choices were confined to integer values, a significant (and intentional) limitation of the choices, in view of the small numbers that were used. Each class meeting was considered a period, and the game extended over several weeks. This

Table 8-2
Average Price, Capacity, and Profit per Firm in Two, Three, Four, and Six Firms

(Trials 10–14)

Measure	More Fixed Costs: $v = 3, f = 5$				More Variable Costs: $v = 7, f = 2$			
	2	3	4	6	2	3	4	6
Price	8.88	9.40	10.10	9.57	10.00	9.27	11.80	9.47
	10.80	9.87	10.65	10.33	11.30	11.13	9.00	10.30
	12.10	8.27	9.40	8.93	12.30	10.00	11.20	10.83
	9.30	9.27	9.65	8.90	10.60	10.00	9.45	9.97
	9.00	10.80	8.75	9.83	10.60	11.13	9.25	10.00
Capacity	9.20	7.53	7.70	7.70	8.10	8.40	5.55	8.90
	9.70	7.27	9.25	7.27	6.10	6.47	7.90	8.00
	5.10	8.73	8.45	8.70	4.90	8.47	8.30	6.10
	8.10	7.93	10.30	8.63	7.80	7.53	9.25	9.87
	9.00	6.27	7.50	7.73	7.20	6.47	12.00	7.83
Profit	1.60	9.93	10.15	10.30	4.40	.27	13.35	−.43
	1.80	11.80	−.30	11.73	12.10	11.67	2.65	5.47
	18.89	−4.00	5.50	4.23	13.80	3.80	7.40	9.00
	7.80	7.93	−4.40	3.83	5.00	5.93	−.80	−2.67
	3.00	12.93	3.20	9.63	8.20	8.40	−8.50	4.97

extended play would destroy some of the control advantages of the experimental setting, but there is no reason to suspect as a result any systematically different effects under one cost condition than another.

Results

One hundred fifty male undergraduates in an intermediate economics class at the University of Virginia served as subjects. The subjects were asked not to attempt collusive arrangements on grounds of fairness (and consistency with prevailing antitrust laws in the U.S.). Payments were promised at the end of the game to one out of five subjects determined by lottery, and on that basis one out of five subjects received his actual earnings in the game. Fourteen periods (or more) were completed in all markets. The five periods from period ten to period 14 were taken as final outcome periods, since play had settled down by then. Price, capacity, and profit averages per firm over those five periods are shown in Table 8-2.

It is possible under each cost condition to test whether smaller N leads to more collusion (smaller capacity, more profit) using the Jonckheere test. [8] A t-statistic approximation for this test [8, 141] is given in Table 8-3 for each variable and each cost condition. The results in Table 8-3 indicate definite interaction between cost condition and number of firms; number of firms has a significant effect on capacity choices and profit under the high variable cost condition, but not under the high capacity cost condition. This is evidence of interaction because the effect of N is altered by the presence of one cost condition rather than the other. The results are broadly consistent with cost variability and number of firm relations indicated in Table 8-1. Table 8-3 shows that N has a significant effect on profit and on capacity choices only in the more variable cost condition, which is represented by the left hand column in Table 8-1. As price went more than 20% above the $v + f$ level under this cost condition, firms would lose their individual motivation to restrain capacity. But in the right

Table 8-3
t-Statistic Approximation to Jonckheere S Test for Effect of N

Measure	Hypothesis	Cost Condition $v = 3$ $f = 5$	$v = 7$ $f = 2$
Capacity ($\bar{k}_N$)	$\bar{k}_2 < \bar{k}_3 < \bar{k}_4 < \bar{k}_6$	$-.32$	1.86^*
Profit ($\bar{\pi}_N$)	$\bar{\pi}_2 > \bar{\pi}_3 > \bar{\pi}_4 > \bar{\pi}_6$	$-.20$	1.86^*

* Significant at 5% level.

hand column of Table 8-1, which represents the high capacity cost condition, a price even 50% above the competitive level could still induce capacity restraint by firms in all four number-of-firm conditions. In this high capacity cost condition, N had no significant effect on profit or capacity level.

Summary

Oligopoly theories have usually emphasized a short-run perspective. Yet with constant long-run marginal costs, when entry is barred and firms are willing to accept a leader's price, capacity expansion from within the industry could still make persistent collusion difficult. We have examined the attractiveness of capacity expansion when a price (perhaps a leader's) is accepted and there is no entry. Individual firm incentive for capacity expansion was found related to the elevel of price and to technology and cost relationships. Persistent collusion was shown to be harder to achieve as total costs depended less on capacity levels and were more variable with output in the short-run. And in this case the number of firms would influence the success of collusion, whereas number of firms would not be so important when capacity costs accounted for a large portion of total costs. Total costs are more variable with output either when expenditures on variable inputs are relatively high, or because technology permits easy adaptation to changing output requirements.

The relation between cost condition and capacity restraint was supported in play of a classroom game. The number of firms affected the amount of cooperation at higher prices when costs were highly variable with short-run output. But when costs depended more on capacity levels, number of firms did not affect amount of cooperation; the cost of capacity discouraged expansion and facilitated cooperation. The behavior revealed in the game suggests that cost variability may be important in the real world.[6] It is conceivable that in the relation of concentration *and* entry barriers to high profitability [1, 9] it is the high capacity cost, not concentration per se that combines with other entry barriers to enhance profits. In any case, capacity cost may have importance not only as an entry barrier, but as an influence on existing firms' behavior as well.

---

[6]A link between cost variability and firm growth is found when entry barriers are very high in [14].

Appendix 8-A: Capacity Cost and Optimal Capacity

Assume the firm faces the demand curve

$$x = X(p) + u \qquad (A1)$$

where x is the quantity demanded, p is the price set by the firm and u is a random term. In this specification of demand the random term is separable so the variance of x does not depend on the price chosen. The firm is assumed to know the distribution function, $g(u)$, so although the firm can not predict x exactly for any p, it does know the probability that x will take any value. The frequency function,

$$G(a) = \int_{-\infty}^{a} g(u) \, du, \qquad (A2)$$

gives the probability that u will not exceed a, and thus the probability that $x \leqslant X(p) + a$.

Consider a simple linear cost function that includes v, as a cost per unit of output actually produced, and f, the cost per unit of capacity, K, which must exist for each unit of x to be produced. Total cost, C, will be:

$$C = (X(p) + u) \, v + Kf. \qquad (A3)$$

Assume that the variable, K, must be chosen before the actual value of u is observed. Then because K in any period represents an upper limit on x, the quantity *actually* supplied in the period, s, will be

$$s = \begin{cases} x \text{ for } X(p) + u \leq K \\ K \text{ for } X(p) + u \geq K. \end{cases}$$

As long as $X(p) + u$ may exceed K, some demand may go unsatisfied. For given values of p and K, the unsatisfied demand that can be expected is

$$D(K, p) = \int_{K-X(p)}^{\infty} (X, (p) + u \qquad (A4)$$
$$- K) g(u) \, du.$$

Expected unsatisfied demand must be subtracted from expected quantity demanded to give expected sales:

$$E(s) = X(p) - D(K, p). \qquad (A5)$$

Expected profit, $E(\pi)$, will now be

$$E(\pi) = pE(s) - vE(s) - fK$$

which, using (A5), can be represented as

$$E(\pi) = (p - v) [X(p) \\ - D(K, p)] - fK. \quad \text{(A6)}$$

Assuming that p is given, an optimal K,K^*, can be obtained by differentiating (A6) with respect to K and setting the result equal to zero:

$$\frac{\partial E(\pi)}{\partial K} = (p - v)[1 - G(K \\ - X(p))] - f = 0.$$

Solving for $G(K - X(p))$, we have

$$G(K^* - X(p)) = \frac{p - v - f}{p - v} \quad \text{(A7)} \\ = 1 - \frac{f}{p - v}$$

Capacity expansion will be restrained when $K > K^*$, because then $G(K - x(p)) > G(K^* - X(p))$. But this means that restraint is in order whenever

$$\frac{1}{G(K - X(p))} < \frac{f}{p - v} \quad \text{(A8)}$$

which resembles the condition for the special case in the text,

$$\frac{1}{1 + N\alpha_i} < \frac{f}{p - v}.$$

References

[1] Bain, J.S., *Barriers to New Competition*. Cambridge: Harvard University Press, 1956.

[2] Cournot, A., *Researches into the Mathematical Principles of the Theory of Wealth*, translated by N.T. Bacon and Irving Fisher. New York: Macmillan Co., 1927.

[3] Dolbear, F.T., et al., "Collusion in Oligopoly: An Experiment on the Effect of Numbers and Information," *Quarterly Journal of Economics*, May 1968, 240-59.

[4] Edgeworth, F.Y., *Papers Relating to Political Economy*, Vol. I. London: Macmillan and Company, 1925.

[5] Fouraker, L.E., and Siegel, S., *Bargaining Behavior*. New York: McGraw-Hill, 1963.

[6] Friedman, James W., "Individual Behavior in Oligopolistic Markets: An Experimental Study," *Yale Economic Essays*, 1963, 359-417.

[7] Johnston, J., *Statistical Cost Analysis*. New York: McGraw-Hill, 1960.

[8] Jonckheere, A.R., "A Distribution-Free k-Sample Test Against Ordered Alternatives," *Biometrica*, 1954, 133-45.

[9] Mann, H.M., "Seller Concentration, Barriers to Entry, and Rates of Return in Thirty Industries: 1950-1960," *Review of Economics and Statistics*, August 1966, 296-307.

[10] Mills, E.S., "Uncertainty and Price Theory," *Quarterly Journal of Economics*, February 1959, 116-30.

[11] Sherman, R., "Capacity Choice in Duopoly," Ph.D. dissertation, Carnegie-Mellon University, 1966.

[12] _____, "Risk Attitude and Cost Variability in a Capacity Choice Experiment," *Review of Economic Studies*, October 1969, 453-66.

[13] _____, "Experimental Oligopoly," *Kyklos*, Fasc. 1, 1971.

[14] _____, "Firm Growth When Entry is Barred," University of Virginia, 1970.

[15] Shubik, M., *Strategy and Market Structure*. New York: John Wiley and Sons, 1959.

117

Part III:
Market Share, Cost Variability, and the Behavior of Real-World Oligopolists

Here a more general model suggests that if new entry is barred, then firm size, price level, and cost function properties will influence firms' capacity expansion incentives. A comparison of samples of firms from industries with and without very high entry barriers confirms implications of the model. Relying on earlier theoretical work by Dorfman and Steiner which can be tested empirically with the cost or payoff structure properties in our model, we find that the recently emphasized advertising and profitability connection may be spurious, and we provide empirical support for an alternative explanation. We show the effect of cost and demand properties on profit risk too, the latter represented by the variance in profit rates. And we indicate the effect of this connection on proper interpretation of earlier empirical studies of how entry barriers, concentration, firm size, and other elements of market structure affect market performance. Finally, the results are reviewed in the context of recent antitrust policy proposals.

Growth of Firms When Entry is Barred

Among firms beyond a minimum efficient size, rate of growth is generally unrelated to firm size. [4, 5, 10, 21] Nevertheless, stochastic models that assume firm size and rate of growth are completely unrelated have had only limited success in predicting the size distribution of firms. [15] So perhaps in special circumstances firm size can affect growth. Our purpose is to identify growth incentives that can plausibly be argued to exist only when barriers to entry are very high, and then test for the effect of these incentives by contrasting samples of firms operating under different entry conditions. Our results indicate that firm size can affect rate of growth more when new entry is barred.

In examining capacity expansion incentives for the firm in an industry when entry is barred we assume homogeneous product, and we assume that price competition is ineffective due to some form of price leadership, or to tacit cooperation at an entry preventing price. [1, 11, 25] We also assume Cournot-like capacity adjustment behavior on the part of individual firms. We find on these assumptions that relative size and technology influence expansion incentives when entry is barred. In particular, a firm may independently refrain from expansion even though price is above long-run marginal cost. On specifying the model and estimating its parameters, we find differences between parameter estimates for 21 firms in industries with very high entry barriers and estimates for 72 firms in other industries.

The capacity adjustment model and its implications for firm growth when entry is barred are discussed first. Next we present estimating equations and state restrictions that are placed on parameter estimates by this capacity adjustment theory. Test results follow, and conclusions are summarized in a final section.

Capacity Choice When Entry is Barred

Shifting attention from price to capacity adjustment can yield interesting hypotheses about industrial organization, but it also requires additional assumptions. First, we rule out the existence of an optimal size and assume constant

Reprinted with permission from "Entry Barriers and the Growth of Firms," *The Southern Economic Journal*, 38 (October 1971), 238-47. I thank William F. Beazer, Bennett T. McCallum, Richard Schramm, Robert Tollison, Rutledge Vining, John K. Whitaker, and Thomas D. Willett for discussions and comments, and Evelyn Glazier and William Johnson for help in gathering data. Financial support by the Wilson Gee Institute for Research in the Social Sciences at the University of Virginia is also acknowledged.

121

average cost (at least over the size range of interest), to make capacity adjustment a genuine option for each firm. There is empirical support for this assumption, [7, 24] and it has served before as a convenient starting point in studies of firm growth.[1] [21] Firms are assumed also to resist price competition (as long as "too much" capacity does not exist), so we need a basis for dividing market quantity among them. We shall assume consumer behavior that will give each firm a market share related to its capacity share. The firm's capacity will determine its market share if consumers choose randomly among firms when price is uniform, provided that any one consumer's chance of encountering a given firm varies directly with the firm's capacity. Since greater capacity can enable a real-world firm to reach and serve more consumers, it seems reasonable to have a larger share in industry capacity enhance a firm's market share.[2] We do not stress an ultimate long-run equilibrium[3] which could be identified under a variety of behavior assumptions, but emphasize instead the process of capacity adjustment. We ask whether firms that forego price action might of their own accord refrain from capacity expansion, even when price is above long-run marginal cost. For if they always expand capacity we can expect eventually a decline in price, by a breakdown of whatever rigid price mechanism is at work.

Now let us make the capacity choice problem explicit. The following variables will be used throughout our analysis:

p = market price

Q = $Q(p)$ = total quantity demanded

v_i = variable cost per unit of output for the ith firm in the short run

f_i = fixed cost per unit of capacity for the ith firm

F_i = $(p - v_i)/f_i$, a cost and price relationship for the ith firm

q_i = the ith firm's output quantity

k_i = the ith firm's capacity level

u = $Q/\Sigma_i k_i$ = utilization of industry capacity

π_i = profit of the ith firm

c_i = $v_i q_i + f_i k_i$ = total cost for the ith firm

α_i = $k_i/\Sigma_i k_i$ = the ith firm's share of industry capacity

G_i = firm rate of growth

G_I = industry rate of growth

---

[1] In addition to being consistent with many observations and theories of firm growth, this assumption facilitates empirical work by requiring only simple linear cost functions for firms.

[2] Capacity share will usually be related to market share in models of spatially separated consumers and firms. Note that firms do not agree on this sharing arrangement; it results from the behavior of buyers who face a uniform price. Explicit sharing agreements among firms are considered by Bennathan and Walters. [2] Other variables, such as advertising, also can influence market share. But considering them would complicate the analysis without adding clear implications for capacity adjustment and firm growth. We emphasize capacity as a determinant of market share because we are inquiring whether existing firms will voluntarily forego capacity expansion, a question that would not even be moot if capacity expansion offered no market share advantage to the firm.

[3] Long-run implications of collusive or other behavior are derived for the size distribution of firms by Worcester. [29]

In Cournot fashion, we assume that the individual firm expects no change in market price despite its own capacity changes, and also that it expects no changes in the capacities of other firms. An individual firm that accepts the going market price faces the problem:

$$\max \ \pi_i = (p - v_i)q_i - f_i k_i \qquad (1)$$

where the only variable it controls is k_i, its capacity level.[4] Substituting for q_i the ith firm's share of market quantity, $Qk_i/\Sigma k_i$, and differentiating partially only with respect to k_i and equating to zero, we obtain the necessary profit maximizing condition,

$$\frac{\partial \pi_i}{\partial k_i} = \frac{\Sigma k - k_i}{(\Sigma k)^2} Q \ (p - v_i) - f_i = 0 \quad (2)$$

Ordinarily, we should expect the firm to expand its capacity if $\partial \pi_i/\partial k_i > 0$, and contract if $\partial \pi_i/\partial k_i < 0$. To simplify (2), we substitute u for $Q/\Sigma k$, α_i for $k_i/\Sigma k_i$, and F_i for $(p - v_i)/f_i$. Then $\partial \pi_i/\partial k_i$ will be less than zero, discouraging the ith firm from expanding, whenever

$$u(1 - \alpha_i)F_i < 1 \qquad (3)$$

It is easy to trace implications of this simple expression. For a small firm, $(1-\alpha_i)$ in (3) will approach 1, and if capacity utilization is high the firm will be motivated to expand as p rises above $v + f$. Capacity restraint develops primarily when a firm or each of several firms has a significant fraction of industry capacity. To show how each firm's gain from expanding capacity changes as his share of total market capacity increases, we differentiate (2) partially with respect to α_i:

$$\frac{\partial^2 \pi_i}{\partial \alpha_i \partial k_i} = -u(p - v_i) < 0$$

The negative sign indicates that gain from capacity expansion declines as share of total market capacity is larger.[5]

---

[4] Strictly speaking, the problem in (1) also requires that output quantity be constrained at not greater than the capacity level: $q_i < k_i$. Under our assumptions, however, and in the price range of interest above the competitive level, it is easy to show that the constraint will not be binding. Firms individually will accept some unused capacity in order to obtain a larger market share.

[5] Cyert and March have pointed out that the observed tendency for dominant firms to decline is difficult for traditional theory to explain. [3] Worcester argued in response that the dominant firm is only a short-run phenomenon, and its decline results because smaller firms and new entrants expand output more than does the dominant firm. [28] Worcester's results relied on the dominant versus minor firm dichotomy, however, with specialized assumptions about the behavior of the dominant firm as price leader, based upon its knowledge of the response of minor firms to its own actions. Our rigid price, market share model implies the same long-run tendency for the dominant firm to decline. For descriptions of the dominant firm model, see Stigler [23], Worcester [28], or Zeuthen [30].

Failure to observe any general association between size of firm and rate of growth does not necessarily rule out capacity restraint by larger firms in the few industries where entry is very difficult. Both Nelson [12, pp. 50-56, 13] and Shepherd [17] have found declines in concentration in industries that grow faster, although Kamerschen has recently shown their findings to be limited to certain periods of time [8] and Weiss has shown that changes in the typical scale must also be considered. [26] The survivor technique permits estimation of an optimal scale of firm (in terms of private cost) by observing changes in the shares of industry output coming from different size classes of firms. [24] Estimates have indicated that average costs are constant over wide ranges of output, because over a considerable range there is no tendency to converge on a 'best' size, but that diseconomies (of very small and very large scale establishments and firms) may exist in some industries. [16, 27] These studies would reveal a tendency of large (small) firms to decline (expand) either because of technological diseconomies (economies) of scale, or because expansion is relatively less (more) attractive to them as expected under our rigid price, no entry model.

Relative size is not the only influence on capacity restraint in (3). Three other factors influence the motive of any one firm to restrain its capacity: (i) the rate of industry capacity utilization, u, (ii) the price level, p, and (iii) technological adaptability and input costs which determine the relative importance of f_i and v_i. That low utilization will lead to capacity restraint is clear from (3) and is intuitively sensible as well. Utilization of capacity surely affects the attractiveness of expansion, even among quite a number of firms when each has a very small share of industry capacity. And a higher price obviously makes capacity expansion harder to resist. For any given u and α_i, an increase in p makes the satisfaction of (3) less likely.[6]

The most interesting of these three other effects on collusion motives is technology, in the form of cost variability over a given period. The value of the left hand side in (3) will be greater, for any price (assuming $p > v + f$) and rate of utilization, as a greater portion of total cost is variable with output quantity. To see this, observe that an increase in v and an equivalent decrease in f will expand the left hand side of (3) by $(1 - u(1 - \alpha_i))$ times the amount of the increase in v. Since $1 - u (1 - \alpha_i) \geq 0$, we know that the left hand side of (3) must then increase. Thus when a greater portion of total cost varies with output quantity, capacity expansion will appear more profitable. On the other hand, when total cost depends less on short-run output, cooperation through restrained capacities will be more attractive.[7] Total costs will vary more with output when

[6]It is possible for an increase in p, which will reduce Q, to be offset by a reduction in capacity utilization, u, but this would occur only with an unusually high-elasticity of market demand.

[7]Variability of short-run total cost affects the attractiveness of price cooperation differently; highly variable total cost tends to encourage price cooperation. See [18, 19, 20]. It should be noted that a uniform short-run time period is assumed for each industry, over which v and f are defined.

technology can adapt easily to changing output requirements, making many inputs variable, or when prices of variable inputs are high enough to make the variable expenditures a larger part of total cost.

The variability of total cost with output (F_i) and the share of industry capacity ($1 - \alpha_i$) enter (3) in a multiplicative way, so their interaction also will be important. Specifically, (3) implies that the differential effect of capacity share will be greater as relatively more costs are variable, and the differential effects of the variability of total cost will be greater when capacity shares are small. To the extent that typical shares of market capacity are inversely related to the number of firms, the number of firms will have a greater differential effect on collusion incentives in industries that have more variable costs.[8] Since this market share model stresses capacity changes rather than short-run conduct, it does not tie concentration measures directly to collusion, despite the appearance of share-of-industry-capacity in (3). Instead, it focuses on capacity expansion motives within an industry. And it suggests that as there are more firms with small shares of industry capacity, their expansion will tend to prevent price from persisting at a level above average cost. Firms with smaller shares of industry capacity and higher values of F_i have stronger incentives to grow.

Hypotheses for the Growth of Firms

When new entry into an industry is possible, the implications from condition (3) are not relevant; p should not rise high above long run marginal cost and remain for very long. Hypotheses derived from (3) can therefore be stated as contrasts between samples from industries with very high entry barriers and samples from other industries. There are advantages in posing hypotheses as such contrasts. Suppose, for instance, that some effects on firm growth other than those suggested in this analysis are captured by the variables we choose. False conclusions could then be drawn if we used a sample of firms taken only from industries with very high entry barriers. By instead comparing industries having very high entry barriers with other industries, we can isolate differential effects of very high entry barriers. In addition, estimation of a relation between firm sizes and absolute rates of growth involves the well known regression bias. [14] Such a bias should not be as important in the difference between samples. Our approach will be to obtain a sample of firms from industries with very high entry barriers and a sample of firms from other industries, and we express hypotheses as contrasts between parameter estimates from the two samples.

Tests can be obtained from condition (3) if we add an assumption that a firm's rate of growth varies with its incentive to expand, represented by E_i. From (2) and (3) we have

---

[8]Support for such an interaction in an experimental market is reported in [20].

$$E_i = (1 - \alpha_i)F_i \qquad (4)$$

and we assume also that

$$G_i = G_i(E_i) \qquad (5)$$

where $dG_i/dE_i > 0$. Of course a desire to expand does not necessarily produce expansion, as Simon has pointed out. [22] Desire cannot ensure ability. But by confining attention to firms above a minimum efficient size we can escape systematic biases in firms' abilities to grow. Moreover, when there is no entry any growth incentives may be expected to persist longer, and thereby induce more growth by the firms experiencing them. Note that we ignore industry utilization of capacity in (4). In gathering data we shall attempt to cover time periods long enough to make unplanned differences in utilization unimportant.

Firms in different industries will have to be pooled, to obtain enough observations to estimate parameters. Before pooling observations across industries we shall normalize them into relatives within each industry. The variable, $1 - \alpha_i$, is already an industry relative because α_i is a share-of-industry capacity measure. To convert cost variability and growth measures[9] into relatives we divide the measure for each firm by its industry average, and we also scale them by averages for the whole sample. Then the content of (3), as altered in (4) and (5), can be expressed in the stochastic form:

$$LN(\bar{G}G_{is}/G_{Is}) = a_{0s}$$
$$+ a_{1s} LN(1 - \alpha_{is}) \qquad (6)$$
$$+ a_{2s} LN(\bar{F}F_{is}/F_{Is}) + v_1$$

where $\overline{G}$ and $\overline{F}$ represent average values of G_i and F_i for the entire sample, v_1 is a random error, and the subscript, s, denotes the sub-sample: H = very high entry barriers, M = substantial or low entry barriers. Since our theory does not specify the relation in (5), we estimate the semi-log form as well:

$$\bar{G}G_{is}/G_{Is} = b_{0s} + b_{1s}LN(1 - \alpha_{is})$$
$$+ b_{2s} LN(\bar{F}F_{is}/F_{Is}) + v_2 \qquad (7)$$

where v_2 is a random error. If (6) and (7) explain growth better for firms in industries with very high entry barriers, the coefficients of $(1 - \alpha_i)$ must be higher there. Thus our theory would restrict parameter estimates so that:[10]

[9] Differences in cost variability across industries cannot be expected to explain growth across industries, and if not removed they might cover up the within-industry effects. The assumption of no coefficient differences necessary for pooling [6, pp. 136-8] was tested for substantial and low entry barrier subgroups and was satisfied.

[10] An alternative test, based more specifically on (5) with E_i as explanatory variable and with a different arrangement for pooling data, is reported in Appendix 9-A.

$$a_{1H} > a_{1M} ; \qquad b_{1H} > b_{1M} \qquad (8)$$

And we have similar restrictions for coefficients of $\overline{FF}_i/F_I$:

$$a_{2H} > a_{2M} ; \qquad b_{2H} > b_{2M} \qquad (9)$$

Results

Our data were selected by taking industries which were classified for the 1950's according to entry conditions by Mann [9] and were found also in the Hymer-Pashigian study [5] as industries which contained four or more firms.[11] Based on the period 1946 to 1955, the Hymer-Pashigian data provided firm and industry growth rates (1955 assets divided by 1946 assets), which were used for G_i's and G_I's. Capacity shares, α_i's, were also taken from Hymer-Pashigian data as the ith firm's assets divided by industry assets. Shares were based on 1955 to avoid the well known regression bias, which would tend to make smaller firms appear to have higher growth rates if the beginning date, 1946, was chosen as the reference date.[12] By using shares at the ending date, 1955, the bias is not avoided, but it is made to work against our hypothesis that smaller firms grow faster. When we compare effects of firm size on growth in samples from different entry conditions, this bias, being present in both samples, will tend to cancel out.[13]

Data for F_i were taken from Moody's Industrial Manual [31] as averages over the four years, 1948-1951, which seemed the most normal reference period between 1946 and 1955.[14] The variable, F_i, or $(p - v_i)/f_i$, is a ratio that was considered to be approximated by the observable values in the ratio: sales less

---

[11] Entry conditions were estimated for 30 industries by Mann. [9] For their study of firm growth, Hymer and Pashigian sorted 1000 largest U.S. firms into industry categories. [5] I am grateful to Hymer and Pashigian for very kindly making available to me all of the large portion of their data still in their possession.

[12] The bias arises from the presence of uncertainty for all variables and is demonstrated for the firm growth context by Prais. [14] Roughly, the problem may be characterized this way. A firm categorized as small at the beginning date is more likely to be unusually small then because of chance. When observed again at the ending date it is apt to be closer to the average size for all firms, so it will appear to have grown at a greater than average rate. If instead firms are categorized according to size at the ending date, the large ones will tend to show higher than average rates of growth, for now they are likely to be unusually large at the ending date in part because of chance. For full treatment see, e.g., [6, p. 148].

[13] As between the two samples, we can expect a stronger bias in the sample from very high entry barrier industries if our theory is correct. For if smaller firms actually do grow faster, the bias from using ending dates to reckon size will be stronger. And the sample from very high entry barrier industries is smaller, which alone leaves more room for the bias. Since we have exposed ourselves to a bias that is unfavorable to our hypotheses, making it stronger in the very high entry barriers sample should assure us of a conservative test.

total variable cost, divided by total fixed costs. Included as fixed costs were selling and general and administrative expense, interest, depreciation, rent, and maintenance. The numerator included the same items plus before-tax profit for the firm, since fixed cost plus profit must equal sales less total variable cost.[15] A number of firms covered by Hymer and Pashigian and from industries classified by Mann had to be dropped for lack of sufficient cost information from Moody's. The sample finally included 93 firms from 13 industries; of these 21 firms were from four industries with very high entry barriers.[16]

Least squares estimates of regression coefficients are reported in Table 9-1,[17] and results of tests for differences between coefficients from different samples are given in Table 9-2.[18] Results are broadly consistent with hypotheses derived

Table 9-1
Effects, by Entry Condition, of Capacity Share and Relative Cost Variability on Relative Firm Growth

| SPECIFI CATION | SAMPLES | | EXPLANATORY VARIABLES | | | STATISTICS |
	ENTRY	N	CONSTANT	$(1-\alpha_i)$	$\overline{FF}_i/F_I$	R_a^2 /Var.
(6)LN-LN	H	21	0.33** (0.14)	0.26 (0.32)	0.73** (0.19)	0.40 0.07
	M	72	0.73** (0.11)	-0.26 (0.26)	0.01 (0.12)	-- 0.09
(7)Semi-LN	H	21	0.95** (0.37)	1.25 (0.81)	2.30** (0.48)	0.52 0.43
	M	72	2.25** (0.28)	-0.40 (0.66)	-0.06 (0.30)	-- 0.58

* One tail significance at .05 test level
** One tail significance at .01 test level

---

[14] Cost data were not available in the 1948-51 period for one firm, Ford Motor Co., because it was not then publicly owned. In the neighboring four year period when such data became available, 1952-1955, Ford had exactly the same cost variability as General Motors, and so the General Motors measure was also applied to Ford for the 1948-1951 period.

[15] Ideally only economic profit, not accounting profit, would be included here in the difference between numerator and denominator. But economic profit is much more difficult to observe and there seems to be no reason why using accounting profit instead will systematically affect the hypothesis tests.

[16] Sample firms and industries are listed by entry condition in Appendix B.

[17] To test for autocorrelation of residuals, observations were ordered by predicted values of the dependent variable. The Durbin-Watson statistic thus obtained indicated no autocorrelation except for the log-log, medium entry barriers case, where the test was indecisive. To test for heteroscedasticity, the variances of the residuals for subsamples that predicted high and low values of the dependent variable were compared using Bartlett's test and found not to be different. The semi-log specification thus appears to satisfy regression assumptions slightly better than the log-log specification.

[18] Our test for differences between coefficients, which is suggested by Johnston, [6, p. 42] requires the same error variance for each sample, an assumption that could not be rejected for either coefficient test.

Table 9-2
Tests of Differences Between Coefficients Based on Entry Condition

SPECIFI-CATION		COEFFICIENTS HYPOTHESIS+	EXPLANATORY VARIABLE	t SCORE
LN-LN	(8)	$a_{1H} > a_{1M}$	$(1-\alpha_i)$	1.92*
	(9)	$a_{2H} > a_{2M}$	$(\overline{F} F_i/F_I)$	3.86**
Semi-LN	(8)	$b_{1H} > b_{1M}$	$(1-\alpha_i)$	1.74*
	(9)	$b_{2H} > b_{2M}$	$(\overline{F} F_i/F_I)$	5.01**

+ Only the alternative hypothesis is given. The null hypoth esis may be obtained by changing "greater-than" to "less-than or-equal-to." This coefficients test is suggested in [6, 42]
   * One tail significance at .05 test level
   ** One tail significance at .01 test level

from the capacity adjustment model.[19] The coefficients of $\overline{FF}_i/F_I$ in Table 9-1 are positive and significant only for the sample of firms from industries with very high entry barriers. The coefficients of $(1 - \alpha_i)$ are not significantly different from zero. But no hypothesis depended on their values relative to zero, and as Table 9-2 shows, they are greater for the very high entry barrier sample as called for by *Hypothesis* (1).[20] And the coefficients of $\overline{FF}_i/F_I$ also are greater for the very high entry barrier sample, as called for by *Hypothesis* (2).

Relative firm size, $(1 - \alpha_i)$, is the weaker of the two independent variables, being more positively related to growth in the very high entry barrier sample but not significant by itself in either case. However, we expect a bias against showing $(1 - \alpha_i)$ positively related to firm growth, because the α_i's are based on the ending date of the period over which growth was observed. Diseconomies of scale also could cause larger firms to expand relatively less, but we doubt that

---

[19] An alternative test, based on a dummy variable for entry condition but with only one explanatory variable, is reported in Appendix 9-A. This test would be more cumbersome in the case of two explanatory variables, and the direct coefficient comparison was used instead.

[20] Some differences between mean values of variables by subsamples could confound this coefficient comparison. For example, if the firms in one subsample tended on average to have larger market shares (smaller $(1-\alpha_i)$'s), but both subsamples had the same average growth rate, the estimated coefficients in the subsample with larger shares might tend to be smaller. Differences in average market shares can be accentuated by the conversion to logarithms too, because the asymmetry that is present in the size distribution of firms can cause geometric means to differ by more than arithmetic means. But mean $LN (1-\alpha_i)$ values are -0.211 for the high entry barriers subsample and -0.120 for the medium barriers subsample. These differences alone would tend to make coefficients for the high entry barriers subsample smaller in absolute magnitude and have the same sign. They therefore would not appear to favor the hypothesis under test, that the coefficient in high entry barrier industries is larger.

diseconomies of scale would exist only in industries with very high entry barriers. Thus, on the whole, the data offer support for the effects on firm growth under very high entry barriers claimed by our simple, near-Cournot, capacity adjustment model. Relative firm size appears to have an effect on growth that would be difficult to detect without contrasting different entry conditions and taking account also of price and cost variability.

It must be admitted that our sample of firms is from only a few industries, over just one time period. Influenced as it is by earlier studies and the availability of data, our sample is not strictly speaking a random one. Other variables which we have not controlled must surely affect the growth of firms, and may change with time. So investigation of a larger sample, over other time periods, with alternative specifications, are all in order. At this point it seems reasonable nonetheless to claim tentatively that very high entry barriers can cause relative size to be a determinant of firm growth.

Summary

Traditional oligopoly theories have been short-run theories. Here we have emphasized a long-run capacity decision when entry is barred, to construct a simple Cournot-like theory of firm behavior. We assumed homogeneous product, lack of price competition, and a sharing of market quantity in proportion to capacity shares. Our assumptions implied that the larger firms would be more likely to restrain their capacities. The tendency to restrain capacity expansion was also stronger as more costs were fixed, possibly with capacity, and not related to short-run output. Moreover, capacity growth decisions depended explicitly on an interaction between relative firm size and cost variability reminiscent of Bain's interaction between the industry variables, concentration and entry condition. [1]

Implications of the model were tested by comparing regression coefficients estimated from a very high entry barrier cross section sample of 21 firms from four industries with those from a substantial and low entry barrier sample of 72 firms from nine industries. Coefficients for relative firm size and cost variability were significantly higher for the high entry barrier sample of firms. The data for these tests came from the 1946-1955 period and are not ideal, but they indicate that different factors affect firm growth when entry barriers are very high. And observed differences seem properly to rest with entry conditions, since other possible causes, such as diseconomies of scale, would be unlikely to exist only when entry barriers were very high.

These results suggest that in certain cases a departure from the law of proportionate affect may be needed to explain the size distribution of firms, a finding of interest partly because the law of proportionate effect is difficult to test by fitting size distributions alone. [15] The results are also in harmony with

Worcester's suggestion that firms enjoying market power, [29] as from barred entry, will tend to become more equal in size than will firms under competitive conditions. And we have a quite general explanation for the decline of dominant firms. Our theory suggests in particular that when entry is difficult, large relative size is undesirable not only because it might foster tacit price collusion among a few firms, but because the large firms will have less *independent* incentive to expand and enforce competition in the long-run as well.

Appendix 9-A: Specifying E_i as the Explanatory Variable

A linear specification of (5) was also estimated. First, E_i was calculated as in (4), and then G_i was regressed on E_i and G_I, G_I being added to remove the effects of industry growth and thus permit pooling across industries. Calculating E_i in advance this way will force exponents of the two terms in (4) to equal one, as specified explicitly by the theory and embodied in condition (3). Entry conditions were represented by the dummy variable:

$$X = \begin{cases} 1 \text{ for very high entry barriers} \\ 0 \text{ for other entry conditions} \end{cases}$$

in the equation

$$G_i = c_0 + c_1 X + c_2 E_i + c_3 X E_i + c_4 G_I + v_3$$

where v_3 is a random error. Our theory requires that the coefficient of E_i be greater when entry barriers are very high, or that $c_3 > 0$. Estimates of the coefficients based on all 93 observations are:

$$G_i = \begin{array}{c} 0.14 - 0.88\,X + 0.04\,E \\ (0.43) \quad (0.45) \quad (0.08) \\ + \ 0.55^{**}\,XE_i + \ 0.93^{**}\,G_I \\ (0.23) \qquad\quad (0.18) \end{array}$$

$$R_a{}^2 = 0.24; \text{Var}\,(v_3) = 0.46$$

*One tail significance at 0.05 test level
**One tail significance at 0.01 test level

The null hypothesis, that $c_3 \leqslant 0$, can be rejected at the 0.01 test level, in favor of the $c_3 > 0$ restriction. Neither autocorrelation nor heteroscedasticity is indicated. When sub-samples were examined separately by entry barrier condition there was no evidence of auto correlation, but heteroscedasticity then appeared in each sub-sample.

Very High Entry Barriers

Autos (3717)
  General Motors
  Ford
  Chrysler
  American Motors (Nash)
Liquor (2085)
  Seagrams
  National Distillers
  Schenley
  Hiram Walker
Cigarettes (2111)
  American Tobacco
  Reynolds
  Liggett and Myers
  Phillip Morris
  Lorillard
Ethical Drugs (2830)
  American Home Products
  Sterling Drugs
  Parke Davis
  Abbott Laboratories
  Rexall Drugs
  Vick Chemical Co.
  Merck and Sharpe and Dohme

Substantial Entry Barriers

Copper (3331)
  Anaconda
  Kennecott
  American Smelting
  Phelps Dodge
  National Lead
  American Metal
  U.S. Smelting
  Revere

St. Joseph
Calumet & Hecla
Bridgeport Brass
Mueller Brass
American Zinc Lead
Magna Cooper
Farm Machinery and Tractors (3820)
  International Harvester
  John Deere
  Allis Chalmers
  Caterpillar
  Oliver
Petroleum Refining (2911)
  Standard Oil, New Jersey
  Socony Vacuum
  Standard Oil, Indiana
  Texaco
  Cities Service
  Standard Oil, California
  Gulf
  Sinclair
  Shell
  Phillips
  Atlantic
  Union
  Tidewater
  Pure
  Standard Oil, Ohio
  Continental
Steel (3310)
  U.S.S.
  Bethlehem
  Republic
  National
  Jones and Laughin
  Youngstown
  American Rolling
  Inland
  Wheeling

Steel (3310) (cont.)
  Crucible

Low or Moderate Entry Barriers

Canned Fruits and Vegetables (2033)
  Heinz
  California Packing
  Libby
  Stokely Van Camp
Glass Containers (3220)
  Owens
  Corning
  Hazel Atlas
  Anchor
Meat Packing (2010)
  Armour
  Swift

Swift
Wilson
Cudahy
Morell
Hygrade
Tobin
Textile Mill Products (2220)
  Celenese Corp.
  J.P. Stevens
  Burlington
  Cannon
  United Merchants
  Textron
  Reeves
Tires and Tubes (3011)
  Goodyear
  U.S. Rubber
  Firestone
  Goodrich
  General Tire

References

[1] Bain, J.S. *Barriers to New Competition.* Cambridge, Mass.: Harvard University Press, 1956.

[2] Bennathan, E., and Walters, A.A., "Revenue Pooling and Cartels," *Oxford Economic Papers*, July 1969, 1961-76.

[3] Cyert, R.M., and March, J.G., "Organizational Factors in the Theory of Oligopoly," *Quarterly Journal of Economics*, February 1956, 44-64.

[4] Hart, P.E., and Prais, S.J., "The Analysis of Business Concentration: A Statistical Approach," *Journal of the Royal Statistical Society*, Ser. A, 1956, 150-81.

[5] Hymer, S., and Pashigian, P., "Firm Size and Rate of Growth," *Journal of Political Economy*, December 1962, 556-67.

[6] Johnston, J. *Econometric Methods.* New York: McGraw-Hill, 1963.

[7] _____. *Statistical Cost Functions.* New York: McGraw-Hill, 1960.

[8] Kamerschen, D.R., "Market Growth and Industry Concentration," *Journal of the American Statistical Association*, March 1968, 228-41.

[9] Mann, H.M., "Seller Concentration, Barriers to Entry, and Rates of Return in Thirty Industries, 1950-1960," *Review of Economics and Statistics*, August 1966, 296-307.

[10] Mansfield, E., "Entry, Gibrat's Law, Innovation, and the Growth of Firms," *American Economic Review*, December 1962, 1021-51.

[11] Modigliani, F., "New Developments on the Oligopoly Front," *Journal of Political Economy*, October 1958, 215-32.

[12] Nelson, R.L. *Concentration in the Manufacturing Industries of the United States*, New Haven: Yale University Press, 1963.

[13] _____, "Market Growth, Company Diversification, and Product Concentration, 1947-1954," *Journal of the American Statistical Association*, December 1960, 640-49.

[14] Prais, S.J., "The Statistical Conditions for a Change in Business Concentration," *Review of Economics and Statistics*, August 1958, 268-72.

[15] Quandt, R.E., "On the Size Distribution of Firms," *American Economic Review*, 1966, 416-32.

[16] Saving, T.R., "The Four-Parameter Lognormal, Diseconomies of Scale, and the Size Distribution of Manufacturing Establishments," *International Economic Review*, January 1965, 105-14.

[17] Shepherd, W.G., "Trends of Concentration in American Manufacturing Industries," *Review of Economics and Statistics*, May 1964, 200-212.

[18] Sherman, R., "Capacity Choice in Duopoly," unpublished doctoral dissertation, Carnegie-Mellon University, 1966.

[19] _____, "Risk Attitude and Cost Variability in a Capacity Choice Experiment," *Review of Economic Studies*, October 1969, 453-66.

138

[20] Sherman, R., "An Experiment on the Persistence of Price Collusion," *Southern Economic Journal*, April 1971, 489-95.

[21] Simon, H.A., and Bonini, C.P., "The Size Distribution of Business Firms," *American Economic Review*, September 1958, 607-17.

[22] Simon, H.A., "Comment: Firm Size and Rate of Growth," *Journal of Political Economy*, February 1964, 81-2.

[23] Stigler, G.J., "The Kinky Oligopoly Demand Curve and Rigid Price," *Journal of Political Economy*, October 1947, 432-449.

[24] ____, "The Economies of Scale," *Journal of Law and Economics*, October 1958, 54-71.

[25] Sylos Labini, P. *Oligopolio e Progresso Tecnico*, Milan 1957, Translated by Elizabeth Henderson, *Oligopoly and Technical Progress*, Cambridge, Mass., 1962.

[26] Weiss, L.W., "Factors in Changing Concentration," *Review of Economics and Statistics*, February 1963, 70-77.

[27] ____, "The Survival Technique and the Extent of Suboptimal Capacity," *Journal of Political Economy*, June 1964, 246-61.

[28] Worcester, D.A., Jr., "Why 'Dominant Firms' Decline," *Journal of Political Economy*, August 1957, 338-46.

[29] ____. *Monopoly, Big Business, and Welfare in the Postwar United States*, Seattle: University of Washington Press, 1967.

[30] Zeuthen, F. *Problems of Monopoly and Economic Warfare*, London: Routhledge and Sons, Ltd., 1930.

[31] *Moody's Industrial Manual*, New York: Moody's Investor Service, 1952-1956.

10 Advertising

Much current empirical work in industrial organization rests on a paradigm that has two main links: (i) determinants of market structure variables, and (ii) effects of market structure variables on behavior. For example, technological determinants of concentration and entry barriers have been associated in turn with high profitability. [2, 16] Advertising does not fit into this paradigm neatly, for it appears as both an aspect of industry behavior and a determinant of market structure as well. [2, 6, 30] Indeed, exactly how advertising is connected to market structure measures has been a subject of controversy. [6, 8, 17, 25, 27] If advertising is accepted as an independent market structure variable it is a very important one, because it has been linked strongly to high profitability. [6] But we shall argue that advertising is not a genuine independent variable; it depends on technological factors and prices, which determine the variability of total cost with output in the short-run.

The variability of total cost with short-run output was captured nicely in Lerner's "measure of monopoly power," [15] which equals price minus marginal cost all divided by price. Total cost varies more as marginal cost is higher. At a profit maximizing equilibrium for the firm, such cost variability also can be linked to both the marginal product of advertising and the price elasticity of demand. If some additional reasonable conditions hold, measures of advertising and cost variability will be related across industries. And cost variability is given by technology, so it seems more apt to be the determinant of advertising than to be determined by it. But cost variability is not related to advertising alone. It also is related to profit when uncertainty is present, through an effect it has on the variance of profit. So cost variability can explain both advertising and profit, and its omission from any study of a relation between them could lead to faulty conclusions. Since cost variability can be represented empirically, these implications need not go untested for lack of data. Here, after we review reasons why cost variability will affect both advertising and profitability, we investigate the relationships empirically. We find that cost variability rather than advertising is a determinant of profitrates in consumer goods industries, and in other industries as well.

Reprinted with permission from "Advertising and Profitability," by Roger Sherman and Robert Tollison, in *The Review of Economics and Statistics*, 53 (November 1971), 397-407. Copyright 1971 by Harvard University Press. We thank William S. Comanor, Bennett T. McCallum, and Dennis C. Mueller for helpful comments, and the Wilson Gee Institute at the University of Virginia and a faculty research grant at Cornell University for financial support.

Cost Variability as Determinant
of Advertising and Profitability

By solving jointly for an optimal advertising budget as well as an optimal price, Dorfman and Steiner illustrated interdependence among the firm's decision variables. [7] They made the quantity that a firm could sell per unit time, q, a function of its price, p, and its advertising budget, s:

$$q = f(p,s).$$

With $f(p,s)$ assumed continuous and differentiable, Dorfman and Steiner showed that an equilibrium for the firm its marginal value product of advertising, μ, would equal (the negative of) its price elasticity of demand, $-\eta$, which would also equal the cost ratio, $p/(p-MC)$, where MC represents marginal cost. The same relation was discussed by Ozga.[1] [18] The reciprocal of this cost ratio, $(p-MC)/p$, is of course Lerner's measure of monopoly power.

If we assume that at any equilibrium the marginal value product of advertising will be decreasing, then a lower value of μ will be associated with a higher advertising budget (at least for one particular firm). From $\mu = p/(p-MC)$ we can expect μ to be lower when short-run marginal cost, MC, is relatively small, so we can also expect higher advertising outlays as total costs are less variable with short-run output. This makes sense intuitively; when added sales will make a higher marginal contribution to profit, the firm should advertise more. The relation may hold for firms within an industry, since they face similar marginal value product of advertising functions, and it might even hold across industries as long as the industries share properties which make their marginal value of advertising functions similar.

The ratio, $p/(p-MC)$, has been applied before by Leontief in an illustrative vein to estimate demand elasticity for steel firms [14] and more recently by Kamerschen in a study of welfare losses due to monopoly. [13] Elasticity was emphasized as a market structure element by Johnson and Helmberger because of its importance along with market share in determining the character of oligopolistic interdependence. [10] More recently, Saving has demonstrated a relationship between concentration and Lerner-type measures of monopoly power. [19] A link between market shares in the form of a concentration measure and $(p-MC)/p$ (called in this case a "price-cost margin") has in turn been well established empirically by Collins and Preston. [4, 5] But interpretation of that link is difficult, as Benishay has claimed, [3] because the $(p-MC)/p$ ratio reflects technology and is not necessarily related to monopoly power.[2] Nevertheless, under static certainty conditions and assuming that firms

---

[1] Advertising was also related to oligopolistic interdependence by Kaldor. [12]

[2] This measure has been criticized in some uses. In particular, see comments by Sylos-Labini, [24, pp. 84-85] who criticizes Lerner, Kalecki, and Machlup for their uses of the ratio. Related problems are discussed by Bain. [1]

maximize profits, a ratio such as $(p–MC)/p$ can be shown to have important associations with demand elasticity, market shares or concentration, and the marginal value product of advertising. Not all of these associations have been recognized in the interpretation of empirical studies.

Cost variability also has been linked to individual behavior in a special case that associated all fixed costs with the level of capacity. High fixed cost (or high capacity cost) led to less capacity expansion and as a result more profit in controlled, two person, prisoner's dilemma type experiments [20] and also in market games. [21] If this behavioral tendency existed also in the real world, we should expect oligopoly firms to achieve greater profitability when costs were less variable with short-run output.

When we drop the certainty assumption a cost variability measure such as $(p–MC)/p$ can be related to profitability without any reference to collusion or monopoly power. Investors are concerned with both the variance and the level of a firm's profitability, and because cost variability can affect the variance of returns under uncertainty, it will affect the level of profitability that is acceptable to stockholders as well. For an illustration of the role of cost variability, consider that if total cost is completely fixed, profits may improve handsomely in periods of high demand, but in periods of low demand losses may be very great. Thus the variance in profit will be high. For a given variance in demand, the variance in profit will be smaller as total costs are more variable with short-run output. We have found empirically that cost variability and profit variance are related in this way. [22] And we know also that stockholders insist on a higher level of profitability when profit variance, sometimes called "profit risk," is high. (e.g., [9]) So again we may expect higher profitability to be associated with lower cost variability in an uncertain environment.

In one of the more successful empirical attempts to untangle the relations among market structure variables, Comanor and Wilson found advertising and capital requirements consistently related to profitability across 41 consumer goods industries. [6] The effect of advertising had been less clear in previous studies. [17, 25] Some of the strong association that Comanor and Wilson observed between advertising and profitability may be due to underestimation of the investment aspects of advertising as Telser [26] and Weiss [28] have argued. But since the consumer-goods industries in the Comanor and Wilson sample might possess similar marginal product of advertising functions, a measure of cost variability should be associated with advertising in their sample. Indeed, cost variability might be an omitted variable that could be leading in the same instances to high advertising and high profitability, since it can be related theoretically to monopoly power and profit variance as causes of high profitability as well.

It is difficult to sort out whether advertising is a market structure variable that helps to *explain* high profitability, possibly because it discourages entry, or whether it is simply a consequence of the degree of cost variability, which could explain advertising and could affect profitability as well. A model of these relationships is difficult to estimate. The dependent profitability variable has two (of several) explanatory variables, advertising and cost fixity, that are highly correlated because one influences the other. We shall take the obvious first step of including a cost variability measure in a test of the already established advertising and profitability relation, to see whether its omission might have invited imputation of too much explanatory power to advertising alone.[3] Relations with other market structure variables may be considered at the same time. First, we shall discuss measures of cost variability and sources of data.

Measures of Cost Variability

Cost variability has two advantages that make it attractive as an element of market structure. First it can be approximated readily for empirical investigation by the ratio of labor and material costs to the value of shipments in *Census of Manufactures* data. Second, it is related to technology and to that extent is a fundamental and presumably exogenous property of firms' environments. Costs vary more with short-run output when technology permits easy adaptation to changing output requirements, so that many inputs are variable. Of course costs will also vary more with short-run output when those inputs that can be varied in the short run have relatively high prices.

We approximate short-run marginal cost using costs that vary with output over a short-run time period. As noted above, variable costs have been used for such an approximation before. [13, 14] A constant short-run marginal cost equal to variable costs is also consistent with the cost function found empirically in most industries by Johnston. [11, p. 163] Substituting variable costs, v, for MC we can obtain for the Lerner measure of monopoly power

$$\frac{p - MC}{p} = \frac{pq - vq}{pq} = 1 - \frac{vq}{pq}$$

where vq/pq is the ratio of variable costs to value of shipments which we shall take as a definition of cost variability. Of course, $1-vq/pq$, which is related directly to the Lerner measure, reflects invariability of total cost in the short run, and we shall call that "cost fixity." Since Lerner's measure was equal to 1 divided by the negative of the price elasticity of demand $(-1/\eta)$, we might expect from $-1/\eta = (pq-vq)/pq$ that as cost is less variable, market demand at equilibrium will be less price elastic. This relationship will not hold perfectly, however, if the threat of entry prevents attainment of a monopoly price, an outcome that seems likely even in some highly concentrated industries. [29]

Further adjustments in this measure are desirable to remove possibly spurious associations between cost fixity and either advertising or profitability. Advertis-

---

[3] Comanor and Wilson cautioned their readers that this might be possible. [6, p. 434]

ing expenditure, s, is contained in and may influence the magnitude of pq. It can be removed and an "advertising adjusted" cost-fixity measure is obtained:

$$\frac{pq - s - vq}{pq - s}, \quad \text{or} \quad 1 - \frac{vq}{pq - s}.$$

Similarly, when profit can be removed from pq, a "profit and advertising adjusted" cost-fixity measure can be obtained:

$$\frac{pq - s - \pi - vq}{pq - s - \pi}, \quad \text{or} \quad 1 - \frac{vq}{pq - s - \pi}.$$

We shall employ adjusted cost-fixity measures as far as it is possible to do so in the empirical work that follows. These adjustments have small effects on most measured values of cost fixity, but they are important because without them high advertising or high profitability could be related to cost fixity not by any causal relation, but simply because profits and advertising expenses are present in both variables.

Profitability is defined as average industry after tax profits divided by stockholders' equity (for firms with at least $500,000 in assets).[4] Elements of market structure which have been linked to profitability include advertising, concentration, economies of scale relative to market size, capital requirements, and growth rate of demand. We represent advertising by the advertising-sales ratio, which appeared in the Comanor-Wilson study to have greater explanatory power than advertising expenditure per firm. For concentration we use the average (over the period) of four-firm sales concentration ratios. Economies of scale, growth rate of demand, and capital requirements estimates were taken from the Bain, Comanor-Wilson, and Mann studies. [2, 6, 16]

Our empirical analysis is based on two samples of industries.[5] We want to consider another sample in addition to Comanor and Wilson's because we expect that with advertising and cost fixity both as explanatory variables, our regression will possess collinearity and may therefore be sensitive to sample coverage. Our second sample is one studied previously by H.M. Mann. [16] An advantage of this sample is that cost fixity can be adjusted for both profit and advertising, whereas only advertising could be removed from cost fixity in the Comanor and Wilson sample. However, the Mann sample is not confined to consumer-goods industries.

---

[4]To avoid attaching undue importance to any relation between cost variability and accounting profit, it is important that a profit-rate such as profit divided by stockholders' equity be estimated. A relatively high value for $(p-v)/p$ may very well be associated with high accounting profit since capital inputs that are not easily varied in the short run may be relatively larger and their "cost" will actually be the return to investors contained in accounting profit.

[5]For sources and other information on the data and variables of both samples, see the appendix.

Our definition of variables and sources for the 41 consumer-goods industries used by Comanor and Wilson [6] correspond to theirs:

a) Profit Rate—profit after taxes as a percentage of stockholders' equity over the 1954-1957 period;

b) Advertising—ratio of advertising expenditure to sales over the 1954-1957 period;

c) Concentration—Stigler's four-firm average concentration ratios;[6]

d) Absolute Capital Requirements—the average output level of plants at minimum efficient size multiplied by the ratio of total assets to gross sales for the industry;

e) Economies of Scale in Production—average plant size among the largest plants accounting for 50 percent of industry output in the relevant market; and

f) Rate of growth in Demand—rate of growth in sales between 1947 and 1957.

For the 25-industry sample originally employed by Mann, [16] our definition and data for the profit rate variable correspond to his:

a) Profit Rate—average rate of return (net income to average net worth) for leading firms in each industry over the 1950-1960 period.

We introduce to the Mann sample the following additional variables from the sources indicated:

b) Advertising—ratio of advertising expenditures to sales over the 1954-1957 period from *Internal Revenue Service Sourcebook of Statistics of Income 1954-1957*;

c) Concentration—average four-firm concentration ratios;

Table 10-1
Advertising-Adjusted Cost Fixity as Simple Linear Predictor of Advertising-Sales Ratio

Number of Industries	Intercept	Advertising-Adjusted Cost Fixity	Advertising-and-Profit-Adjusted Cost Fixity	R_a^2/S.E.	d.f./F
(1) 41	−0.019[a]	0.24[b]		0.42	39
(C-W)	(−1.90)	(5.52)		0.024	30.49[b]
(2) 25	0.016		0.150[a]	0.08	23
(Mann)	(0.85)		(1.73)	0.044	2.99

t values are given in parentheses.
[a] One tail significance at 0.05 test level.
[b] One tail significance at 0.01 test level.

---

[6]Comanor and Wilson use several additional specifications of the concentration variable.

d) Absolute Capital Requirements—taken from a variety of sources (see appendix) but generally conforms to the Comanor-Wilson definition—the average output level of plants at minimum efficient size multiplied by the ratio of total assets to gross sales for each industry; and

e) Economies of Scale in Production—taken from a variety of sources (see appendix) but generally conforms to the Comanor-Wilson definition—average plant size among the largest plants accounting for 50 percent of industry output divided by total output in the relevant market.

This amended Mann sample must be applied and interpreted cautiously since data available for some variables and industries are imperfect (see appendix). Data are not always at the same level of industry aggregation. For example, profit data are for the leading firms, while advertising and cost-variability data cover the entire industry.

In all cases, our measure of cost fixity is from the *Census of Manufactures*.

Results

As a preliminary observation, we note that advertising-adjusted cost-fixity could serve as a good predictor of advertising-sales ratios in either sample. The simple linear relations are shown in Table 10-1. The relationship is stronger in the sample of consumer-goods industries, where similarity in marginal product of advertising values is more likely. Our inability to remove profit from the cost-fixity measure also might enhance the relationship in the consumer-goods industries sample, but the advertising adjustment should prevent any very substantial spurious relation. Simple correlation coefficients between possible market structure elements and profit rates are shown in Table 10-2. A high correlation between cost-fixity measures and profitability is evident in the Comanor-Wilson sample. It is not as strong in the Mann sample, where no market structure variable has a significant correlation with profit rate. Of course tests using simple correlation coefficients are not really appropriate here, and they would be especially treacherous for samples of moderate size such as the Mann sample.

Now let us examine the effect of cost fixity on profitability in the presence of other market structure variables. We first examine the 41-industry sample, where it was possible to remove advertising (but not profit) from the cost-fixity measure.[7] Multiple regression equations in linear form are reported in Table

---

[7]Profit data could not be obtained for this sample on the same basis as other variables. In the Mann sample, where the profit adjustment is made, it is imperfect because it is based on profit-rates for a subset of larger firms. But any resulting bias should weaken the relation between cost fixity and profitability because these profit-rates are probably high, so the adjustment is overdone.

Table 10-2
Simple Correlation Coefficients Between Profit Rates and
Elements of Market Structure

Independent Variable	Comanor-Wilson 41-Industry Sample	Mann 25-Industry Sample
Advertising-Sales	0.42 [b]	0.30
Profit and Advertising Adjusted Cost Fixity	—	0.33
Advertising Adjusted Cost Fixity	0.46 [b]	—
Concentration	0.33 [a]	0.31
Capital Requirements	0.43 [b]	0.11
Economies of Scale	0.26	0.33
Rate of Growth of Demand	0.17	—

[a] Significance at 0.05 test level.
[b] Significance at 0.01 test level.

10-3. Equation (1) shows the advertising-sales ratio to be an important determinant of profits, along with absolute capital requirements, as Comanor and Wilson found. [6] When cost fixity is included as $1-vq/(pq-s)$ (the advertising adjusted form) in Equation (2), however, it has a significant effect on profit while the advertising sales ratio no longer does. Moreover, if advertising-sales is now omitted and the cost-fixity measure is retained, as in Equation (3), practically no explanatory power is lost. And direct replacement of advertising by the cost-fixity measure (Equation (3) versus Equation (1)) improves the explanatory power of the equation considerably.

Aside from its relationship with advertising-sales, the cost-fixity variable is not related strongly to the other independent variables. The highest simple correlation coefficient between cost fixity and any other explanatory variable was -0.096 with concentration. Evidence of some multicollinearity was found among capital requirements, concentration, and economies of scale, however, and will be discussed below in connection with logarithmic specification of equations.

Similar results are obtained from the 25-industry Mann sample, and they are presented in Table 10-4. Advertising is not an important determinant of profit-rate across these industries, nor is any other single market structure variable. Profit data for these industries permit adjustment of the cost-fixity measure to remove profit as well as advertising and obtain a profit and advertising adjusted cost-fixity measure. The adjusted cost-fixity measure greatly improves the explanatory power of the equations. In its presence absolute capital requirements and concentration explain slightly more of the profit-rate as well. Thus in addition to explaining a significant portion of profitability, a cost-fixity variable may also permit more efficient estimation of other market structure effects.

Table 10-3
Linear Multiple Regression Equations Explaining Profit Rates Over 41 Consumer Goods Industries

	Intercept	Advertising-Sales Ratio	Advertising Adjusted Cost Fixity	Four-Firm Concentration	Economies of Scale	Capital Requirements	Growth of Demand	R_a^2/S.E.	d.f./F.
(1)	0.047[b] (4.00)	0.513[b] (3.17)		0.001 (0.03)	0.085 (0.58)	0.000274[b] (2.70)	0.231 (1.02)	.33 .031	35 4.96[b]
(2)	0.021 (1.32)	0.175 (0.840)	0.175[a] (2.36)	−0.014 (−0.45)	0.179 (1.25)	0.000295[b] (3.17)	0.24 (1.10)	.41 .029	34 5.60[b]
(3)	0.017 (1.114)		0.217[b] (4.05)	−0.018 (−0.57)	0.219 (1.63)	0.000294[b] (3.18)	0.242 (1.14)	.41 .029	35 6.64[b]

t values are given in parentheses.
[a] One tail significance at 0.05 test level.   [b] One tail significance at 0.01 test level.

Table 10-4
Linear Multiple Regression Equations Explaining Profitability Over 25 Mann Industries

	Intercept	Advertising Sales Ratio	Profit and Advertising Adjusted Cost Fixity	Four-Firm Concentration	Economies of Scale	Capital Requirements	R_a^2/S.E.	d.f./F
(1)	0.085[b] (4.69)	0.20 (1.28)		0.023 (0.76)	0.203 (0.87)	0.00004 (0.68)	.05 .033	20 1.337
(2)	0.057[b] (2.55)	0.113 (0.73)	0.129[a] (1.85)	0.032 (1.11)	0.18[a] (1.82)	0.071 (1.211)	.16 .031	19 1.884
(3)	0.057[b] (2.57)		0.144[a] (2.198)	0.036 (1.275)	0.197 (0.908)	0.064 (1.122)	.18 .031	20 2.275

t values are given in parentheses.
[a] One tail significance at 0.05 test level.   [b] One tail significance at 0.01 test level.

Equations specified in logarithmic form do not give completely equivalent results. In the 41-industry Comanor and Wilson sample, shown in Table 10-5, logarithmic specification returns importance for influencing profit-rates to concentration and capital requirements. This result may be due in part to multicollinearity among variables, however, which makes their product, as brought out in logarithmic form, more important.[8] When concentration is omitted to reduce multicollinearity (concentration has simple correlation coefficients of 0.52 with capital requirements and 0.57 with scale economies) in Equations (4), (5), and (6), cost fixity again has a significant coefficient while advertising-sales does not. Rate of growth of demand also has a significant coefficient when concentration is not present. In the Mann sample no significant results remain after logarithmic transformations. Multicollinearity becomes more serious. But even after concentration is omitted (concentration has simple correlation coefficients of 0.31 with capital requirements and 0.45 with scale economies) in Equations (4), (5), and (6), there is little improvement. While we have no very good reason for presuming a multiplicative specification, we must acknowledge that results are sensitive to specification.

To test for heteroscedasticity, industry data were ordered according to value of shipments and subjected to Bartlett's test for uniform variance. While heteroscedastic errors were not found in the Mann sample, their presence in the Comanor and Wilson sample was indicated for important equations in both linear and logarithmic specifications. In an effort to remedy this violation of our statistical assumptions, we carried out weighted regressions using the square root of industry value of shipments to weight the observations. This weighting was used successfully by Comanor and Wilson to adjust for heteroscedasticity. [6, pp. 435-436] Results for weighted regressions, which now satisfy the homoscedasticity assumptions, are reported in Table 10-7.

The weighted regressions give results that generally are consistent with indications from the unweighted regressions. The cost-fixity measure remains highly significant and still robs the advertising-sales ratio of much of its power to explain relative profitability. In linear form the presence of cost fixity appears to strengthen the roles of concentration, capital requirements, and economies of scale in explaining relative profitability. In the logarithmic specifications cost fixity and rate of growth of demand are the only independent variables that appear statistically significant. Overall explanatory power is improved in all cases in Table 10-7 as a greater fraction of the error is now explained.

On the whole the technological variable, cost fixity, thus plays an important role in explaining advertising expenditures, and it also accounts better for industry profitability. When it is included along with advertising-sales in a

---

[8]Part of the collinearity is due to the method of measuring scale economies. Comanor and Wilson showed that capital requirements and economies of scale explained much of observed concentration. [6, p. 435, n. 38] Of course Bain has shown that concentration and entry barriers are more important when they occur together, [2] but it is hard to test for that here when they tend often to occur together.

Table 10-5
Logarithmic Multiple Regression Equations Explaining Profit Rates Over 41 Consumer Goods Industries

	Intercept	Advertising Sales Ratio	Advertising Adjusted Cost Fixity	Four-Firm Concentration	Economies of Scale	Capital Requirements	Growth of Demand	R_a^2/S.E.	d.f./F
(1)	−0.506	0.033		−0.544[a]	0.083	0.000271[b]	0.240	.27	34
	(−0.74)	(0.38)		(−2.20)	(0.84)	(2.71)	(1.41)	.48	3.84[b]
(2)	−0.479	−0.033	0.268	−0.449[a]	0.071	0.000232[a]	0.233	.28	33
	(−0.71)	(−0.32)	(1.24)	(−1.75)	(0.720)	(2.23)	(1.38)	.48	3.50[b]
(3)	−0.430		0.231	−0.456[a]	0.064	0.000239[a]	0.228	.30	34
	(−0.66)		(1.27)	(−1.81)	(0.68)	(2.38)	(1.38)	.47	4.29[b]
(4)	−0.519	0.049			−0.013	0.000107	0.345[a]	.19	35
	(−0.722)	(0.54)			(−0.14)	(1.52)	(2.01)	.51	3.23[a]
(5)	−0.479	−0.049	0.381[a]		−0.006	0.000092	0.309[a]	.23	35
	(−0.69)	(−0.47)	(1.79)		(−0.06)	(1.34)	(1.84)	.49	3.39[a]
(6)	−0.405		0.392[a]		−0.018	0.099	0.304[a]	.25	35
	(−0.60)		(1.84)		(−0.20)	(1.50)	(1.84)	.49	4.28[b]

t values are given in parentheses.
[a] One tail significance at 0.05 test level.
[b] One tail significance at 0.01 test level.

Table 10-6
Logarithmic Multiple Regression Equations Explaining Profit Rates Over 25 Mann Industries

	Intercept	Advertising Sales	Profit and Advertising Adjusted Cost Fixity	Four-Firm Concentration	Economies of Scale	Capital Requirements	R_a^2/S.E.	d.f./F
(1)	-1.772[b]	0.071		0.047	0.063	0.033	.09	20
	(-5.27)	(1.29)		(0.35)	(0.78)	(0.70)	.28	1.61
(2)	-1.517[b]	0.068	0.021	0.047	0.06	0.035	.05	19
	(-5.22)	(1.20)	(0.32)	(0.35)	(0.72)	(0.72)	.29	1.25
(3)	-1.657[b]		0.032	0.06	0.10	0.017	.03	20
	(-6.16)		(0.49)	(0.44)	(1.31)	(0.36)	.29	1.18
(4)	-1.530[b]	0.072			0.071	0.036	.13	21
	(-5.87)	(1.35)			(0.94)	(0.79)	.27	2.20
(5)	-1.502[b]	0.070	0.021		0.068	0.038	.09	20
	(5.35)	(1.26)	(0.32)		(0.88)	(0.81)	.28	1.60
(6)	-1.642[b]		0.032		0.112	0.02	.07	21
	(-6.283)		(0.50)		(1.61)	(0.44)	.29	1.56

t values are given in parentheses.
[a] One tail significance at 0.05 test level.
[b] One tail significance at 0.01 test level.

Table 10-7
Linear and Logarithmic Weighted Regression Equations Explaining
Profit Rates Over 41 Consumer-Goods Industries

Intercept	Advertising Sales	Advertising Adjusted Cost Fixity	Four-Firm Concentration	Economies of Scale	Capital Requirements	Growth of Demand	R_a^2/S.E.	d.f./F
Linear Specification:								
(1) 653.90[a]	0.615[b]		0.078[b]	0.163	0.173[b]	0.280	.90	35
(1.793)	(3.031)		(2.872)	(1.477)	(3.439)	(1.519)	1187.62	60.38[b]
(2) −133.88	−0.066	0.264[b]	0.050[a]	0.168	0.186[b]	0.180	.94	34
(−0.423)	(−0.324)	(5.162)	(2.325)	(1.195)	(4.847)	(1.274)	902.24	91.63[b]
(3) −133.77		0.254[b]	0.051[b]	0.163[a]	0.186[b]	0.181	.94	35
(−0.428)		(6.601)	(2.444)	(1.995)	(4.926)	(1.299)	890.63	112.82[b]
Logarithmic Specification:								
(4) 2.622	0.098		0.064	0.022	0.067	0.678[b]	.74	34
(0.970)	(0.946)		(0.287)	(0.191)	(0.626)	(4.861)	.564	19.010[b]
(5) −4.275	−0.008	0.751[b]	0.074	0.058	0.005	0.400[b]	.81	33
(−1.378)	(−0.767)	(3.418)	(0.380)	(0.577)	(0.053)	(2.731)	.492	22.766[b]
(6) −3.900		0.666[b]	0.073	0.039	0.018	0.402[b]	.80	34
(−1.281)		(3.524)	(0.379)	(0.401)	(0.191)	(2.762)	.489	27.535[b]

t values are given in parentheses.
[a] One tail significance at 0.05 test level.
[b] One tail significance at 0.01 test level.

regression equation, cost fixity robs advertising-sales of significant explanatory power. And when used in place of advertising-sales in two samples of 41 and 25 industries, it explains a greater amount of variation in industry profit-rates for linear, although not for logarithmic, specifications. If advertising-sales were an important cause of profitability beyond its ordinary role as sales stimulant, as an entry barrier would be for example, it might have continued to have a significant coefficient even in the presence of cost fixity. But we must admit that our test of this added effect of advertising is biased against revealing it, because of collinearity with the cost-fixity variable which will increase the standard error of its regression coefficient. We tentatively conclude that cost-fixity explains profitability better than advertising, and it appears to influence advertising too. But there may be an additional effect of advertising on profitability which we cannot detect. This effect must be much smaller, however, than the Comanor and Wilson findings indicated.

One other shortcoming of our analysis should be made clear. In both of our samples for the linear specification we found cost fixity related more strongly than advertising-sales to profitability. But in each case some data imperfections could contribute to this result. In the Mann sample, although cost fixity can be adjusted (albeit imperfectly) to remove both profit and advertising, the sample is not confined to consumer goods industries, and in consumer goods industries the coefficient for advertising-sales might be more significant. In the Comanor-Wilson sample we have only consumer goods industries, but here the cost-fixity measure could not be adjusted to remove profit. As a result it could be easier to find as significant the coefficient for cost fixity.

Summary

We have defined short-run total cost variability as a ratio of variable costs divided by the value of shipments, and short-run cost-fixity as one minus that ratio. Variable costs are those costs that vary with changes in output over a specific calendar time period, such as one year. A measure of this kind can be related clearly to more classical influences on firm behavior which involve relations in static certainty models between price and marginal cost, such as Lerner's measure of monopoly power, $(p-MC)/p$. It also is related to profit variance in uncertainty models, and in turn to profitability. Cost variability was not correlated highly with economies of scale, concentration, or capital requirements variables. It appears as a distinctly separate variable that offers precise theoretical implications.

Cost variability was shown able to predict advertising-sales ratios and to reduce the advertising-sales measure to an insignificant role in explaining profit rates. Being a technologically determined variable, especially after adjustment to remove the effects of profit or advertising expenditures, cost variability would seem to be the genuine explanatory variable in the relationship, making advertising a dependent variable. This is not to say that advertising is irrelevant; an industry that has a very high level of advertising expense surely will be more difficult to enter, and our tests were biased against detection of such a role for advertising. However, we have shown that plausible, largely technological conditions can invite firms to engage in heavy advertising, and we argue that these conditions, *not advertising itself*, should be examined for their effect on profitability and market performance. A high level of advertising in an industry may be viewed as a symptom, not necessarily of disease, but rather of a condition that complicates the functioning of competitive process.

Appendix 10-A: Data

Comanor-Wilson Sample

The variables are defined and discussed in the text. Data on all variables except cost fixity and concentration are from Comanor and Wilson, [6] whose generosity in supplying unpublished data is acknowledged. The Comanor and Wilson study of forty-one consumer-goods industries contains an appendix which discusses in detail the derivations of the data for their variables. Sources of data appear in Table 10-8. Observations for all variables in the forty-one industry Comanor and Wilson sample, ordered by value of shipments from lowest to highest, appear in Table 10-9.

Mann Sample

The variables are defined and discussed in the text. Table 10-10 lists the source of data.

Cost variability data have been normalized for the element of profit (π) contained in value of shipments. Absolute accounting profits taken from the *Internal Revenue Service Source Book of Statistics of Income—1954* were deducted from value of shipments in the following expression: $1-vq/(pq-\pi)$. To relate industries defined by the Census Bureau to those of the Internal Revenue Service for the following industries, Internal Revenue Service industry profits were allocated according to percent of industry output accounted for by

Table 10-8
Sources of Data: Comanor-Wilson Sample

Variable	Source
a) Profit rate	*Internal Revenue Service Source Book of Statistics of Income.* Average values for 1954–1957.
b) Advertising — sales ratio	*Internal Revenue Service Source Book of Statistics of Income.* Average values for 1954–1957.
c) Concentration	George J. Stigler, *Capital and Rates of Return in Manufacturing Industries*, pp. 206–215.
d) Absolute capital requirements	*1954 Census of Manufactures and Internal Revenue Service Source Book of Statistics of Income.*
e) Economies of scale relative to market	*1954 Census of Manufactures.*
f) Rate of growth of demand	*Internal Revenue Service Source Book of Statistics of Income.*
g) Cost fixity	*1954 Census of Manufactures.*

Table 10-9
Average Profit Rates (1954-1957)

Industries	Profit Rate (per cent)	Advertising Expenditure (per cent)	Advertising Adjusted Cost Fixity (per cent)	Concentration (per cent)	Absolute Capital Requirements (millions)	Economies of Scale (per cent)	Growth in Demand (ratio 1957/1947)
1) Furs	5.7	1.0	25	3.3	0.16	0.71	0.80
2) Motorcycles and Bicycles	5.2	1.1	13	46.2	6.66	12.49	1.14
3) Hats	1.6	2.2	17	53.6	3.57	10.36	0.50
4) Venetian Blinds	9.3	1.6	17	19.0	1.30	3.29	1.03
5) Millinery	−1.3	0.8	20	7.0	0.18	0.38	1.32
6) Carpets	4.5	2.0	19	56.0	21.24	7.74	2.07
7) Costume Jewelry	1.4	4.0	18	18.9	0.59	0.65	1.23
8) Jewelry	5.3	3.2	19	35.2	4.56	3.92	0.96
9) Wines	7.3	5.2	24	32.2	7.04	4.17	2.01
10) Watches and Clocks	1.9	5.6	18	42.2	17.53	8.33	1.11
11) Cigars	5.3	2.6	20	42.3	5.35	2.00	0.58
12) Cereals	14.8	10.3	28	81.4	36.51	19.46	1.43
13) Hand Tools	11.4	4.2	24	35.2	16.60	3.89	1.54
14) Perfumes	13.5	15.3	43	24.4	10.94	2.63	2.34
15) Distilled Liquor	5.0	2.1	36	69.3	14.67	4.16	1.38
16) Electrical Appliances	10.3	3.5	25	42.9	21.20	9.98	1.39
17) Books	10.1	2.4	32	20.8	7.20	1.77	2.33
18) Soaps	11.7	9.2	34	65.1	18.71	3.92	1.46
19) Household Service Machinery	7.3	1.9	22	44.7	45.01	6.41	2.22
20) Confectionery	10.6	3.5	19	34.4	10.30	6.68	1.15

21) Soft Drinks	10.0	6.2	24	10.2	0.75	8.23	1.98
22) Sugar	5.8	0.2	11	65.8	31.01	6.47	1.14
23) Periodicals	11.7	0.2	33	31.6	22.37	2.38	1.93
24) Cigarettes	11.5	4.8	32	83.0	99.59	7.62	1.70
25) Drugs	14.0	9.9	44	32.8	46.45	4.63	2.56
26) Instruments	12.0	2.0	26	47.0	28.42	6.63	2.25
27) Footwear	**7.6**	**1.5**	**18**	28.6	2.00	0.30	1.13
28) Tires and Tubes	10.2	1.4	21	77.0	61.43	5.00	1.57
29) Malt Liquors	7.2	6.8	32	25.5	20.28	2.32	1.32
30) Grain Mill Products	7.0	1.9	09	28.8	4.18	0.98	1.04
31) Paints	9.9	1.5	27	35.0	8.67	2.40	1.58
32) Knit Goods	3.8	1.3	15	16.6	2.02	1.26	1.34
33) Radio, Television and Phonograph	8.8	2.2	18	46.8	20.37	2.71	15.22
34) Furniture	9.7	1.5	18	19.8	2.26	2.25	1.42
35) Bakery Products	9.3	2.9	17	28.8	2.57	8.30	1.69
36) Men's Clothing	5.9	1.2	14	14.1	1.73	0.60	1.19
37) Canning	6.4	2.9	17	30.6	6.72	1.36	1.89
38) Women's Clothing	6.1	1.8	18	8.2	0.46	0.30	1.20
39) Dairy Products	7.9	2.2	14	38.2	2.09	14.21	1.16
40) Meat Packing	4.6	0.6	04	35.6	9.46	0.67	1.27
41) Motor Vehicles	15.5	0.6	11 [a]	80.1	375.00	7.50	2.31

[a] For 1958.

Table 10-10
Sources of Data: Mann Sample

Variable	Source
a) Profit rate	Mann [16].
b) Advertising-sales ratio	*Internal Revenue Service Source Book of Statistics of Income 1954–1957.*
c) Concentration	*Concentration Ratios in Manufacturing Industries: 1958.* Average four-firm concentration ratios.
d) Absolute capital requirements	Bain [2, pp. 158–159]; Comanor and Wilson [6]. *1954 Census of Manufactures*; and *Internal Revenue Service Source Book of Statistics of Income 1954.* Average values for 1950–1960.
e) Economies of scale relative to market	Bain [2]; Comanor and Wilson [6]; and Mann [16, p. 301].
f) Cost fixity	*1954 Census of Manufactures and Internal Revenue Service Source Book of Statistics of Income 1954–1957.*

the census industry: chewing gum, flat glass, aluminum reduction, biscuits, tractors, glass containers, rayon, and flour. Cost variability data were also normalized for advertising expenditure(s) to obtain the following expression: $1-vq/(pq-s-\pi)$. Absolute advertising expenditure data were taken from the *Internal Revenue Service Source Book of Statistics of Income–1954-1957.* To relate Census Bureau industries to those of the Internal Revenue Service in the following industries, the advertising expenditure adjustment required allocation of Internal Revenue Service advertising expenditure data according to the percent of industry output accounted for by the census industry: flat glass, biscuits, tractors, glass containers, and flour. Also, advertising expenditure data for the chewing gum industry are taken from Mann, [16, p. 303] and advertising expenditure data for the aluminum reduction industry are computed for the smelting and refining of all non-ferrous metals.

Capital requirements data are from Bain, [2, p. 158-159] and are adjusted by 1954 employment ratios in the following industries: flat glass, aluminum reduction, biscuits, petroleum refining, steel, tractors, cement, rayon, gypsum products, metal containers, and bituminous coal; and from Comanor and Wilson, [6] in the following industries: automobiles, chewing gum (confectionery), cigarettes, ethical drugs, liquor, soap, tires and tubes, shoes, canned fruits and vegetables, meat packing, flour, beer, and baking. The capital requirement estimate for the glass container industry is derived via the technique described in Comanor and Wilson. [6, p. 429]

Advertising-sales ratios were derived by taking the average of absolute advertising expenditures by Internal Revenue Service industry over the 1954-1957 period as a proportion of value of shipments of Census Bureau industries (s/pq). The above discussion of the allocation of Internal Revenue

Table 10-11
Average Profit Rates (1950-1960)

Industries	Average Profit Rates (per cent)	Profit-Adjusted and Advertising-Adjusted Cost Fixity (per cent)	Capital Requirements (millions)	Concentration (per cent)	Advertising s/pq (per cent)	Economies of Scale (per cent)
1) Chewing Gum	17.5	39	10.30	87	8.0	6.68
2) Gypsum Products	14.4	06	5.00	89	5.0	2.06
3) Flat Glass	18.8	23	47.00	91	1.6	10.00
4) Rayon	8.5	11	93.00	78[c]	1.6	5.00
5) Aluminum Reduction	10.2	16	63.00	83	6.2	4.50
6) Glass Containers	13.3	21	30.50	61	1.7	1.50
7) Liquor	9.0	27	14.67	62	7.9	4.16
8) Cement	15.7	38	24.00	32	3.1	0.95
9) Biscuits	11.4	31	9.50	68	3.1	1.50
10) Soap	13.3	18	18.71	88	18.7	3.92
11) Metal Containers	9.9	12	15.10	80	0.4	1.17
12) Cigarettes	11.6	19	99.59	81	10.5	7.62
13) Ethical Drugs	17.9	36	46.45	26	12.6	4.63
14) Beer	10.9	25	20.28	28	10.6	2.32
15) Tires and Tubes	13.2	14	61.43	77	3.1	5.00
16) Shoes	9.6	16	2.00	29	1.6	0.30
17) Flour	8.6	01	4.18	39	1.7	0.98
18) Bituminous Coal	8.8	25	30.00	27[d]	0.09	1.50
19) Tractors	8.8	14	83.70	72	3.1	12.50
20) Baking	11.0	15	2.57	21	3.1	8.30
21) Canned Fruits and Vegetables	7.7	15	6.72	29	2.8	1.36
22) Meat Packing	5.3	25	9.46	37	0.6	0.67
23) Petroleum Refining	12.2	01	265.00	33	1.3	1.75
24) Steel	10.8	16[a]	465.00	54	1.2	1.75
25) Automobiles	15.5	06[b]	375.00	75	0.63	7.50

[a] For 1955.
[b] For 1958.
[c] From Bain, *Barriers to New Competition*, p. 45.
[d] Computed by per cent of industry output accounted for by three largest firms (by asset) — *Census of Mineral Industries — 1958*.

Service advertising expenditures to Census Bureau industries and the derivation of the advertising expenditure estimates for the chewing gum and aluminum reduction industries applies to this variable as well.

Economies of scale data for the beer, liquor, meat packing, canned fruits and vegetables, flour, baking products, chewing gum (confectionery), cigarettes, drugs, soaps, tires and tubes, shoes, and automobile industries are from data supplied by Comanor and Wilson, op. cit. Estimates for the cement, tractors, petroleum refining, steel, metal containers, gypsum products, and rayon industries come from averaging Bain's estimates of "percentage of national industry capacity contained in one plant of minimum efficient size." See Bain. [2, p. 72] Estimates for the flat glass, aluminum reduction, biscuits, glass containers, and bituminous coal industries are derived by translating the scale-barrier ranking given by Mann, [16, p. 301] into Bain's classification scheme. [2, pp. 103-104]

Observations for all variables in the twenty-five industry Mann sample, ordered by value of shipments from the lowest to the highest, appear in Table 10-11.

References

[1] Bain, J.S., "The Profit Rate as a Measure of Monopoly Power," *Quarterly Journal of Economics* 55 (Feb. 1941), 271-293.

[2] _____, *Barriers to New Competition* (Cambridge, Mass.: Harvard University Press, 1956).

[3] Benishay, H., "Concentration and Price-Cost Margins: A Comment," *Journal of Industrial Economics*, 16 (Nov. 1967), 73-74.

[4] Collins, N.R., and L.E. Preston, "Concentration and Price-Cost Margins in Food Manufacturing Industries," *Journal of Industrial Economics*, 15 (July 1966), 226-242.

[5] Collins, N.R., and L.E. Preston, "Price-Cost Margins and Industry Structure," *Review of Economics and Statistics* 51 (Aug. 1969), 271-286.

[6] Comanor, W.S., and T.A. Wilson, "Advertising, Market Structure, and Performance," *Review of Economics and Statistics*, 49 (Nov. 1967), 423-440.

[7] Dorfman, R., and P.O. Steiner, "Optimal Advertising and Optimal Quality," *American Economic Review*, 44 (Dec. 1954), 826-836.

[8] Ekelund, R.B., Jr., and C. Maurice, "An Empirical Investigation of Advertising and Concentration: Comment," *Journal of Industrial Economics*, 19 (Nov. 1969), 76-84.

[9] Fisher, I.N., and G.R. Hall, "Risk and Corporate Rates of Return," *Quarterly Journal of Economics*, 83 (Feb. 1969), 79-92.

[10] Johnson, A.C., Jr., and P. Helmberger, "Price Elasticity of Demand as an Element of Market Structure," *American Economic Review*, 57 (Dec. 1967), 1218-1221.

[11] Johnston, J., *Statistical Cost Analysis* (New York: McGraw-Hill, 1960).

[12] Kaldor, N., "The Economic Aspects of Advertising," *Review of Economic Studies*, 18 (Jan. 1950), 1-27.

[13] Kamerschen, D.C., "An Estimation of the 'Welfare Losses' from Monopoly in the American Economy," *Western Economic Journal*, 4 (Summer 1966), 221-236.

[14] Leontief, W., "Elasticity of Demand Computed from Cost Data," *American Economic Review*, 30 (Dec. 1940), 814-817.

[15] Lerner, A.P., "The Concept of Monopoly and the Measurement of Monopoly Power," *Review of Economic Studies*, 1 (June 1934), 157-175.

[16] Mann, H.M., "Seller Concentration, Barriers to Entry, and Rates of Return in Thirty Industries," *Review of Economics and Statistics*, 48 (Aug. 1966), 296-307.

[17] Mann, H.M., J.A. Henning and J. W. Meehan, Jr., "Advertising and Concentration: An Empirical Investigation," *Journal of Industrial Economics*, 16 (Nov. 1967), 34-39.

[18] Ozga, S.A., "Imperfect Markets Through Lack of Knowledge," *Quarterly Journal of Economics*, 74 (Feb. 1960), 29-52.

[19] Saving, T.R., "Concentration Ratios and the Degree of Monopoly," *International Economic Review* (Feb. 1970), 139-146.

[20] Sherman, R., "Risk Attitude and Cost Variability in a Capacity Choice Experiment," *Review of Economic Studies*, 36 (Oct. 1969), 453-466.

[21] _____, "An Experiment on the Persistence of Price Collusion," *Southern Economic Journal*, 37 (April 1971).

[22] _____, and R. Tollison, "Technology, Profit Risk, and Assessments of Market Performance," *Quarterly Journal of Economics* 86 (Aug. 1972).

[23] Stigler, G.J., *Capital and Rates of Return in Manufacturing Industries* (Princeton: Princeton University Press, 1963).

[24] Sylos-Labini, P., *Oligopoly and Technical Progress*, translated by E. Henderson (Cambridge, Mass.: Harvard University Press, 1962).

[25] Telser, L.G., "Advertising and Competition," *Journal of Political Economy*, 72 (Dec. 1964), 542-544.

[26] _____, "Discussion," *American Economic Review*, 59 (May 1969), 121-123.

[27] _____, "Another Look at Advertising and Concentration," *Journal of Industrial Economics*, 18 (Nov. 1969), 85-94.

[28] Weiss, L.W., "Advertising, Profits, and Corporate Taxes," *Review of Economics and Statistics*, 51 (Nov. 1969), 421-430.

[29] Wenders, J.T., "Entry and Monopoly Pricing," *Journal of Political Economy*, 75 (Oct. 1967), 755-760.

[30] Williamson, O.E., "Selling Expense as a Barrier to Entry," *Quarterly Journal of Economics*, 77 (Feb. 1963), 112-128.

11

Assessments of Market Performance

Over the past twenty years many studies of industrial organization have associated market structure variables with industry profitability.[1] Only recently has evidence also established a link between risk and industry profitability,[2] a link suggesting that to the extent technological (or other) factors have systematic effects on both risk and market structure, results of some of these industrial organization studies could have been wrongly interpreted. For example, higher risk rather than concentration alone might account for high profitability observed in some industries. While it is doubtful that many of the well established associations between market structure variables and profitability can be explained away by risk, some consideration of risk effects is in order. And if risk and market structure variables are confounded, the existing tacit separation of finance from industrial organization may no longer be advisable.

A technological property that can be linked theoretically to profit risk is production flexibility with respect to changes in output. This flexibility can be interpreted as a short-run "cost variability" measure, and is apt to influence the extent to which any variability or instability in output quantity will be carried over as instability in profits.[3] Depending on the

Reprinted with permission from "Technology, Profit Risk, and Assessments of Market Performance," by Roger Sherman and Robert Tollison, *Quarterly Journal of Economics*, 86 (August 1972), 448-62. Copyright 1972 by Harvard University Press. We are grateful to Edward A. Manfield, Bennett T. McCallum, and Dennis C. Mueller for helpful comments, and to the Wilson Gee Institute for Research in the Social Sciences of the University of Virginia and a Faculty Research Grant from Cornell University for financial support.

[1] Bain may be credited with stimulating much of this empirical work. See J.S. Bain, "Relation of Profit Rates to Industry Concentration: American Manufacturing, 1936-1940," *Quarterly Journal of Economics*, LXV (Aug. 1951), and *Barriers to New Competition*, Cambridge, Mass.: Harvard University Press, 1956. We cannot list all contributions here, but recent ones include H.M. Mann, "Seller Concentration, Barriers to Entry, and Rates of Return in Thirty Industries," *Review of Economics and Statistics*, XLVIII (Aug. 1966), 296-307, and W.S. Comanor and T.A. Wilson, "Advertising, Market Structure, and Performance," *The Review of Economics and Statistics*, XLIX (Aug. 1967), 319-31.

[2] See I.N. Fisher and G.R. Hall, "Risk and Corporate Rates of Return," *Quarterly Journal of Economics*, LXXXIII (Feb. 1969), 79-92, F.D. Arditti, "Risk and the Required Return on Equity," *Journal of Finance*, XXII (March 1967), 19-36; G.R. Conrad and I.H. Plotkin, "Risk/Return: U.S. Industry Pattern," *Harvard Business Review*, XLVI (Mar.-Apr. 1968), 90-99; and P.H. Cootner and D.M. Holland, "Risk and Rate of Return," Massachusetts Institute of Technology DSR Project No. 9565, Feb. 1964.

[3] Early descriptions of this effect of technology on profit variability are given by G.J. Stigler, "Production and Distribution in the Short-Run," *Journal of Political Economy*,

risk attitude of the individual decision maker, such cost variability has been shown to affect individual price and capacity choice behavior in an experimental setting, and it has also been linked to advertising expenditure and profitability.[4] Cost variability can easily be represented empirically if short-run average variable cost is constant over a relevant range of outputs, and because it is not subject to sampling effects as variance measures are, it might serve as a convenient surrogate for profit variance.

Our purposes here are, first, to show how a largely technological property, the extent to which a firm's total cost can be adjusted in the short-run as its output varies, is related to profit risk, and second, to sketch the importance of this relationship to the interpretation of firm and industrial organization studies. Our reasons for seeking such relationships should be clear. Cost variability and profit risk might affect the average level of profitability under competitive circumstances, so if they are related systematically to market structure variables that have been associated empirically with average profitability, conclusions drawn about those market structure variables reflecting market power could be wrong. The (omitted) cost variability or profit risk variable might account instead for high profitability.

We begin by developing the relation between a defined measure of short-run cost variability and measures of profit risk. This relation is tested and supported empirically. Next, we investigate whether firm size and profitability relationships are due to effects of profit risk and cost variability. We find that, if anything, including cost variability or profit risk will tend to *strengthen* the relationship between firm size and profitability. Advantages of the cost variability measure over a profit risk measure also are noted here. Finally, we search for possible correlations between cost variability and those market structure variables that have been found associated with profitability. We find none that is strong enough to suggest that the omission of profit risk or cost variability has caused incorrect imputation of profitability to market structure measures. Indeed, omitting a measure of cost variability may have made such relationships *harder to detect*.

Cost Variability and Profit Risk-Theory

We shall take the variance in profitability as a measure of profit risk. This is a convenient measure that has been used in one way or another by practically all

(June 1939), and A.G. Hart, *Studies in Business Administration*, Vol. 11, No. 1, University of Chicago Press, 1940. More recent elaborations are contained in D. Vickers, *The Theory of the Firm: Production, Capital, and Finance*, New York: McGraw-Hill, 1968, Ch. 4, and C.A. Tisdell, *The Theory of Price Uncertainty, Production, and Profit*, Princeton, N.J.: Princeton University Press, 1969, Ch. 6. See also E.S. Mills, "Uncertainty and Price Theory," *Quarterly Journal of Economics*, 73 (Feb. 1959), 116-30, and R.R. Nelson, "Uncertainty, Prediction, and Competitive Equilibrium," *Quarterly Journal of Economics*, 75 (Feb. 1961), 41-62.

[4] See Chapters 7, 8, and 10.

investigators.[5] Such a measure has been specified in two ways, one emphasizing profit instability over time and the other emphasizing profit differences among firms across an industry. In the first case instability is measured for each firm as the variance about its own earnings trend over time, and the average of such variances for firms within an industry is then taken as a measure of industry risk. In the second case variance of earnings among firms in cross section about an industry average is taken as the measure. The latter measure has been published in two sources for a number of industries.

Cost variability also may be defined in several different ways, all of which assume that we can agree on a single short-run time period. Short-run cost variability depends on the flexibility of technology together with the relative prices of variable inputs. We say the flexibility of technology is high when output can be altered in the short run by adjusting variable factors without any serious declines in their marginal products. Flexibility also will tend to be higher as more inputs are variable in the short run. Cost variability will be high when flexibility is high, so long as the variable inputs account for a substantial fraction of total cost. Indeed, most researchers have found it convenient to define high flexibility as a low *rate of change* of marginal cost, although it also can be defined in terms of the level of marginal cost relative to price. To illustrate, in Figure 11-1, cost curves MC_v and AC_v describe the more flexible plant.[6] Comparable average cost curves can also be obtained up to a capacity limit by assuming constant marginal cost up to that capacity point, as illustrated in Figure 11-2,[7] and this cost function is of the type observed for most industries by Johnston.[8] In either Figure 11-1 or Figure 11-2 the more flexible AC_v case will have a higher fraction of total costs varying in the short-run than the AC_n case. In the Figure 11-2 case, marginal cost equals short-run average variable cost and may be approximated by measures of labor and material inputs.

With x representing quantity sold, p price, π profit, vx variable cost, and F fixed cost, we have

(1) $$\pi = (p - v)x - F$$

The variance in profit, σ_π^2, will then depend on the variance in quantity sold, σ_x^2:[9]

---

[5]This measure is not free of criticism. W.A. Morton argues in effect that higher mean profitability will cause a higher variance of profitability. See W.A. Morton, "Risk and Return: Instability of Earnings as a Measure of Risk," *Land Economics*, XLV (May 1969), 229-61.

[6]See Stigler, op. cit., p. 317, for an analysis in which the firm chooses an optimal degree of flexibility. A tradeoff is posed between flexibility and minimum cost because the more flexible cost curve is assumed to have a higher minimum cost point than the less flexible one.

[7]Stigler, op. cit., p. 309, describes this as a divisible but unadaptable plant.

[8]See J. Johnston, *Statistical Cost Functions*, New York: McGraw-Hill, 1960, p. 168.

[9]In order to obtain this simple relation between quantity sold and profit variances, we must assume that the random term is independent of x and p, as when the random term is simply added to a linear demand curve.

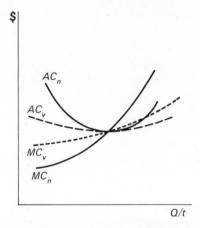

Figure 11–1. Total Cost Variability with Increasing Marginal Cost.

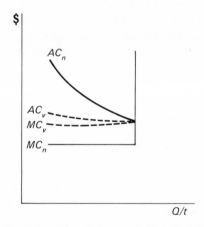

Figure 11–2. Total Cost Variability with Constant Marginal Cost.

$$(2) \qquad\qquad \sigma^2{}_\pi = (p - v)^2 \ \sigma^2{}_x$$

From (2) it is obvious that for given $\sigma_x{}^2$, greater cost variability (a larger v relative to p) will reduce profit risk (σ^2_π). Thus low cost variability, which we shall call "cost fixity," will tend to *increase* profit risk. The relation in (2) can be complicated when capacity limits exist causing the distribution of x to be truncated because orders cannot always be filled. But even here the same general relation may be expected, although its form will change. Because it prevents realization of some potential large quantities, the capacity limit will introduce negative skew in the distribution of quantity sold. However, the short-run capacity limit will also encourage price increases when greater quantities are demanded, so higher profits can still be expected from higher demand conditions. By itself this will add positive skew to the distribution of profits, and it should tend to offset the negative skew caused by truncation of the quantity sold distribution.

Cost Variability and Profit Risk-Evidence

In examining the relationship between cost fixity and profit risk we shall assume that variability in demand across industries is not systematically related to cost fixity. More precisely, we assume that cost fixity is not chosen to any important extent *in response* to demand variability, but is instead exogenously determined by technology and input prices. To the extent that firms depart from this assumption and tailor their cost fixity to the demand instability that they encounter, the relationship we expect will be weakened and will be more difficult to detect. For example, if managements acting in behalf of risk averse stockholders attempted to reduce profit instability when demand was unstable by choosing very flexible technology, we might find the least cost fixity in industries with the most unstable profits—the opposite of what we expect to find.[10]

From Equation (2) we expect $(p - v)^2$ to be related to σ^2_π. The expression, $p - v$ represents an assignment, to each unit, of costs that do not vary with output. Rather than use the absolute magnitude of $p - v$, we shall begin with the *proportion* of total costs that do not vary, $(p - v)/p$, so that absolute sizes of firms will not determine outcomes. Then different industries may be compared. From (1), $p - v = (F + \pi)/x$. We substitute for this the normalized expression, $(F + \pi) / (F + \pi + vx)$. Since $F + \pi + vx = px$,

---

[10] We do not rule out all effects in the other direction, but rather we assume them to be small. Management's response to profit risk is much more likely to come through financing decisions (e.g., debt versus equity) than through choice of technology. To treat properly such financial decisions, a simultaneous equations problem ought to be considered, possibly as set out by D.C. Mueller, "The Firm Decision Process: An Econometric Investigation," *Quarterly Journal of Economics*, 81 (February 1967), 58-87.

$$(F + \pi)/(F + \pi + vx) = (px - vx)/px,$$

which is equivalent to $(p - v)/p$. We then remove π from numerator and denominator to prevent any possibly misleading association that would be due only to the appearance of profit in both cost fixity and the profit variance. Our final cost fixity measure is $F/(F + vx)$. It will be observed empirically by taking value of shipments for px and labor and materials categories for vx from the *Census of Manufactures*, and then eliminating profits to obtain F and $F + vx$.[11]

Only the intraindustry cross section of profit variance is readily available from published sources.[12] A profit variance among firms in many industries was provided by Conrad and Plotkin from Standard and Poors *Compustat Annual Industrial Tape*, 1966 edition, for the years 1950-1965.[13] They added fixed interest charges to net income to obtain earnings before interest was deducted; this way a firm's capital structure would not affect its profit variance. Their main measure was expressed as the variance in profit percentages of total market values of firms about industry averages, which we shall identify as $\sigma^2_{\pi_i/m}$. A second measure of profit variance among firms was provided for eleven industries by Fisher and Hall.[14] They calculated variances in rates of return on net worth about industry averages, which we shall identify as $\sigma^2_{\pi/nw}$, from a sample of firms in the *Fortune 500* listing for the period from 1957-1964. Interest payments were not included in profit, and so capital structure will also affect profit risk as measured in this way. We did not include the aerospace industry in our study because of its special relations with the government; the

---

[11] We included nonproduction as well as production labor in vx on grounds that factory support labor also can be varied with output. And we examined one of our samples (the 10-industry Fisher and Hall sample) two ways using only production labor in vx one time and both production and nonproduction labor in vx the other time. The results were very similar. The short-run variability of labor costs deserves more attention, nevertheless. For one examination, see G.E. Delehanty, *Nonproduction Workers in U.S. Manufacturing*, Amsterdam: North-Holland Publishing Company, 1968. For the subsample of firms in drugs, automobiles, chemicals, office machines, electrical machinery and appliances, petroleum, rubber, food, steel, and textiles industries, data for profit adjustments were taken from I.N. Fisher and G.R. Hall, "Risk and the Aerospace Rate of Return," Rand Corporation Memorandum RM-5440-PR (Dec. 1967), 6. Profit data were estimated from IRS *Statistics of Income Sourcebook* (1957 to 1964) for the other industries included, which were cigarettes, liquor, aluminum, cement, containers (metal and glass), shoes, beer, and bituminous coal.

[12] The theoretical relation between cost fixity and profit variance that is described above for one firm can be related more easily to the intertemporal variability of profits measure than to the cross-sectional intraindustry measure which we use here because it is more readily available. The two measures are correlated, though only imperfectly. There are other difficulties with the intertemporal measure as well. Professors Joyce and Vogel have shown that changes in length of the time period over which the variance is calculated will affect the rankings of firms. See J.M. Joyce and R.C. Vogel, "The Uncertainty in Risk: Is Variance Unambiguous," *Journal of Finance*, 25 (Mar. 1970), pp. 127-34.

[13] Conrad and Plotkin, op. cit., pp. 93-96.

[14] Fisher and Hall, "Risk and the Aerospace Rate of Return," Rand Corporation, RM-5440-PR (December 1967), p. 34.

ten industries included are listed in n. 11 together with the additional eight industries examined with the Conrad and Plotkin profit variance data. Note that these data cover different periods of time, no one of which comprises just "good years" or "bad years." So a relationship which might arise only in a sample of extreme periods is not apt to emerge here.

Results of the simple regressions of $F/(F + vx)$ on profit instability are summarized in Table 11-1. Using either measure of across industry profit instability, a relation is found with the short-run cost fixity measure, although the cost fixity coefficient is significant only in the larger sample. Capital structure would affect profit risk in the smaller sample where interest payments were taken away from earnings before return on investment was calculated. This might be the reason that cost variability does not explain profit risk as well in this sample, since managers presumably could tailor their financing to modify profit risk. When capital structure effects are removed by including interest payments in the 18 industry sample, cost fixity is related significantly to profit risk. But because the differences in sample sizes also could account for differences in the strength of results, it is not possible to judge the precise effect capital structure has.

Table 11-1

Cost Fixity as Determinant of Profit Risk

Dependent Variable	No. of Industries	Constant	$F/ (F + vx)$	R^2adj.	F
$\sigma^2_{\pi_i/m}$	18	0.017* (1.54)	0.091** (2.06)	.16	4.24*
$\sigma^2_{\pi/nw}$	10	0.029** (2.23)	0.084* (1.66)	.16	2.75

(t statistics in parentheses)
*One tail significance at 0.10 test level
**One tail significance at 0.05 test level

Cost Variability, Profit Risk, and Firm Size

Could the association repeatedly found between firm size and profitability be explained by a systematic relation between profit risk or cost fixity and firm size?[15] Profit risk and firm size are difficult to interpret alone because of an observed sampling effect that leads to some interdependence between profit risk

[15] A considerable literature has grown around the question whether firm size and profitability are related. For an early study, see S.S. Alexander, "The Effect of Size of Manufacturing Corporation on the Distribution of the Rate of Return," *Review of Economics and Statistics*, 31 (August 1949), 229-35. More recent studies, which give further references to earlier work, are M. Hall and L. Weiss, "Firm Size and Profitability," *Review of Economics and Statistics*, 49 (August 1967), pp. 319-31, and M. Marcus, "Profitability and Size of Firm: Some Further Evidence," *Review of Economics and Statistics*, 51 (February 1969), 104-7.

and size of firm or number of observations. Hall and Weiss noted that very little systematic relationship remained between size and the profitability variance sum of squares for firms beyond $200 million in assets.[16] Of the industry samples examined here, only one (the drug industry with average assets of $169 million per firm) has average assets per firm of less than $200 million. And these industry samples each contain about the same number of firms, so sample sizes also should not cause differences in profit variability. In comparing size and cost fixity, of course, there is less reason to expect such a heteroskedasticity problem.

A comparison can be made from the I.N. Fisher and G.R. Hall data, which represent a 20% to 25% subsample of the Hall and Weiss data and are drawn mostly from the same years (1956-1962 for Hall and Weiss; 1957-1964 for Fisher and Hall). We shall compare average firm size with profit risk by industry, since Marcus has shown that very little of the association shows up *within* industries.[17] Average firm sizes for the Fisher and Hall industries were obtained by averaging 1957 and 1964 assets from the *Fortune 500* list for those firms in the ten industry Fisher and Hall sample used above. The profit divided by net worth measure of profitability, used in both studies, is regressed on cost fixity and average firm size with the results presented in Table 11-2.

The simple correlation between $F/(F + vx)$ and average firm assets is -0.60. This alone would suggest that risk does not tend to be greater for larger firms to account for their greater profitability. Any relation which does exist runs in the *opposite* direction instead and therefore strengthens the independent influence of size on profitability. In Table 11-2 the presence of $F/(F + vx)$ brings out a relation between size and profitability and at the same time accounts for a

Table 11-2
Average Firm Size, Cost Fixity, and Profit Risk as Determinants of Profitability (Profit/Net Worth)

No. of Inds.	Constant	Assets	$F/(F + vx)$	$\sigma^2_{\pi/nw}$	Concentration	R^2adj.	F
10	0.071*** (3.422)	0.046 (0.886)		1.144*** (4.145)	−0.021 (−0.566)	.63	6.06**
10	0.028 (0.957)	0.138** (1.993)	0.212*** (3.575)	−	0.054 (1.407)	.54	4.53*
10	0.103*** (2.982)	−0.009 (−0.104)	−	−	0.034 (0.547)	−	.15

(*t* statistics in parentheses)
*One tail significance at 0.10 test level
**One tail significance at 0.05 test level
***One tail significance at 0.01 test level

[16]See, e.g., Hall and Weiss, op. cit., pp. 323-24.
[17]See Marcus, op. cit.

significant portion of the profitability itself. When profit risk appears in the equation with this sample, it explains even more of the profitability of firms, and it also makes firm size and profitability positively related. We can conclude that the firm-size and profitability relation is not explained by an association between inter-industry risk and inter-industry average firm size. On the contrary, industries with larger firms seem more profitable in this sample *only* when the *negative* relation between firm size and profit risk, or firm size and the lack of short-run cost variability, is also taken into account.[18]

Note that a systematic relationship between firm size and properties of the cost function can be an influence in the imperfect relation that has been observed between profit variance measures and firm size when only sampling effects were considered as causes. Viewing large firms as larger samples of small units actually explains too much of the observed decline in variance with firm size.[19] A decline in cost fixity with the increase in firm size would also tend to reduce variance, at least of the profit measure, and so it would account for even more of the decline in profit variance.[20] We have not attempted to trace further the causes of this change in cost fixity with firm size. It may be related to the degree of vertical integration, or having a large fraction of total cost fixed in the short run may be inimical to growth beyond a certain firm size. In any case, a measure of cost fixity might serve conveniently as a surrogate for profit risk, because it is relatively free of the sampling problems which seriously complicate the interpretation of profit variance.

Links Between Market Structure and Market Performance

Several studies have shown that profit risk affects profitability just as investment theories that assume a tendency of investors toward risk aversion would predict (see n. 2 for references). Since measures of profitability have served often as dependent indicators of market performance in studies linking market structure variables to performance, it is appropriate to ask whether these market structure

---

[18]No heteroskedasticity or autocorrelation was apparent for either of the first two equations in Table 11-4, although the sample size is so small that tests of these assumptions are weak. However, the third equation in Table 11-4, which has no cost variability or profit variance term, gives evidence of poor specification; with data ordered by value of shipments, positive serial correlation and borderline heteroskedasticity are both present.

[19]See, e.g., Hall and Weiss, op. cit.

[20]This relationship may be quite complicated, however. Mansfield has pointed out in the context of firm growth that lack of independence among the smaller units considered as pooled into a larger firm could account for the incomplete explanation that sampling gives of changes in variance by size of firm. See E. Mansfield, "Entry, Gibrat's Law, Innovation, and the Growth of Firms," *American Economic Review*, LII (December 1962), 1034. Diwan recently presented evidence that the elasticity of substitution of a firm's production function first increases and then decreases as the firm grows. See R.K. Diwan, "About the Growth Path of Firms," *American Economic Review*, LX (March 1970), 30-43. Systematic effects of size on cost behavior is made plausible by such evidence.

variables are correlated with profit risk. If they are, relationships observed between market structure and profitability could be due not to market structure, but rather to the omitted profit risk variable. The same is true for cost fixity. If correlated with, say, concentration, cost fixity could be accounting for profitability differences that formerly might have been imputed to concentration. Moreover, profit risk or cost fixity could cause profit rate differences under *competitive* market processes without resort to any inference of market power that is usually drawn from an association of concentration with profitability.[21]

We shall search for possible effects of cost fixity in the recent replication of Bain's analysis carried out by H.M. Mann.[22] The Mann study examined profitability in 25 industries which were classified according to entry condition. Entry barriers and concentration together were associated with high profitability. We have added observations on additional market structure variables for this sample.[23] For the industries in the sample we obtained measures of cost variability with the purpose of searching for any relationships between these measures and market structure variables. Adequate profit risk measures were not available for these industries, and in any case they would present an interpretation problem because sample size effects by industry would be more serious in this sample.

Cost variability was estimated by taking labor and materials from the *Census*

---

[21]Professors Caves and Yamey have already argued, in the context of Fisher's and Hall's results, that differences in concentration may lead to risk differences. See R.E. Caves and B.S. Yamey, "Risk and Corporate Rates of Return: Comment," *Quarterly Journal of Economics*, LXXXV (August 1971), 513-17 (and Reply). We ask instead whether risk differences could have affected the associations observed before between concentration (or other market structure variables) and profitability. This seems the more appropriate empirical question since stockholders may be expected to respond consistently to realized risk, whether it results from normal competitive process or oligopolistic behavior. Tackling either question is difficult empirically because observable profit variances contain sampling as well as risk effects.

[22]Mann, op. cit.

[23]Capital requirements data were taken from Bain, *Barriers to Entry*, pp. 158-159, and adjusted by 1954 employment ratios in the following industries: aluminum reduction, petroleum refining, steel, cement, metal containers, and bituminous coal; and from unpublished data kindly supplied to us by Comanor and Wilson, op. cit., in the following industries: automobiles, cigarettes, ethical drugs, liquor, tires and tubes, shoes, canned fruits and vegetables, meat packing, flour, beer, and baking. The capital requirement estimate for the glass container industry is derived by a technique explained in Comanor and Wilson, op. cit., p. 429. Advertising-sales ratios were derived by taking the average over the 1954-1957 period of absolute advertising expenditures by Internal Revenue Service industry as a proportion of value of shipments of Census Bureau industries. Economies of scale data were taken from Comanor and Wilson, op. cit., for these industries: beer, liquor, meat packing, canned fruits and vegetables, flour, baking products, chewing gum (confectionary), cigarettes, drugs, soaps, tires and tubes, shoes, and automobiles. Estimates for the cement, tractors, petroleum refining, steel, metal containers, gypsum products, and rayon industries were obtained by averaging Bain's estimates of "percentage of national industry capacity contained in one plant of minimum efficient size." See Bain, *Barriers to New Competition*, p. 72. Estimates for the flat glass, aluminum reduction, biscuits, glass containers, and bituminous coal industries were derived by translating the scale-barrier ranking given by Mann, op. cit., p. 301, into Bain's classifications.

of Manufactures as variable cost and dividing it by value of shipments from the same source. Two additional adjustments were made to the ratio thus obtained. First, profits were again subtracted form value of shipments in order to avoid any built-in link with profitability.[24] Second, advertising expenditures also were removed from the value of shipments, in this case to avoid a spurious link between the cost variability measure and the advertising-sales ratio.[25] The resulting ratio of variable cost to other costs, $vx/(F + vx)$, was then subtracted from one to make it a measure of cost fixity, $F/(F + vx)$, which is expected to be related positively with profit.

Table 11-3 presents partial correlation coefficients between market structure variables and either cost fixity or profit risk, so we can see whether each market structure variable is related either to cost variability or to profit risk after the effects of the other market structure variables have been removed. Since we are concerned here with whether the omission of cost fixity might have invited false imputation of its effects to other variables, we note associations of even such

Table 11-3
Partial Coefficients of Correlation Between Individual Market Structure Variables and Cost Fixity

Market Structure Variable	Partial Correlation with Cost Fixity
Advertising/Sales	0.407
	(1.99)**
Concentration	0.077
	(0.35)
Capital Requirements	−0.307
	(−1.44)*
Scale Economies	−0.076
	(−0.34)

(*t* statistics in parentheses)
*Two tail significance at 0.20 level
**Two tail significance at 0.10 level
***Two tail significance at 0.05 level

---

[24]To accomplish this adjustment, absolute accounting profits taken from the *Internal Revenue Service Source Book of Statistics of Income—1954* were deducted from value of shipments. To relate Internal Revenue Service data on profits to those industries defined by the Census Bureau, Internal Revenue Service industry profits were allocated according to per cent of industry output accounted for in the following Census industries: chewing gum, flat glass, aluminum reduction, biscuits, tractors, glass containers, rayon, and flour.

[25]The advertising expenditure adjustment for the Mann sample required allocation of Internal Revenue Service advertising expenditure data according to the per cent of industry output accounted for in the following Census industries: flat glass, biscuits, tractors, glass containers, and flour. Advertising expenditure data for the chewing gum industry were taken from Mann, op. cit., p. 303, and advertising expenditure data for the Aluminum Reduction industry is for the smelting and refining of all non-ferrous metals.

modest strength as to be significant at only the 0.20 level. We see that when cost is highly fixed in the short-run, advertising tends to be higher. Capital requirements are related negatively to cost fixity, but not at a significant level.

From the partial correlation coefficients in Table 11-3, we can anticipate effects of introducing a cost fixity measure as explanatory variable into a regression of profitability on market structure variables. First, since cost fixity and an advertising-sales ratio measure are highly correlated, if cost fixity and profitability are positively related we should expect a *reduction* in the explanatory power of the advertising-sales ratio when cost fixity is introduced.[26] We also should expect that capital requirements might *increase* in importance, since it is negatively related to cost fixity although not at a high level of significance. We can see these effects in our sample by regressing profitability on market structure variables with and without the cost fixity measure. On adding cost fixity to the original 25 industry Mann sample we see in Table 11-4 that cost fixity itself is very highly related to profitability. In the presence of cost fixity, the advertising-sales ratio becomes less important while capital requirements appears much more closely related to profitability than it did before. When cost fixity is present, economies of scale also appear to be slightly more important. Thus, whatever effect capital requirements and economies of scale had before will be increased when cost fixity is considered, and cost fixity itself explains a large fraction of the sum of square deviations in profitability.

Table 11-4
Adding Cost Fixity to a Regression of Profitability on Market Structure Variables

N	Const.	Cost Fixity	Adv./ Sales	Concent.	Capital Reqmts.	Econ. Scale	R^2adj.
25	0.08 (4.69)***		0.20 (1.28)	0.02 (0.76)	0.04 (0.68)	0.20 (0.88)	.05
25	0.04 (2.01)*	0.20 (3.07)***	0.02 (0.14)	0.02 (0.66)	0.09 (1.71)*	0.25 (1.27)	.33

(*t* statistics in parentheses)
*One tail significance at 0.10 test level
**One tail significance at 0.05 test level
***One tail significance at 0.01 test level

---

[26]The effect of advertising on profitability is eliminated when cost fixity is introduced in a sample of consumer goods industries. See Chapter 10. Advertising and cost fixity should be so related according to the relation between the marginal value product of advertising and cost fixity derived from a firm's profit maximizing conditions in R. Dorfman and P.O. Steiner, "Optimal Advertising and Optimal Quality," *American Economic Review*, 44 (December 1954), pp. 826-36. Thus the strong relationship between advertising and profitability found by W.S. Comanor and T.A. Wilson, op. cit., should not be interpreted as a cause-effect relationship; the omitted cost fixity variable could lead both to high advertising and high profitability. For another view, see W.S. Comanor and T.A. Wilson, "On Advertising and Profitability," *Review of Economics and Statistics*, 53 (November 1971), pp. 408-410.

Fisher and Hall recently have added some market structure measures to their original regression of firm profitability on intertemporal profit variance and profit skew.[27] And their strong positive relation between profit risk and profitability remains. In the presence of profit risk and other variables in their sample, concentration will continue to be related significantly to profitability. Whether concentration will continue to be related positively to profitability after a profit risk measure is allowed for must await the development of more complete data series for profit risk.

Note that the measure of cost fixity we have constructed is very similar to the one that Collins and Preston called the "price-cost margin" and found correlated with concentration.[28] The difference is that we attempted to remove profit to obtain only the ratio of fixed to total costs. Collins and Preston regarded their price-cost margin as a dependent performance measure whereas we view our ratio as one that is given largely by technology and as an influence on profit risk; we view cost fixity as an *explanatory* variable. Although we lack the large number of observations available to Collins and Preston in their study of four-digit industries, the apparent lack of strong association between concentration and our cost variability ratio suggests that omission of these same profit and advertising elements from the price-cost margin would destory its association with concentration. In any case, a link between price-cost margin and concentration should not be taken as an indication that cost variability and concentration are similarly related.

Thus we conclude that since cost fixity is positively related to profitability and yet *not* positively correlated with concentration, capital requirements, or economies of scale, its omission from market structure-performance studies is unlikely to have caused improper imputation of influence on profitability to other variables. On the contrary, a modest negative relation between cost fixity and capital requirements indicates that capital requirements may be even more important in explaining profitability than has appeared before. Cost fixity is positively related to advertising-sales, and it will reduce that variable's importance in explaining profitability. Cost fixity itself also appears as a very important determinant of profitability. We cannot be sure that cost fixity has its effects solely through the greater variance in profit that it may cause, but it does appear as an important determinant of industry performance. It is related to profit risk theoretically and empirically, and yet is free of sample size effects, which complicate interpretation of the profit variance.

---

[27] See I.N. Fisher and G.R. Hall, "Risk and Corporate Rates of Return: Reply," *Quarterly Journal of Economics*, LXXXV (August 1971), 518-22.

[28] See N.R. Collins and L.E. Preston, "Price-Cost Margins and Industry Structure," *Review of Economics and Statistics*, 51 (August 1969), 271-86, and "Concentration and Price-Cost Margins in Food Manufacturing Industries," *Journal of Industrial Economics*, 15 (July 1966), 226-42. See also criticism by H. Benishay, "Concentration and Price-Cost Margins: A Comment," *Journal of Industrial Economics*, 16 (November 1967), 73-74.

Summary

We have shown that a measure of short-run cost fixity is theoretically and empirically associated with profit risk. Since profit risk is known to affect the level of profitability, cost fixity will also be a cause of profitability, and if positively associated with market structure variables migh diminish their power to explain profitability. Although cost variability is related to profitability, it is not highly correlated with market structure variables except for advertising-sales and in that case the relation can be explained at the level of the firm by the Dorfman-Steiner optimal level of advertising conditions. However, cost variability and profit risk are related to firm size in a way that tends to strengthen rather than reduce the previously noted relation between firm size and profitability.

We thus find earlier studies have not wrongly imputed to market structure 'causes' profitability that is due instead to profit risk or to technology in the form of short-run variability. This does not mean that profit risk can be ignored in market structure-performance studies. The sum of squared deviations in profit-rates may be reduced by the presence of cost-variability or profit risk in test equations, and the explanatory power of other variables may be affected as a result also. So although profit risk or cost variability is not apt to have confounded earlier studies, we nevertheless would urge that measures of profit risk be taken into account in future market structure-performance studies, possibly by the more convenient cost-variability surrogate suggested here.

12 Implications for Antitrust Policy

We have focused carefully and deliberately on the reward structure faced by each firm in an oligopoly market. And in doing so we have found that the rewards to alternative capacity and price choices can influence the degree of competitiveness that is to be expected among firms making those choices, even when the reward structure is complicated by interdependence among the firms. More dispersion in equilibrium values may be observed in oligopolies than in clearly competitive markets, but the predictability of average outcomes can be established nonetheless. Thus oligopoly markets can be analyzed much as competitive markets are, with hypotheses about firm behavior being traced from properties of a cost-reward structure assuming the profit maximizing goal, and without need of specialized oligopoly behavior theories. So the apparent indeterminancy of oligopoly is merely troublesome, not debilitating; oligopolies can be studied empirically. Indeed, because greater dispersion of outcomes must be expected in oligopolies, proportionately more empirical work is appropriate there.

Although its origin lies more in efforts to deal with difficult problems of public policy than in testing oligopoly theories, the field of industrial organization has contributed much empirical evidence about the performance of oligopoly markets. The great importance of entry barriers has convincingly been established by Joe Bain, and effects of other operational aspects of market structure, such as concentration, also have been identified.[1] Indeed, a coherent set of empirical relationships now is accepted by most students of industrial organization.[2] Our aim here has been to add more subtle relationships by focusing on existing firms in markets that are difficult to enter, where the existing firms can influence industry performance. Constant long-run average cost gives the existing firms an opportunity to expand and thus perhaps to destroy any prospect of cooperation at a high price. Alternatively, the firms may resist expansion. They then can depart with impunity in several different ways from the competitive behavior benchmark, setting higher prices, competing more by advertising and sales promotion, perhaps even wasting resources by careless management, and very probably earning higher rates of return on invested capital than firms in more competitive industries.

When capacity as well as price choices are taken into account, the cost-reward structure faced by an individual firm depends on market structure variables, such

---

[1] Earlier results are available in [2] and [3], and more recent studies are [4, 14, 24].

[2] A review and summary of empirical results is provided in [33]. See also [21] and [25].

x

177

as market share, which are of interest to industrial organization economists and antitrust authorities. Since reward structure in turn can influence behavior, even where decisionmakers are interdependent in mixed-motive conflict situations, this dependence of a firm's reward structure on its industry's market structure is important. It means that the firm's *independent* actions should be expected to change as market structure changes. Aside from the extreme case of monopoly, no effect of market structure on the independent behavior of firms is presumed in current antitrust law,[3] which regards collusive action as the main threat that an oligopoly market holds against competitive performance. Our analysis calls instead for explicit concern with market structure because of its effect on the cost-reward structure of individual firms and, hence, their behavior. Antitrust policy should be concerned with the cost-reward structures of firms, and should not attempt solely to root tacit and active collusion from oligopoly markets as if collusion were the only cause of poor industry performance.

Here we shall review the payoff structure faced by one firm in an oligopoly market. Because it is assumed to have constant average cost,[4] the firm can choose its capaciy as well as its price. We shall elaborate also the terms in which payoff structure can be characterized in real-world oligopolies. Finally we shall review antitrust policy implications and proposals, and provide at the end a brief summary of our main recommendation.

The Reward Structure for an Oligopolistic Firm

Constant long-run average cost for existing firms in many manufacturing industries makes their behavior almost as important as new entry in determining market performance. For the firms can change scale and expand, and the new capacity they add to their industry will bring pressure to lower price and expand quantity demanded, very much like that created by new entrants. To be sure, new entry will tend to reduce market shares and will also increase the probability that the industry will have at least one aggressive risk-taker. But even without new entry, the capacity choice opportunity of existing firms broadens the scope of their interdependence, and exacts long-run as well as short-run requirements from firms that wish to exploit their protection from new entry. This framework seems to reveal much better than has the short-run framework along the way in which psychological factors can influence decisions in mixed-motive conflict situations. And it also can pose well the fundamental economic cost-reward structure faced by oligopolistic firms.

---

[3]Current U.S. antitrust law is presented in [18]. The Sherman Act is concerned exclusively with monopolization and collusion. The Clayton Act deals with individual firms' practices that are presumed to be monopolistic, such as tie-in sales, exclusive dealing, and price discrimination.

[4]See Chapter 4.

A firm's prospect for gain by expanding capacity can depend on many things. We have characterized the firm's reward structure here in a simple way, and found that relative firm size can influence the incentive to expand. A firm that has a large market share will be more reluctant to expand because it will feel the disadvantages of a lower capacity utilization and lower market price that will necessarily follow. A small firm will not appreciate such effects, however, and may expand whenever price rises above average cost. If the cost associated with a unit of capacity is very high, relative to other costs, expansion will be less attractive to the firms, for unused capacity will involve greater sacrifice then. Indeed, the cost variability relation can affect reward structure in many ways, as seen in Part II. Of course a low elasticity of market demand also could discourage expansion, especially by a large firm, because it would make a greater price reduction necessary in order to clear the market of expanded output.

The effect of relative size on the capacity expansion incentive is felt by each firm *independently* through its own cost-reward structure, and capacity restraint does not really require any tacit collusion among firms. We have used the word, "collusive," to describe market outcomes that were not truly competitive, but these outcomes do not require the sort of tacit collusion presumed in oligopoly markets and examined in Part I. Each firm can see its own interest, and that interest calls for cooperative rather than competitive action. In essence, the capacity decision permits a Cournot-like quantity adjustment, where market share exercises a clear effect on each firm's behavior. Operationally, concentration measures may typify the large-firm market shares in an industry, and thus can capture in part this independent incentive effect. If a few firms in an industry have large market shares they will resist expansion and will be able to maintain higher prices. Recent findings indicate, however, that market share serves even better than concentration to indicate effects on profitability, a result that is consistent with our simple capacity choice model.[5]

The relationship between price and marginal cost also will affect advertising, because it influences the profitability of advertising. The sale of one additional unit contributes more toward profit as the difference between price and marginal cost is greater, and so all other things equal, it is reasonable to expect more advertising then, as the empirical results of Chapter 10 suggest. Moreover, when price is high, firms might compete by advertising rather than price. Doing so could limit the amount of their excess profit, though. And so high advertising need not be associated with high profit. The consumer is not necessarily ideally served either, simply because profit is not excessively high, for price and advertising might still remain higher than they would be if new entry was easier.

A greater difference between price and marginal cost also can make the variance of profit, called profit risk, larger, because any fluctuations in quantity will then tend to produce greater fluctuations in profit. But there seems to be no

---

[5] See [7] and [24].

strong positive correlation between concentration and profit risk.[6] Indeed, in examining effects of profit risk we found no reason here for questioning the results of previous industrial organization studies linking concentration and entry barriers to profitability merely because they failed to consider profit risk. If anything, the presence of profit risk may make the capital requirement entry barrier more important, possibly because high profit risk makes raising capital more difficult.

Although profit risk is not related to concentration, there is some evidence that in the U.S., employment instability *is* related to concentration.[7] In its response to demand shifts, the firm with some monopoly power can trade-off between profit risk and employment instability, which we might call employment risk.[8] So a link between concentration and employment risk tells us firms that have market power may resolve this trade-off more favorably for owners than for workers. The firm can raise price when demand is high and lower price when demand is low, in order to make output and employment more stable. But such responses will tend to make profit fluctuations greater. By keeping price constant (or even raising it slightly when demand is low and lowering it when demand is high), the firm can keep profit risk small, but it must then experience greater fluctuations in employment. There is evidence that profit risk and employment risk both will affect the value of the firm,[9] and if the firm has power to set its own price we may expect it to choose a response that will maximize its value. If capital markets reflect risks and returns more precisely than labor markets, which seems plausible, the cost of profit risk may appear greater to the firm.[10] The relationship between these observations and the "administered pricing" controversy should be obvious.[11]

Some of the main effects of market structure variables on an individual oligopolist's incentives to increase price, restrain capacity, and advertise heavily

---

[6]See [29], as well as Chapter 11. In Chapter 11 the cost function property of cost fixity, which correlates with profit risk and is the Lerner measure of monopoly power purged of profit, was not related significantly with concentration. The variance of profit was not related to concentration in [29] until a possibly inappropriate adjustment [13] was made for "excessive" withdrawals in small firms, and even then there was no significant relation when war years were not involved. (See also more recent evidence by Stigler on the relation between concentration and profit-rate. [30]) A slight negative relation was found between concentration and the residual variance in profit rates for a sample of 116 British firms. [20]

[7]See the evidence provided by D. Stanton Smith. [28] This point is still open to question. Some conflicing evidence has suggested there is less instability of employment in concentrated industries, [8, 32] but it is based on less complete measures of work instability such as new hires, layoffs, and quit rates, which would be lower for concentrated industries because they tend to employ more skilled workers. Smith used the variance in total hours worked as his employment stability measure.

[8]See [22].

[9]A higher average wage is required by workers when employment risk is higher. [28] And a higher rate of return is required by investors when profit risk is higher. [1, 5, 6, 9]

[10]Of course this conclusion applies only in market economies where terms of employment may be changed unilaterally by the firm, and it should not be expected in countries such as Spain or Japan where employee tenure arrangements are common.

[11]For recent comment on this controversy, and some further references, see [17] and [31].

are shown in Table 12-1. The ratio of fixed cost to total cost, $f/(f+v)$, reflects "cost fixity" and is related to Lerner's measure of monopoly power but with profit omitted from both numerator and denominator. The reciprocal of the absolute value of demand elasticity, $1/|\eta|$, is equal to Lerner's measure at the firm's profit maximizing equilibrium, except for the extent to which the threat of new entry discourages full exploitation of monopoly power in setting a high price.[12] The $k/\Sigma k$ term represents market share. A reduction in all capacities can increase the incentive to raise price, so even though high cost fixity discourages a high price directly, it may invite it over the long-run by encouraging capacity restraint.

The well established importance of entry condition applies also, of course, for if new entry is not inhibited, any excess profit that is won by cooperative behavior will be bid away by new entrants who will expand industry capacity. But if entry barriers make new entry difficult, the payoff structure faced by individual firms may invite either cooperative or competitive behavior. The ultimate outcome will be influenced by relative firm sizes, cost variability, and the extent of product differentiation, with capacity levels important but influenced also by capacity cost and cooperation prospects.

Thus, in considering real-world measures of market structure, we can see how they affect the reward structure seen by an individual firm. Capacity expansion incentive can depend on market share and cost variability as well as on demand elasticity, which is much more difficult to measure. The firms with large market shares will feel and *independent* incentive to restrain capacity expansion through their own reward structure for alternative actions, and may reach a higher price without any genuine collusion. Cost variability also can influence advertising and profit risk, variables that need to be untangled before definitive cause-effect relations can be established with profitability. There also is a possibility that the firm with market power may exploit it not merely by obtaining a higher profit level, but also by reducing fluctuations in profit at the cost of greater employment instability, and in other ways as well.

Table 12-1
Effects of Market Structure Variables on Firm Behavior Incentives

Effect on	Parameter Increased		
Incentive to	$f/(f+v)$	$1/\eta$	$k/\Sigma k$
Raise Price	−	+	+
Limit Capacity	+	+	+
Advertise More	+	+	?

[12] Full monopoly power probably can seldom be exploited. See [34].

Antitrust Policy Implications

Market share has served as an operational antitrust policy measure of monopoly power ever since Judge Hand's decision rested so heavily on it in the Alcoa case.[13] But no routine or systematic account is taken of market share in antitrust policy, except in extreme monopoly cases and in connection with specific merger proposals, where merger guidelines of the Antitrust Division of the Justice Department are expressed in terms of market shares.[14] Antitrust policy is most effective against well defined collusive practices, such as price fixing, but it has been almost helpless against cases of possible tacit collusion by a few firms in concentrated industries, and it has failed altogether to deal with perverse aspects of entirely independent behavior by firms that enjoy large shares of their markets.

That profit rates are higher in concentrated industries is now quite well established, [33] and the fact has led many observers to urge that high levels of concentration be prevented by explicit legislation.[15] It has been difficult politically to adopt such a policy, however, in part because some scope has existed for arguing the other way. Large firms are claimed to be more efficient [16] and more able to carry out innovations. [10, 23] And in addition it is claimed that undesirable behavior by large firms in concentrated industries already is within the reach of the Sherman Act, so that new legislation is not needed. [19] Our results, including especially the dampened *independent* incentive for firms with large market shares to grow and expand when properties of their cost functions would permit it, clearly favor the legislated control of market share, and they serve specifically to undercut the arguments that have been offered against it.

No reliable evidence shows very large firms to be more efficient in the many industries that are not regulated monopolies. As noted in Chapter 4, to the extent that cost functions can be identified they show scale economies only at quite small scales, and beyond some particular size in most industries average cost is constant. Moreover, Bain has shown that concentration is well above the level needed to enable firms to reach the minimum efficient scale in many industries. [2] More recent studies show the same result; [26] concentration could be reduced considerably without creating any higher costs of production for firms. What empirical evidence we have also shows the largest firms do not undertake proportionately more research, and they may even innovate less than more moderate sized firms. [15, 35] The fact that firms with large market shares have an independent incentive to restrain growth makes them apt to have higher prices and smaller outputs without collusion that would violate any existing

---

[13] *United States vs. Aluminum Company of America*, 148 F. 2nd 416 (2nd Cir., 1945).

[14] The Antitrust Division of the Justice Department issued guidelines in May of 1968 to indicate the types of mergers it would oppose. Many of the guideline definitions were expressed in terms of market shares.

[15] The first proposal of this sort was H.C. Simons'. [27] See also [12].

antitrust law, so new rules against unnecessarily large market shares become appropriate.

The argument by Posner that undesirable behavior by large firms could be attacked under the Sherman Act assumed throughout that independent behavior was a sufficient goal, and that only actively or tacitly collusive behavior needed to be prevented. [19] But attention to the payoff structure faced by firms shows that relative size can affect independently taken decisions, not only through its effect on the relative rewards that interdependent firms see for cooperative versus competitive behavior, but also through the gains they perceive to be available from expansion. Independent responses to the cost-reward structure can affect industry performance, and yet they do not raise any questions under the Sherman Act or the Clayton Act. In order reliably to prevent contrived scarcity by a few large firms in oligopolistic industries, new legislation therefore is appropriate, legislation which deals explicitly with relative firm size and denies market shares well beyond those needed to exhaust enconomies of scale in an industry.

Several practical proposals to limit concentration have been made.[16] One recent one is contained in "The White House Task Force Report on Antitrust Policy," which was the work of a Presidential commission chaired by the Dean of the University of Chicago Law School, Phil C. Neal. [37] Based on the original Kaysen and Turner proposal, [12] it called on the Antitrust Division of the Justice Department and the Federal Trade Commission to bring dissolution suits against the leading firms in an industry if its top-four-firm concentration ratio was persistently above 70 percent and its total annual sales exceeded $500,000,000. The firms in the industry each were to reduce their market shares below 12% unless they could establish that doing so would increase their average costs, by denying them scale economies. The study of antitrust enforcement sponsored by Ralph Nader [11] made similar, but more severe proposals, calling for dissolution if top-four-firm concentration was above 50 percent, and extending jurisdiction to industries with only $50,000,000 in annual sales if concentration was above the 50 percent level for a long time. An absolute limit on firm assets of $2 billion also was proposed (regulated monopolies excepted). And the Nadar proposal suggested that divestiture automatically be required within three to five years after a suit was filed, with no economies of scale defense allowed.

Empirical studies repeatedly have shown stronger relations between concentration and profit rate when concentration is high. [3, 14, 32, 33] Large market shares will interfere with the independent incentives firms face to pursue socially desirable behavior, and legislation drawn to prevent them where they offer no offsetting economy is entirely appropriate. A modest proposal such as the 12 percent market share limit of the Neal report proposal offers a suitable treatment of the problem, for it will prevent the independent firm incentives

---

[16]See [11, 12, 37]. Different types of policy are proposed in [19] and [36].

from straying very far away from competitive market ones. The proposal can even be improved by omitting the requirement that industry concentration persistently be above 70 percent before action can be taken. The market share of an individual firm influences its reward structure, and when the share is large it will tend to entice the firm away from competitive behavior. Such an effect itself should be controlled, quite apart from industry concentration. Moreover, antitrust policy cannot easily be applied to industries, and reference to industry variables only complicates orientation toward the proper ultimate subject of any policy action, the individual firm. It might be advisable to have some total industry sales requirement that must be met before a suit is contemplated, if only to center attention on the most significant problems and permit more scope for one firm dominance in new product industries. But an additional concentration requirement is unnecessary and would complicate enforcement of the act, so it should not be imposed.

Our psychological findings showed that some individuals will respond with more risk-taking and competitive behavior than others in the mixed-motive conflict that characterizes oligopoly markets. Because one aggressive firm can force competitive behavior on all the others in its industry, we need only focus on the likelihood of having at least one aggressive firm. And we can expect this likelihood to be greater as there are more firms in an industry. An upper limit on market share should increase the number of firms that can influence industry price and output, and so it should increase also the likelihood of having at least one aggressive risk-taker. It is true that if the absence of one aggressive risk-taker led clearly to anticompetitive results, traditional antitrust law might be able to reach the tacitly cooperative firms. But anticompetitive results are not always apparent. An upper limit on market share could help to enforce competition and thus reduce the temptation to cooperate tacitly that arises in oligopolistic markets.

Without new antitrust legislation, relatively large firms will be left in their present situation, where their independent actions may be critized even though they violate no law, and where they may be attacked, somewhat unpredictably, only when their departures from a competitive benchmark of performance take the most extreme forms. Furthermore, efforts to contain the law-abiding but unwanted behavior of large firms in the absence of direct remedies may press antitrust authorities to emphasize other measures, such as merger controls, which alone are unnecessary and even undesirable.[17] Dissolution is a more extreme and potentially very costly remedy that antitrust authorities have been most reluctant to impose. On the other hand, a well defined legislated market share maximum is fair and feasible. It also will enlist the cooperation of the firms themselves in remedying the problems of industrial concentration, for to serve their stockholders best, and still comply with the market share limits, managers of successful firms must choose an optimal time and form for

[17]For this argument, see [35].

voluntary dissolution, something they should be able to do with far less cost than the antitrust authorities could.

Summary

We have demonstrated that the reward structure faced by an individual firm can be expected to influence its behavior, at least probabilistically. Economic variables will influence that reward structure; the effects of market share and cost variability have been emphasized here. As a firm's market share becomes large it is invited to behave less in harmony with social goals and less like a competitive firm. No provision of present antitrust laws takes account of this effect of market share on independent incentives, and market structure problems also remain unsolved. Our main recommendation is that the reward structure faced by independent firms be controlled through a structural antitrust law that places an upper limit on market shares, and thereby deals directly with problems of firm and industry performance that now are attacked, if at all, by means of extreme remedies and inappropriate antimerger policy.

References

[1] F.D. Arditti, "Risk and the Required Return on Equity," *Journal of Finance* 22 (March 1967), 19-36.

[2] J.S. Bain, "Economies of Scale, Concentration, and the Condition of Entry in Twenty Manufacturing Industries," *American Economic Review* 44 (March 1954), 15-39.

[3] _____, *Barriers to New Competition* (Cambridge, Mass.: Harvard University Press, 1956).

[4] W.S. Comanor and T.A. Wilson, "Advertising, Market Structure, and Performance," *The Review of Economies and Statistics* 49 (August 1967), 319-31.

[5] G.R. Conrad and I.H. Plotkin, "Risk/Return: U.S. Industry Pattern," *Harvard Business Review* 46 (March-April 1968), 90-99.

[6] P.H. Cootner and D.M. Holland, "Risk and Rate of Return," Massachusetts Institute of Technology DSR Project No. 9565, February 1964.

[7] J.A. Dalton and David W. Penn, "The Quality of Data as a Factor in Analysis of Structure-Performance Relationships," Washington, D.C.: Staff Report of the Federal Trade Commission, 1971.

[8] C.E. Ferguson, *A Macroeconomic Theory of Workable Competition* (Durham, N.C.: Duke University Press, 1964).

[9] I.N. Fisher and G.R. Hall, "Risk and Corporate Rates of Return," *Quarterly Journal of Economics* 82 (February 1969), 79-92.

[10] J.K. Galbraith, *The New Industrial State* (Boston, Mass.: Houghton Mifflin Co., 1967).

[11] M.J. Green, ed., *The Closed Enterprise System* (Washington, D.C.: Center of the Study of Responsive Law, 1971).

[12] C. Kaysen and D.F. Turner, *Antitrust Policy: An Economic and Legal Analysis* (Cambridge, Mass.: Harvard University Press, 1959).

[13] R.W. Kilpatrick, "Stigler on the Relationship Between Industry Profit Rates and Market Concentration," *Journal of Political Economy* 76 (May-June 1968), 479-88.

[14] H.M. Mann, "Seller Concentration, Barriers to Entry, and Rates of Return in Thirty Industries," *Review of Economics and Statistics* 48 (August 1966), 296-307.

[15] E. Mansfield, "Industrial Research Expenditures: Determinants, Prospects, and Relation to Size of Firm and Inventive Output," *Journal of Political Economy* 72 (August 1964), 319-40.

[16] J.S. McGee, *In Defense of Industrial Concentration* (New York: Praeger Publishers, Inc., 1971).

[17] G.C. Means, "The Administered-Price Thesis Reconfirmed," *American Economic Review* 62 (June 1972), 292-306.

[18] A.D. Neale, *The Antitrust Laws of the United States* (London: Cambridge University Press, 2nd ed., 1970).

[19] R.A. Posner, "Oligopoly and the Antitrust Laws: A Suggested Approach," *Stanford Law Review* (June 1969), 1562-1606.

[20] J.M. Samuels and D.J. Smyth, "Profits, Variability of Profits, and Firm Size," *Economica* N.S. 35 (May 1968), 127-39.

[21] F.M. Scherer, *Industrial Market Structure and Economic Performance* (Chicago, Ill.: Rand McNally and Company, 1970).

[22] R. Schramm and R. Sherman, "Advertising to Manage Profit Risk," mimeographed, Cornell University, 1972.

[23] J. Schumpeter, *Capitalism, Socialism and Democracy* (New York: Harper and Row, 1972).

[24] W.G. Shepherd, "The Elements of Market Structure," *Review of Economics and Statistics* 54 (February 1972), 25-37.

[25] R. Sherman, *The Economics of Industry* (Boston, Mass.: Little, Brown and Company, 1973).

[26] _____ and R. Tollison, "Public Policy Toward Oligopoly," *Antitrust Law and Economics Review* 4 (Summer 1971), 77-90.

[27] H.C. Simons, *Economic Policy For a Free Society* (Chicago, Ill.: University of Chicago Press, 1948).

[28] D.S. Smith, "Concentration and Employment Fluctuations," *Western Economic Journal* 9 (September 1971), 267-77.

[29] G.J. Stigler, *Capital and Rates of Return in Manufacturing Industries* (Princeton, N.J.: Princeton University Press, 1963).

[30] _____ , *The Organization of Industry* (Homewood, Ill.: Richard D. Irwin, 1968).

[31] _____ and J.K. Kindahl, *The Behavior of Industrial Prices* (New York: Columbia University Press, 1970).

[32] L.G. Telser, *Competition, Collusion and Game Theory* (Chicago, Ill.: Aldine Atherton, 1972).

[33] L.Weiss, "Quantitative Studies of Industrial Organization," Ch. 9 in Michael D. Intriligator, ed., *Frontiers of Quantitative Economics* (Amsterdam: North Holland Publishing Co., 1971).

[34] J.T. Wenders, "Entry and Monopoly Pricing," *Journal of Political Economy* 75 (October 1967), 755-60.

[35] O.E. Williamson, "Innovation and Market Structure," *Journal of Political Economy* 73 (February 1965), 67-73.

[36] "The Report of the President's Task Force on Productivity and Competition," G.J. Stigler, Chairman (Washington, D.C.: Congressional Record-Senate, June 16, 1969, pp. S6473-80).

[37] "The White House Task Force Report on Antitrust Policy," P.C. Neal, Chairman (Washington, D.C.: Bureau of National Affairs, 1969).

Index

About the Author

Roger Sherman was born in 1930 in Jamestown, New York. He is now Professor of Economics at The University of Virginia, where he has been a member of the faculty since 1965. He studied mathematics as an undergraduate at Grove City College (B.S. 1952), finance at Harvard University (M.B.A. 1959), and economics at Carnegie-Mellon University (M.S. 1965 and Ph.D. 1966). He served as a U.S. naval officer from 1952 to 1956 and in various management positions with the IBM Corporation between 1956 and 1962. He was Visiting Fellow in Economics at the University of Bristol during 1968-1969 and Fulbright Lecturer at Autonomous University of Madrid in 1972.